Studying Ethnic Minority and Economically Disadvantaged Populations

Methodological Challenges and Best Practices

Studying Ethnic Minority and Economically Disadvantaged Populations

Methodological Challenges and Best Practices

George P. Knight, Mark W. Roosa, and
Adriana J. Umaña-Taylor

American Psychological Association · *Washington, DC*

Published by
American Psychological Association
750 First Street, NE
Washington, DC 20002
www.apa.org

To order
APA Order Department
P.O. Box 92984
Washington, DC 20090-2984
Tel: (800) 374-2721; Direct: (202) 336-5510
Fax: (202) 336-5502; TDD/TTY: (202) 336-6123
Online: www.apa.org/books/
E-mail: order@apa.org

In the U.K., Europe, Africa, and the Middle East, copies may be ordered from
American Psychological Association
3 Henrietta Street
Covent Garden, London
WC2E 8LU England

Typeset in Minion by Circle Graphics, Inc., Columbia, MD

Printer: Courier Westford, Westford, MA
Cover Designer: Naylor Design, Washington, DC
Technical/Production Editor: Harriet Kaplan

The opinions and statements published are the responsibility of the authors, and such opinions and statements do not necessarily represent the policies of the American Psychological Association.

Library of Congress Cataloging-in-Publication Data

Knight, George P., 1950-
  Studying ethnic minority and economically disadvantaged populations : methodological challenges and best practices / George P. Knight, Mark W. Roosa, and Adriana J. Umaña-Taylor.
    p. cm.
  Includes bibliographical references and index.
  ISBN-13: 978-1-4338-0474-8
  ISBN-10: 1-4338-0474-3
  1. Social sciences—Research—United States—Methodology. 2. Minorities—Research—United States. 3. Poor—Research—United States. 4. Marginality, Social—Research—United States. I. Roosa, Mark W. II. Umaña-Taylor, Adriana J. III. Title.

  H62.5.U5K65 2010
  305.5'69072—dc22
                              2009002141

British Library Cataloguing-in-Publication Data
A CIP record is available from the British Library.

Printed in the United States of America
First Edition

Contents

Preface   *vii*

1. Introduction to Studying Ethnic Minority
    and Economically Disadvantaged Populations   3

2. Sampling, Recruiting, and Retaining Diverse Samples   29

3. Ethical Issues   79

4. Measurement and Measurement Equivalence Issues   97

5. Translation Processes Associated With Measurement
    in Linguistically Diverse Populations   135

6. Putting Research Into Action: Preventive
    Intervention Research   167

Epilogue   191

References   197

Index   215

About the Authors   223

Preface

Ethnic minority and economically disadvantaged populations have consistently been underrepresented in most social science research. Given the changing demographics of the United States, there appears to be some movement toward a greater research emphasis on these populations. The focus on gaining more support for research on these populations represents a substantial opportunity to move the field forward with respect to an understanding of diversity and a more nuanced understanding of human behavior and outcomes. Unfortunately, there is a relative dearth of information on the unique methodological challenges associated with conducting research with ethnic minority and economically disadvantaged populations. In our own efforts over the years teaching research methods to graduate students or mentoring students involved in our research on ethnic minority and economically disadvantaged populations, we have been frustrated by the challenge in accessing the sparse and difficult-to-find literature on methods that have been demonstrated to be most effective with these populations. This book evolved from many discussions in which we shared these frustrations with each other and with like-minded colleagues. The purpose of this book is to provide a comprehensive single resource for the lessons learned from research with ethnic minority and economically disadvantaged populations, to describe the unique methodological issues researchers face, and to provide some best practice guidance for how to address these challenges.

We decided to write this book because we believe that there is an emerging interest, as a result of the population dynamics of the United States, in research on ethnic minority and economically disadvantaged populations. In addition, there is now a greater awareness of disparities with respect to health care as well as educational and occupational opportunities experienced by many ethnic minority and economically disadvantaged groups than in the past. For these reasons, we think this volume is timely. Furthermore, on the basis of our individual and collective histories of conducting research with ethnic minority and economically disadvantaged populations, we believe that our experiences in dealing with the associated methodological challenges put us in a position to provide an initial volume on this topic. Perhaps most relevant are our experiences in maintaining a longitudinal and representative sample of Mexican American participants, many of whom reside in low-income communities. Hence, the methodological challenges and the best practices for addressing these challenges that are described in this volume are based, wherever possible, on the empirical literature and on our research experiences and attempts to address these challenges as we experienced them.

This volume is intended for social scientists interested in conducting research with ethnic minority and economically disadvantaged populations. Although we come to this subject with a background in psychological research, and although some of the examples we cite involve measures of psychological constructs, the methodological challenges and best practices we discuss are applicable to most social sciences. Many, if not all, of these methodological challenges and best practices apply to broader forms of cross-cultural and cross-group research efforts. Furthermore, although our examples most often involve Latino populations because of our personal research experiences and the relatively little published information about methodological details in research with other groups, these methodological challenges and best practices apply to a wide range of ethnic minority and economically disadvantaged populations.

This book is not intended to be an extensive volume on research methods in general but an extension for readers with a broader background in research methods or a supplement to a general text on research methods. Furthermore, although many, if not most, of the research methods issues we discuss may apply to broader forms of cross-cultural and cross-group research efforts, we have chosen to focus on ethnic minority and economically disadvantaged groups within the United States. We made this decision because the U.S. population has been changing, and is continuing to change, in relatively dramatic ways. The ethnic minority and economically disadvantaged populations within the United States have become very large. Indeed, many, if not most, of the individuals in many of our largest cities are ethnic minority persons and/or economically disadvantaged. This dramatically changing nature of the U.S. population is in part responsible for the burgeoning interest in research on ethnic minority and economically disadvantaged populations. We believe that addressing these issues is critical if we are going to develop a better understanding of the role of ethnic and economic diversity in many of the challenges facing society, families, and individuals today and to expand social and psychological theories to apply to these often-neglected populations.

These methodological challenges may appear daunting to some readers and may lead them to wonder if a career studying these populations is really for them. We would urge readers who come to this conclusion to reconsider their point of view. Given the blossoming interest in research on ethnic minority and economically disadvantaged populations, an awareness of these methodological challenges and best practices may represent substantial opportunities to contribute to this literature in a way that may make an important difference in our understanding of processes in psychology and other social sciences. Each of the authors of this volume has managed to develop a rewarding career out of our interests in studying these populations, and along the way we also have encountered many colleagues and graduate students interested in studying these populations. Furthermore, in pursuing these research interests, we have confronted and tried to address some of the methodological challenges and identify the best practices for addressing these challenges. Hence, some of our research has been distinctly methodological in nature. We believe that it is generally best to embed methodological research within studies of broad psychological and social science substantive issues and processes. We hope that others will find our discussion of the relatively unique methodological challenges associated with studying ethnic minority and economically disadvantaged populations practically useful, will embed the investigation of methodological issues within their own research, and ultimately will improve on our best practice suggestions.

In chapter 1, we discuss the goals of this volume with regard to the future of research on ethnic minority and economically disadvantaged populations as well as our desire to provide summaries of the best practice approaches for dealing with some of the relatively unique methodological issues researchers in this area face. We discuss the current and changing nature of the ethnic and economically disadvantaged populations of the United States. We also describe the four basic types of research designs commonly used to study these populations, with a focus on the challenges associated with the use of each type of research design.

In chapter 2, we discuss sampling, recruitment, and retention issues, including the importance of representative sampling and the implications of ethnic and economic diversity for representative sampling. For example, if one takes a relatively broad perspective on what constitutes an ethnic group (e.g., when studying Latinos or Asian Americans), representative sampling creates challenges in terms of ensuring the appropriate representativeness of persons from each country of origin that is considered a part of that broader perspective. Similarly, representative sampling creates challenges associated with the within-group diversity created by differing levels of connection to the mainstream society when one takes a relatively broad perspective on what constitutes an ethnic group (e.g., when studying Latinos or Asian Americans) or when one takes a narrower perspective (e.g., when studying Mexican Americans or Chinese Americans). The confounding of an individual's economic resource base with ethnicity creates additional sampling challenges. In addition to discussing these issues in chapter 2, we present strategies for selecting, recruiting, and retaining representative samples in cross-group comparative designs, within-group designs, national sample designs, and inadvertently diverse designs that include ethnic minority and economically disadvantaged participants.

In chapter 3, we discuss the ethical issues associated with examining ethnic minority and economically disadvantaged samples. Historical events demonstrate that ethical issues and legal protections of research participants are of particular concern when research includes or focuses on these populations. Ethnic minorities have consistently been underrepresented in research from which they might benefit (e.g., medical research, research to guide policy or interventions). Although changes in federal policies have improved the situation, concerns remain. Economically disadvantaged and ethnic minority groups have been exploited and abused in research (e.g., the use of deliberate deception, active and passive denial of access to medical care, inadequate informed-consent procedures). Although some scholars dismiss past abuses of the rights of these populations in research as historical anomalies, more recent research suggests that considerable room for improvement remains. Researchers may have difficulty conveying basic concepts and rights contained in informed-consent forms (e.g., research vs. intervention or therapy, the right to skip questions or stop participating in a study without penalty) because of differences in power or status between researchers and ethnic minority and economically disadvantaged populations; cultural beliefs about appropriate or ideal power relations among many immigrant populations; challenges of communicating with persons with different reading levels, which are more common among these groups; and challenges in communicating concepts such as freedom of choice to persons who have immigrated from countries where there may be little individual freedom. Researchers need to be aware of these challenges and of strategies for communicating these ideas more clearly to targeted populations. In this chapter, we provide a brief history of ethical problems in research experienced by ethnic minority or economically disadvantaged populations, a discussion of the ethical issues that are more common in research with these populations, and provide ethical guidelines for future research with these groups.

In chapter 4, we discuss the measurement issues associated with examining ethnic minority and economically disadvantaged samples in cross-group comparative designs, within-group designs, national sample designs, and inadvertently diverse designs. We discuss the basics of

measurement and the measurement implications when samples are ethnically or linguistically diverse and/or economically disadvantaged. The
need for representative samples, regardless of whether one takes a relatively broad perspective or a more narrow perspective on what constitutes
an ethnic group, creates challenges for measurement that are problematic
in each of these types of research designs. For example, if measures of target constructs do not comparably assess the respective underlying constructs equivalently across different ethnic or economic groups, then
observed differences or similarities may be a function of measurement
issues instead of a reflection of actual ethnic minority or economic group
differences in the underlying constructs. We describe strategies for developing culturally sensitive or culturally appropriate measures, including
the use of qualitative methods. We also discuss the implications of ethnic
and economic diversity for making scientific inferences regarding both
mean-level differences and similarities and differences and similarities in
the relations among psychological constructs across groups. In chapter 4,
we also describe the importance of measurement equivalence and the relation between measurement equivalence and factorial invariance, and we
describe the analytical methods available to make scientific inferences
regarding measurement equivalence and factorial invariance.

In chapter 5, we discuss translation issues and describe how the
need for representative samples of ethnic minority and economically
disadvantaged populations creates challenges that require measures to
be administered in multiple languages. We discuss the linkages between
the quality of the translation of measures and the credibility of the scientific inferences based on the use of these translated measures.
Although there have been substantial developments in the recommended procedures for translating measures and broader research protocol materials, we suggest that there are still reasons that these
procedures can fail us in creating equivalent measures across languages.
We suggest that the current state-of-the-art methods used to evaluate
the translation of measures are inadequate and that the translation of
measures be approached as a special case of evaluating measurement
equivalence. That is, we contend that at a minimum, researchers should
conduct the types of analyses designed to assess cross-group measure-

ment equivalence to also evaluate the degree of cross-language measurement equivalence for translated measures. Finally, we discuss translation issues associated with examining ethnic minority and economically disadvantaged samples in cross-group comparative designs, within-group designs, national sample designs, and inadvertently diverse designs, and we end the chapter with a discussion of recommendations for best practices.

In chapter 6, we discuss the implications of research findings for applied or translational research with ethnic minority and economically disadvantaged samples. The field of preventive intervention science currently is limited with regard to prevention efforts with ethnic minority or economically disadvantaged populations. Most preventive interventions are designed without attention to cultural differences or diversity in socioeconomic class, and thus there is a need to adapt, develop, and test approaches with diverse populations that hold promise as preventive interventions. Cultural competency is an important aspect of this process. Researchers must consider adaptations that are culturally relevant and attractive to the groups in question and consider culturally appropriate methods of delivering these programs. We review the state of the field with regard to preventive intervention research with ethnic minority and economically disadvantaged populations, discuss the need to increase prevention efforts with diverse populations, present culturally competent strategies for adapting existing programs to diverse groups, and provide an overview of challenges inherent in such adaptations. We offer best practice recommendations for how to create a culturally/economically adapted prevention/intervention program.

Much of our understanding of these best practice approaches to addressing the methodological challenges associated with studying ethnic minority and economically disadvantaged populations was acquired through interactions with collaborating colleagues. These colleagues deserve much of the credit for useful ideas we present in this volume. We greatly appreciate our collaborations with the following faculty, postdoctoral fellows, and graduate student colleagues: Edna Alfaro, Janette Beals, Mayra Bámaca, Martha E. Bernal, Ginger Lockhart Burrell, Carlos O. Calderón, Gustavo Carlo, Maria Elena De Anda, Khanh T. Dinh, Shiying Deng,

Juliana Deardorff, Larry Dumka, Camille Garza, Nancy A. Gonzales, Nancy Hill, Ryan P. Jacobson, Liliana Lengua, Vera A. Lopez, Freda Liu, Michelle Little, Sandra H. Losoya, Rajni L. Nair, Armando Pina, Hazel Prelow, Rae Jean Proescholdbell, Leticia Reyes, Sonia Y. Ruiz, Jenn-Yun Tein, Marisela Torres, Kimberly Updegraff, Jaimee Virgo, Scott Weaver, Rebecca M. B. White, and Jennifer Wood. We also thank Kristen Judd for her editorial assistance as well as Tyler Aune and the anonymous reviewers for their valuable suggestions. Finally, we are most grateful to all the families who have participated in our research and to our community partners who have given us terrific advice and made much of our research possible; we have learned so much from their selflessness and generosity, and we hope this book accurately reflects the many lessons they have taught us.

Studying Ethnic Minority and Economically Disadvantaged Populations

Methodological Challenges and Best Practices

1

Introduction to Studying Ethnic Minority and Economically Disadvantaged Populations

This book is designed to serve as a supplement to standard research methods texts by providing some guidance regarding the unique challenges researchers face in studying ethnic minority and economically disadvantaged populations. Too often, standard methods texts spend little time discussing the additional challenges involved in conducting high-quality research with these populations, despite the fact that most procedures were developed in the process of conducting research with middle-class European American samples. Our intention is for readers to gain an understanding of the methodological challenges researchers have faced when studying diverse populations, learn best practices for conducting such research, and develop an informed perspective that will facilitate their ability to critically evaluate research conducted with ethnic minority and/or economically disadvantaged populations. We hope that researchers and students will benefit by using this book as a resource that describes these challenges and that the best practice guidance we provide helps them address these challenges and move social science research forward.

There has been a slow but steady growth in the research base on ethnic minority and economically disadvantaged populations in the United States for the past couple of decades (see Quintana et al., 2006; Roosa, Deng, Nair, & Burrell, 2005; Spencer & McLoyd, 1990). However, the growth in this research base has not kept pace with the dynamic changes in the U.S. population over the same time period. That is, despite the changing demographic trends in the United States, much of the current research continues to underrepresent ethnic minority and economically disadvantaged populations or overrepresent selected subgroups of these populations (e.g., inner-city residents, English-speaking immigrants; see L. Case & Smith, 2000; Cauce, Ryan, & Grove, 1998; Flaskerud & Nyamathi, 2000).

Even though ethnic minority and economically disadvantaged populations have been underrepresented in the research literature, decades of research have shown the importance of identifying and understanding differences in psychological and social science processes that occur in different cultural groups or different social classes (e.g., Baldwin, Baldwin, & Cole, 1990; Rogoff, 2003). Cultural differences between ethnic groups are reflected in differing values that shape parenting goals and how children are socialized as well as how groups judge whether individuals are successful (e.g., Rogoff, 2003; Roosa, Morgan-Lopez, Cree, & Specter, 2002). Although methods of dealing with poverty, such as the use of and reliance on the extended family, may appear similar across cultures at a superficial level, they are often quite different in structure and management across cultural groups (e.g., Harrison, Wilson, Pine, Chan, & Buriel, 1990). Within the United States, parenting practices vary among ethnic and racial groups, but more important than mean-level differences are the differences in the relations between specific parenting practices and outcomes for children across groups (Broman, Reckase, & Freedman-Doan, 2006; Ruiz, Roosa, & Gonzales, 2002). Predictors of substance use among adolescents differ across racial and ethnic groups (Bryant, Schulenberg, O'Malley, Bachman, & Johnston, 2003). Similarly, income differences between families, even families from the same ethnic or racial group, also are related to both mean-level differences in specific parenting practices and to differing relations between parenting practices and child outcomes. For example, Baldwin et al. (1990) showed that children of low-income African American families in high-risk communities were more likely to be successful (i.e., have a high level of cognitive competence) if parents were highly restrictive and used more severe punishment, parenting approaches that were ineffective or counterproductive in middle-income African American families. This small sample of results from a variety of studies over the past 2 decades and many more like them, combined with the increasing diversity of the U.S. population, have convinced us that many more social scientists will likely begin conducting research with ethnic minority and economically disadvantaged groups with three goals in mind: to (a) correct errors in theories that were developed without the benefit of information about these populations, (b) provide a scientific foundation for more effective social services as well as intervention and prevention programs, and (c) guide the development of more inclusive and effective public policies.

There may be several reasons for the historical underrepresentation of ethnic minority and economically disadvantaged populations in the research literature. One possibility is that many researchers may have avoided studying these populations because of the associated challenges that we describe in this book. It also is possible that common practices by journal editors and grant review panels supported this underrepresentation. The reviewers for the major journals and funding agencies may not have fully appreciated the efforts necessary to address the demands associated with the study of ethnic minority and economically disadvantaged populations. This, in turn, may have led researchers to avoid such research endeavors or to the diversion of research on ethnic minority and economically disadvantaged populations to specialty journals, which often are considered of a lower status compared with major journals. Indeed, there has been a trend toward the development of specialty journals or the publication of special issues of the major journals as outlets for research on ethnic minority and economically disadvantaged populations. Some researchers feel that although the editors of major journals and funding agencies ascribe to the desire for submissions focused on these populations, the methodological challenges associated with conducting such research often become the basis for negative publication or funding decisions. Some also feel that diversion to publication in specialty journals or special issues has assigned this research to a second-class status. That is, journal editors and funding agencies may not have adequately credited researchers who study these populations for addressing the associated methodological challenges. Another possibility is that some researchers who study ethnic minority and economically disadvantaged populations have not adequately made a case for the importance of their research. We have seen this in submissions to journals or funding agencies that essentially argue that it is important to study some effect in a particular ethnic or economic population simply because it has not been demonstrated in such a population in the previous literature. Such a justification does not consider the unique nature of the ethnic or economic population or the potential commonalities these populations share with the more typical populations represented in the major journals. Such a justification is not likely to appear sufficiently important to warrant publication in the major journals or funding from granting agencies. Instead, although replications of studies of particular theoretical relations with samples that are not middle class and European American are justifiable in many cases, researchers need to make a strong case a priori for why results would be expected to differ, or not differ, for a particular ethnic group or for economically disadvantaged people and why answering the research question is of substantive concern for the field and, ultimately, for advancing science.

Even in the light of this underrepresentation, we and many other scholars have made a career out of research focused on the unique aspects, or common aspects, of ethnic minority and economically disadvantaged populations. Furthermore, there appears to be a shifting interest toward research on these populations. Perhaps this increasing interest is a function of the changes in the nature of the population of the United States. Indeed, we have reached the point at which many, if not most, of the individuals in the largest U.S. cities, where many of the major research universities are located, are members of ethnic minority groups and/or are economically disadvantaged. Researchers are beginning to discover that our understanding of some important psychological or social science processes may not generalize to ethnic minority and economically disadvantaged populations. They also are increasingly questioning whether the processes they are studying operate in the same manner in ethnic minority and economically disadvantaged populations, and they are discovering that their sampling strategies are leading them to encounter more ethnic minority and economically disadvantaged participants in their research simply because of changing population demographics. The changing population demographics of the United States and much of the rest of the world appear to be leading to a greater appreciation for research focused on ethnic minority and economically disadvantaged populations. It is also very likely that the interest in research including participants from these populations will continue to accelerate and that this interest will result in more researchers designing studies that involve sampling and assessments of these populations. These research interests, and the desire to make sound scientific inferences based on data obtained from these diverse populations, will ultimately require that researchers interested in this area of study, especially novice ones, address methodological issues that they may not have been dealt with in the past. Attending to these methodological issues will be critical if we are going to develop a better understanding of the role of ethnic and economic diversity in psychological and social processes. Hence, this may be an ideal time not only for young scientists who are beginning a career studying ethnic minority and economically disadvantaged populations but also for established scholars who are increasingly considering issues related to ethnicity and economic disadvantage in their research.

We hope that this book will create a greater appreciation for the challenges associated with studying ethnic minority and economically disadvantaged populations. Furthermore, we provide what we consider to be best practice recommendations for dealing with these challenges. However, we hope that researchers, journal editors, and funding agencies understand that the research context often makes full compliance with these best practice recommendations impossible and that the best one can do is to make incremental approximations to these recommendations. Nevertheless, we hope that our discussion and recommendations will move social science researchers forward in their understanding of ethnic minority and economically disadvantaged populations, including an increased emphasis on developing improved methods for research with these populations.

Many of the recommendations we make in this book are based on our own experiences over many years in conducting research with ethnic minority and economically disadvantaged populations, in particular Latino populations. Where possible, we have incorporated the empirical evidence regarding the importance of these methodological issues and the utility of our recommendations. Unfortunately, there is relatively little published empirical research related to many of these issues. Hence, one of the major goals of this volume is to identify methodological topics that we hope others will deem deserving of empirical research aimed at improving methods for research with ethnic minority and economically disadvantaged populations. In addition, we believe that such methodologically driven research has the potential to enhance our understanding of the role of ethnicity and economic disadvantage in social science processes, and we hope that a discussion of these challenges will lead to a greater appreciation on behalf of editorial boards and review panels.

The research focusing on ethnic diversity in the United States generally characterizes this diversity in one of three ways. The first includes studies of groups of individuals within the United States with family origins in vastly different regions of the world. Hence, some researchers may study pan-ethnic groups such as Latinos, African Americans, Asian Americans, American Indians, or European Americans. These pan-ethnic studies sample participants from multiple countries of origin (e.g., Mexican Americans, Cuban Americans, Guatemalans, and Colombians) or Indian tribes but who are considered to have some general similarity. The second type of diversity research studies groups within a particular pan-ethnic group, with a focus on individuals from specific countries of origin. For example, although some researchers study Latinos (i.e., a pan-ethnic group), others study a subset of the Latino population from a single country of origin, such as Mexican Americans. Similarly, although some researchers study pan-ethnic American Indians, others study Cherokee Indians. The third and final type of diversity research includes studies of groups of individuals within a more specific ethnic group, focusing on these individuals' degree of connection to that specific ethnic group and/or the mainstream culture. For example, although some researchers may study Mexican Americans, others may study recent immigrants from Mexico. Still other researchers may study individuals who vary in regard to, for example, generation of family immigration from Mexico, region of immigration from within Mexico, *enculturation* (i.e., the process of socialization and adaptation to the ethnic culture) among Mexican Americans, *acculturation* levels (i.e., the process of adaptation to the mainstream culture of the United States) among Mexican Americans, or the *ethnic identity* (i.e., sense of belonging or identity achievement) of Mexican Americans.[1]

---

[1]We do not mean to imply that the mainstream culture is homogeneous. Indeed, the behaviors, attitudes, and values of the mainstream culture are derived from the cultural elements that immigrants brought to the United States. Historically, however, these behaviors, attitudes, and values have been based primarily on immigrants from European countries.

Much of the research that focuses on economically disadvantaged populations in the United States does not acknowledge within-group diversity but instead focuses on individuals who are living in poverty compared with those who are not living in poverty. However, research acknowledging the within-group diversity among economically disadvantaged populations in the United States generally focuses on comparisons between subgroups living at different levels of poverty (e.g., the very poor, those living on incomes below 50% of the federal poverty level, those living on incomes from 51% to 100% of the poverty threshold; Brooks-Gunn, Klebanov, Liaw, & Duncan, 1995) or variations in adaptation to poverty (e.g., Conger & Conger, 2002; Werner & Smith, 1992). Still other research focuses on comparisons between members of different ethnic groups living in poverty, between single- and two-parent families living in poverty, and between families in poverty living in rural and urban areas (Amato & Zuo, 1992; Cunradi, Caetano, Clark, & Shafer, 2000; McLanahan, 1985).

POPULATION CHARACTERISTICS AND CHANGE

From 1990 through 2000, the United States experienced a dramatic total population increase of 32.7 million (U.S. Census Bureau, 2001c). This was the largest numerical increase during any 10-year span in American history, and it occurred because of net population gains associated with immigration (compared with migration from the United States to other countries) and birth rates (compared with death rates). The West and South experienced the most growth, and the Midwest and Northeast had minimal growth. The second-largest increase in the U.S. population (28.0 million; U.S. Census Bureau, 2001c), in contrast, occurred between 1950 and 1960 and was largely the result of the post–World War II baby boom.

In this book, we define *ethnic minorities* as those persons whose families have a relatively recent origin from outside the United States (e.g., Hmong Americans) and/or who represent a relatively small proportion of the overall population (e.g., Navajo). Although the United States is a nation of immigrants, there is substantial variability in the degree to which the families with histories in other countries have become embedded in the mainstream culture. Because of this, we have chosen to focus on several select pan-ethnic groups, including Latinos, African Americans, and Asian Americans. In addition, American Indians have become an ethnic minority group because of the great population change that has occurred since the United States was formally established. Although we have chosen to focus mostly on four pan-ethnic groups in this volume, the methodological challenges and best practices we describe likely apply to other minority groups as well. For example, these challenges may be even more difficult to address if one were interested in studying the American Amish population. Understanding the nature of the population dynamics surrounding these groups is essential for understanding the utility of research on these ethnic minority groups and for understanding why researchers are going to increasingly be exposed to the challenges associated with studying these populations.

Latinos

The record-breaking recent population growth of the United States varied not only by region but also, greatly, by ethnicity. The Latino[2] population increased by 57.9%, from 22.4 million in 1990 to 35.3 million in 2000, compared with an increase of 13.2% for the total U.S. population (U.S. Census Bureau, 2001b). In 2000, Latinos made up 12.5% of the U.S. population, with persons of Mexican origin being the largest Latino group, representing 59.3% of the Latino population, or 7.4% of the U.S. population (U.S. Census Bureau, 2004c). The Latino population also grew by 53% (7 times faster than the rest of the national population) in the 1980s and by 61% in the 1970s (U.S. Census Bureau, 1993c). The primary factors contributing to this tremendous growth in the Latino population are a higher birth rate than the rest of the U.S. population and immigration from Mexico, the Caribbean, and Central and South America.

Furthermore, the Latino population is on average younger and economically more disadvantaged than the rest of the U.S. population (U.S.

---

[2]Although the terms *Latino* and *Hispanic* are occasionally used to refer to slightly different groups, in general both are used to refer to all persons from, or with family origins from, Latin America. We use the term *Latino* exclusively throughout this book.

Census Bureau, 2004c). In 2000, the median age for Latinos was 26 years, compared with 35.4 years for the United States as a whole. The median reported income for Latino families in 1999 was $34,400, compared with $50,000 for all U.S. families. Among the Latino population, 22.6% lived in poverty, compared with 12.4% of the total population. The proportion of Latinos under age 18 years who were living in poverty in 1999 was higher than the proportion among most other minorities in the United States (U.S. Census Bureau, 2004c). Latinos are more likely than the general population to be living in married-couple households (55.1% vs. 52.5 %), but 17.3% live in a household headed only by a female, and 8.3% live in a household headed only by a male (U.S. Census Bureau, 2004c). Latinos are the majority population group in several large cities, including East Los Angeles, California (98.6% of the population); Laredo, Texas (94.1%); Hialeah, Florida (90.3%); and Miami, Florida (65.8%; U.S. Census Bureau, 2001b). Furthermore, Los Angeles, Houston, Chicago, San Antonio, and Phoenix have the largest Mexican American populations among major U.S. cities (U.S. Census Bureau, 2001b).

There are two very important ways in which the Latino population is diverse, particularly when compared with the U.S. population in general. First, Latinos in the United States come from a broad range of countries of origin. The countries or regions of origin of the families of these individuals are as follows: Mexico for nearly 21 million (7.4% of the U.S. population), Puerto Rico for more than 3.4 million (1.2%), Cuba for nearly 1.3 million (0.4%), Central America for more than 1.8 million (0.6%), South America for nearly 1.5 million (0.5%), and the Dominican Republic for more than three quarters of a million (0.3%). Furthermore, the recent growth in these Latino populations is substantial (U.S. Census Bureau, 2001b). From 1990 to 2000 the estimated growth rates by country of origin were as follows: 52.9% for Mexican Americans (i.e., individuals of Mexican origin), 24.9% for Puerto Ricans, 18.9% for Cuban Americans, and 96.9% for Latinos who reported other countries of origin. Although these groups are all considered Latino, they come from cultures that are discernibly different in some important aspects (e.g., variations in Spanish spoken, the legal status of their immigrants in the United States, cultural variations).

Second, Latinos in the United States have a broad range of exposure to the mainstream U.S. culture and their own ethnic cultures. For example, 53% of the increases in the Latino population just described are the result of immigration to the United States (U.S. Census Bureau, 2001b). The remaining 47% of the increases are the result of the difference between birth and death rates among Latinos whose families have been in the United States for more than one generation. Regardless of their generation of immigration to the United States, Latinos experience a process of dual cultural adaptation (see Gonzales, Fabrett, & Knight, in press) that is inherent in the processes of acculturation and enculturation. Variations in family histories, including differences in the circumstances or reasons leading to their family's immigration to the United States (e.g., political upheavals, lack of educational opportunities, lack of employment opportunities), differences in the length of time (i.e., years and generations) their family has been in the United States, and differences in the nature of the communities in which these families reside (e.g., ethnic enclaves vs. more integrated communities), enhance the diversity in the Latino population of the United States. One very limited, but clear, indication of this diversity pertains to Latinos' language use and capabilities. In 2000, more than 75% of Latinos reported speaking a language other than English at home, with 99% of these persons reporting Spanish as the language spoken at home (U.S. Census Bureau, 2003, 2004c). Approximately 40% of all Latinos reported speaking English less than "very well" (U.S. Census Bureau, 2004c). Furthermore, there is considerable variability across Latino groups. For example, more than 90% of Dominicans and Central Americans reported speaking a language other than English at home, and 57% of Central Americans reported speaking English less than "very well," whereas only 26% of Puerto Ricans reported speaking English less than "very well" (U.S. Census Bureau, 2004c).

African Americans

African Americans also experienced a larger growth rate than the total population of the United States in the 1980s and 1990s. The African American population increased by 15.6%, from 30 million in 1990 to

34.7 million in 2000, making up 12.3% of the total population (U.S. Census Bureau, 2001a). The rate of growth for African Americans was not as dramatic as that of Latinos in the 1980s, but the African American population grew by 13%, 33% faster than the national rate (Bureau of the Census, 1993b). In 2000, the median age for African Americans was 30.4, compared with the national median of 35.4 (U.S. Census Bureau, 2005). In 1999, the median income of African American families was $33,300, compared with $50,000 reported by all U.S. families. Furthermore, twice as many African Americans reported living in poverty (25%) than other groups in the total U.S. population (12%; U.S. Census Bureau, 2005). African Americans are much less likely to be living in married-couple households compared with the general population (32% vs. 52.5 %); 30% live in a household headed only by a female, and just under 6% live in a household headed only by a male (U.S. Census Bureau, 2005). Hence, the percentage of households maintained by a female only is nearly three times the corresponding proportion of all households in the United States.

The African American population in the United States is also diverse. Although a large percentage (94%; U.S. Census Bureau, 2005) of these individuals were born in the United States, U.S. Census Bureau (2005) estimates indicate that in 2000, foreign-born African Americans hailed primarily from the Caribbean (60%), Africa (24%), and Central and South America (12%). Although these individuals are often considered members of the same ethnic minority group, they come from countries and cultures that are distinctly different. Because of variability in the length of time these individuals and their families have been in the United States and in the degree to which different communities in the United States may be supportive of African American cultures, these individuals are likely variable in their connection to the mainstream culture. The unique history of segregation and discrimination experienced by African Americans (e.g., Massey & Denton, 1987), largely because of slavery, and the nature of the impact African Americans have had on the mainstream culture of the United States, likely influences the nature of these individuals' connection to the mainstream culture. A majority of African Americans live in the South (U.S. Census Bureau, 2001a), and although there

has been considerable housing integration, continuing negative stereo-
types and discrimination may have limited the economic gains of African
Americans (e.g., Farley, 1997).

Asian Americans

The third largest ethnic minority population in the United States, that of
Asian Americans, has also experienced a larger increase in growth than the
total population. The Asian American population increased by 48%, from
6.9 million in 1990 to 10.2 million in 2000, making up 3.6% of the total
population (U.S. Census Bureau, 2002). The Asian American population
also grew by 99% in the 1980s (from 3.5 million to 6.9 million; U.S. Census
Bureau, 1993a). In 2000, the median age for Asian Americans was 33 years,
only 2 years younger than national median of 35. The median income for
Asian American families ($59,300) is more than $9,000 higher than the
median for all U.S. families ($50,000). Furthermore, the poverty rate for
Asian Americans (12.6%) is similar to that for the rest of the U.S. population
(12.4%: U.S. Census Bureau, 2004a). Asian Americans are more likely to be
living in married-couple households compared with the general population (60% vs. 52.5 %), 8.8% live in a household headed only by a female, and
4.5% live in a household headed only by a male (U.S. Census Bureau, 2004b).

Asian Americans in the United States also come from a broad range
of countries of origin (U.S. Census Bureau, 2004b): China for more than
2.8 million (1.02% of the U.S. population), the Philippine Islands for
nearly 2.4 million (0.85%), India for more than 1.8 million (0.66%),
Korea for more than 1.2 million (0.44%), Vietnam for more than 1.2 million (0.43%), Japan for nearly 1.2 million (0.41%), and at least six other
Asian countries for approximately 1.5 million (0.45%). Asian Americans
also have a variety of family histories, a wide variety of reasons for immi-
grating to the United States, differences in the length of time (i.e., years
and generations) their families have been in the United States, and differences in the nature of the communities in which their families reside.
Asian Americans come from cultures that vary considerably, and they differ in their connection (e.g., acculturation and enculturation status) to the
mainstream and ethnic cultures in important ways.

As with Latinos, English is not the predominant language spoken in Asian American homes. Of the 9.5 million Asians aged 5 and over, 79% speak a language other than English at home, and about 40% speak English less than "very well" (U.S. Census Bureau, 2003, 2004b). Furthermore, there is considerable variability across Asian American groups (U.S. Census Bureau, 2004b). For example, the proportion of Asian Americans who speak a language other than English at home ranged from 47% for Japanese Americans to 96% for Hmong Americans. More than 90% of Cambodians, Hmong, Laotians, Pakistanis, and Vietnamese Americans reported speaking a language other than English at home. Japanese Americans were the only Asian Americans among whom more than 50% who reported speaking only English at home. Vietnamese Americans had the highest proportion (62%) who reported speaking English less than "very well." In most Latin American countries, Spanish is the official language, and indigenous languages are relatively rare; that is, Latino immigrants generally share a somewhat common language despite local variations in usage. In contrast, each Asian country has an official language not shared by other countries, and almost all have multiple indigenous languages. This diversity in spoken language has important implications for research practices that focus on Asian Americans.

Geographical Diversity

Four states (California, Hawaii, New Mexico, and Texas) and the District of Columbia now have more ethnic minority residents than European American residents. Members of ethnic minority groups represent approximately 77% of the resident population in Hawaii, 70% in the District of Columbia, 57% in New Mexico, 56% in California, and more than 50% in Texas (U.S. Census Bureau, 2001b, 2001c). Members of ethnic minority groups represent approximately 40% of the statewide populations in five additional states (Arizona, Georgia, Maryland, Mississippi, and New York). Ethnic minorities are now the majority in almost one third of the most populous counties and in nearly 10% of all counties in the United States (S. Roberts, 2007). Furthermore, the U.S. Census Bureau

(2004a) predicted that ethnic minorities will represent half of the U.S. total population sometime around the year 2050.

Economic Diversity

In 2000, approximately 31.1 million people in the United States reported living in poverty (incomes below the federal poverty line; U.S. Census Bureau, 2001d). Between 2001 and 2005, the total national poverty rate increased to 37 million people, approximately 12.6% of the total U.S. population (U.S. Census Bureau, 2006). It is estimated that 25% of all children in the United States are living in poverty (Carnegie Task Force, 1994) and that a vast majority of these children are living in families headed by a single mother (U.S. Census Bureau, 1995).

Many African Americans and Latinos, some subgroups of Asian Americans, and many of the members of other ethnic minority groups (e.g., American Indians) residing in the United States are also overrepresented in the portion of the population that is economically disadvantaged. The U.S. Census Bureau (2007) indicated that of all individuals living in poverty, 87.4% were born in the United States, 4.9% were foreign-born naturalized citizens, and 7.7% were foreign born but not U.S. citizens. Although there is some variability by gender and nativity, African Americans, American Indians, Latinos, and some Asian populations are underrepresented among individuals who complete a high school or college education, whereas many Asian American groups and European Americans are overrepresented (Farley, 1997). The economic disparity among ethnic minority or racial groups is in part a function of the relative proportion of single-parent households headed by a female (Farley, 1997). This overlap of ethnic minority status and low-income populations represents a major challenge for researchers; in many research designs, ethnicity and social class or income are highly confounded.

Although ethnic minority status is sometimes confounded with economically disadvantaged status, this is not always the case. In this volume, we describe the methodological challenges and best practices associated with studying ethnic minority and economically disadvantaged populations. When these two status variables are confounded, the methodological challenges and associated best practices are based on being both an ethnic minority and being economically challenged. When one is studying members of an ethnic minority group who are not economically disadvantaged, then the methodological challenges and associated best practices are a function of the target population's ethnic minority status. When one is studying economically disadvantaged individuals who are not members of an ethnic minority group (e.g., European Americans living in poverty), then the methodological challenges and associated best practices are a function of the target population's low socioeconomic status.

FOUR COMMON RESEARCH DESIGNS

Although there are many specific types of research designs that have included samples from ethnic minority and economically disadvantaged populations, for our purposes we categorize these designs into four types: (a) *cross-group comparative designs,* (b) *within-group designs,* (c) *national sample designs,* and (d) *inadvertently diverse designs.* Researchers who use these four types of designs generally start out with quite different research goals and thus frequently make quite different methodological decisions that have important implications for the scientific conclusions that can be drawn. Furthermore, although researchers who use these designs may start out with specific research goals, methodological decisions and limitations may limit the degree to which these original goals are achievable. Hence, it is important to understand the differing original goals associated with these types of research designs and the methodological issues associated with the ways in which ethnic minority and economically disadvantaged populations are included, because these may influence the accuracy of the scientific conclusions regarding the role of ethnicity or economic class in the psychological or social science processes under investigation.

Cross-Group Comparative Designs

Researchers using cross-group comparative designs generally want to make a comparative judgment about the relative nature of two or more ethnic or economic groups. These comparisons may be of mean levels on some psychological or social science construct or of the relations between two or more constructs. For example, R. E. Roberts, Roberts, and Chen (1997) compared the prevalence of adolescent depression among nine ethnic groups to determine whether members of specific ethnic groups were at elevated risk for depression. Similarly, on the basis of previous work that had identified Mexican Americans to be at increased risk for depressive symptoms, Joiner, Perez, Wagner, Berenson, and Marquina (2001) compared Mexican American adolescents' levels of depressive symptoms with those of African American, European American, Puerto Rican, and American Indian adolescents. In cross-group comparative designs, the hypotheses driving the research may emphasize either similarity or difference across ethnic or economic groups. For example, whereas R. E. Roberts et al. were primarily interested in exploring whether rates of depression were similar or different across ethnic groups, Joiner et al. expected Mexican Americans to have significantly higher levels of depressive symptomatology, perhaps because of the contexts in which they live.

Regardless of the nature of the specific comparative hypotheses, researchers must strive to sample each ethnic minority or economic group representatively and to assess or measure the relevant construct or constructs equivalently in each group (we discuss these issues further later in this volume). That is, any deviation from representative sampling, or any difference across ethnic minority or economic groups in the degree of representativeness of the sample, creates a methodological confound and the possibility of an alternative explanation of any observed difference or similarity across groups. Similarly, any difference in the accuracy of measurement of the relevant constructs also creates a methodological confound and the possibility of an alternative explanation of any observed difference or similarity across groups. Furthermore, given that a substantial segment of several of these ethnic populations may not be fluent in English, the translation of measures and the task of ensuring the equivalence of those translations become essential.

Within-Group Designs

Researchers using within-group designs generally want to examine psychological or social science processes within a specific ethnic or economic group. The impetus for this may be that the processes being examined have been identified in other ethnic or economic groups and the researcher is interested in the generalizability of findings from the research on other ethnic minority or economic groups to the ethnic minority or economic group of interest. For example, the rationale for the Tuskegee study of syphilis in the Black male was to determine whether the disease process would be the same as that documented in a preceding study in Norway with White males (Jones, 1981). Alternatively, the psychological or social science issue or process of interest may be unique to a particular ethnic minority or economic group and be based on the theoretical and empirical understanding of the nature of this specific group. For example, because findings have indicated that suicide attempt rates are highest among Latina adolescents, researchers developed a conceptual model that focused on the unique sociocultural processes of suicide attempts for Latinas (Zayas, Lester, Cabassa, & Fortuna, 2005). Variables such as familism, acculturative stress, and migration are central to the model and are considered unique to this particular population and essential to understanding this process among members of this specific group.

Regardless of the nature of the specific within-group hypotheses, researchers must strive to sample the ethnic minority or economic group of interest representatively and to accurately assess or measure the relevant construct or constructs in that group. Although this sounds relatively straightforward from a methodological perspective, that is not always the case. Given the breadth of the definition of what constitutes an ethnic or economic group, and the heterogeneity within such groups, representative sampling and accurate measurement can be very challenging. Research with American Indians represents an extreme example of the difficulties researchers can face when sampling within a pan-ethnic group. For example, Clifton (1989) described how the number of American Indian and Alaska Native persons in the United States varies systematically with changes in the benefits associated with being a member of these ethnic groups. The U.S. Department of Education (1982, cited in Norton & Manson, 1996) identified nearly 70 different operational definitions of *American Indian* or *Alaska Native.* Furthermore, Norton and Manson (1996) indicated that there are more than 250 federally recognized tribes,

209 Alaska Native villages, 65 communities that have tribal status within the state in which they are located but are unrecognized by the federal government, and several dozen American Indian and Alaska Native communities that have not been formally recognized. Hence, researchers focusing on American Indians must deal with the very broad range of definitions of the tribal membership and a tremendous range of different tribal cultures. This degree of diversity can make representative sampling at the pan-ethnic level almost impossible, and it can introduce significant variability into psychological or social science processes, both of which can lead researchers to draw inaccurate conclusions.

Some researchers have argued that they used a within-group design even though they defined the group at a level that allows members to be diverse in both country/culture of origin and their degree of connection/adaptation to the mainstream. The most common examples of such pan-ethnic research include studies of Asians, Latinos, or American Indians that either overlook differences in national origins, cultural traditions, and language or that treat such differences as though they were trivial. In doing this, researchers are assuming that there is some common characteristic or experience among all members of these broadly defined groups that justifies defining them as members of a single group. We think it is extremely difficult to make a cogent argument that Chinese immigrants are highly similar to Hmong immigrants, or that people with backgrounds from the Dominican Republic are similar to people with Cuban backgrounds, or that members of the Cherokee Nation are similar to Alaska Natives. Hence, in studies of broadly defined pan-ethnic groups researchers need to be concerned with the representativeness of the participant sampling from each country of origin or tribal group if those researchers want to make scientific inferences about such a broadly defined ethnic group. These researchers also need to be concerned about the equivalence of the assessments or measurements of the construct or constructs of interest across participants from different countries of origin in general, but this concern becomes even more acute when assessment is conducted in differing languages as well (Umaña-Taylor & Fine, 2001). Similarly, studies of a select socioeconomic status group need to be concerned with the representativeness of sampling of the diverse participants within that group and with the equivalence of measures across this diversity. Any deviation in representativeness of sampling or equivalence in the measurement of constructs may limit the accuracy of scientific inferences either by biasing observed means on the constructs of interest or by biasing the observed relations among constructs.

Researchers examining within-group hypotheses in a more narrowly defined specific ethnic group (e.g., Hmong Americans) need to be aware that even these groups are more diverse and less homogeneous than is often assumed. For example, members of the Mexican American or Chinese American populations, or any other cultural group that has a history of immigration (voluntary or forced), differ in their degree of adaptation or connection to the mainstream culture of the United States. This diversity is often studied under the rubric of *acculturation* (or *acculturation and enculturation*), *biculturalism,* or *ethnic identity* (e.g., M. E. Bernal & Knight, 1993; Berry, 2006; Gonzales, Knight, Morgan-Lopez, Saenz, & Sirolli, 2002; Tsai, Chentsova-Dutton, & Wong, 2002).

Mexican Americans, Chinese Americans, and members of most other ethnic and economic groups are also diverse in their fluency with the English language. Hence, diversity exists even within a more narrowly defined ethnic group, and the methodological demands associated with sampling and measurement noted among more broadly defined ethnic groups applies equally well among more narrowly defined ethnic groups. Indeed, these difficulties may be quite serious and relatively intractable even within a narrowly defined ethnic group. For example, language fluency or degree of adaptation to the mainstream U.S. culture may affect the likelihood that specific individuals within a narrowly defined ethnic minority or economic group may be identified for participation, or willing to participate, in research endeavors.

National Sample Designs

Researchers using national sample designs generally want to examine psychological or social science processes in a sample that is as representative as possible of the U.S. population. Because these types of research designs are usually time consuming and expensive, the relatively high resource demands often lead research teams to make decisions that limit the degree to which the resulting data sets can accurately address comparative or within-group research questions. That is, although the samples in these types of designs may be reasonably representative of the broader U.S. population, select subsamples may not be highly representative of the corresponding subpopulations. Nevertheless, because these types of research designs often have large samples, some researchers use the resulting data sets to try to make comparisons across ethnic minority or economic groups or to test hypotheses about the relations among constructs within an ethnic group, even though these studies may not have been originally designed for these purposes. For example, the National Longitudinal Study of Adolescent Health (Add Health; see UNC Carolina Population Center, n.d.) assessed a "nationally representative" sample of 90,118 students from 145 middle, junior high, and high schools with an in-school assessment battery.[3] This was followed with an in-home assessment of 20,745 adolescents and family members that oversampled Cuban Americans, Puerto Ricans, Chinese Americans, and highly educated African Americans. In the in-home interview portion of the study, however, the absence of American Indians, Mexican Americans (or any Latino groups other than Cuban Americans and Puerto Ricans), and any Asian American groups other than Chinese Americans limited the opportunities to study some select groups or to make pan-ethnic comparisons. The oversampling of highly educated African Americans also compromises the generalizability of findings involving these data.

Furthermore, as far as we know, there were no in-home assessments in any language other than English in the Add Health study. Hence, the Latino and Asian American samples are not fully representative of these ethnic populations, a limitation that further threatens the accuracy of any scientific inferences made from comparisons between or within these groups. Although the primary goal of these research designs usually is to obtain a sample that is as representative of the U.S. population as possible, it is impractical to translate and administer all measures in every lan-

---

[3]Add Health data are available from the Sociometrics Corporation, 170 State Street, Suite 260, Los Altos, California 94022-2812. Telephone: (650) 949-3282. E-mail: socio@socio.com

guage preference that exists within the United States. As a result of this impracticality, national sample designs generally administer all measures in English. This means that some segments of the ethnic groups in the United States (i.e., individuals who do not speak English well or who are not comfortable speaking English) are excluded from the sample and that some individuals may have completed measures in English even if they have limited English proficiency. Furthermore, individuals in some economic groups may complete measures that use a level of the English language that is not completely concordant with their normal level of English use. This typical limitation associated with national sample designs threatens the comparability of the representativeness of samples of different ethnic groups as well as the accuracy of ethnic minority or economic group comparisons. In addition, to the degree that different proportions and different segments of each ethnic group are excluded because of their lack of fluency with English, the ethnic groups in these national sample designs do not equally represent their respective ethnic segments of the U.S. population, and these comparisons are confounded with a whole host of demographic variables associated with fluency in English.

Conducting assessments only in English also limits the accuracy of within-group tests of the relations among constructs, because specific segments of an ethnic population are not represented in the samples. The exclusion of segments of the ethnic population from the ethnic sample limits the variability in any construct associated with English fluency. This restriction of range may itself be sufficient to attenuate observed relations among constructs. However, if the constructs one is examining are themselves related to English fluency or to the myriad related demographic variables (e.g., acculturation, socioeconomic status), then the relations between these constructs can be upwardly or downwardly biased. For example, if one is interested in assessing the relation between familism values and family conflict among Latinos, excluding families in which some potential participants do not speak English or are uncomfortable speaking English may limit the variability of the results if monolingual Spanish speakers adhere more fully to a more traditional Latino value system. This limitation in the observed variability in a sample of English-fluent Latinos may in turn attenuate the observed correlation between familism values and family conflict.

The relatively high resource demands associated with national sample designs also often lead research teams to attempt to measure as many constructs as possible. Given that these data sets are frequently designed to become available to researchers all over the world, the research teams can, appropriately, try to create a data set that can be used to address a wide array of research questions. The attempt to measure a large number of constructs leads to the use of measures with as few items as is possible. Often the result is a one-, two-, three-, or four-item measure of relatively complex constructs, some of which may themselves be multidimensional in nature and thus require a higher order factor structure. For example, three items in the Add Health study can be used to assess family conflict: one regarding the adolescent's conflict with the mother, one regarding the adolescent's conflict with the father, and one regarding interparental conflict. Similarly, the Add Health study includes one item to assess the support adolescents receive from peers. Of course, these national sample designs sometime have focal goals, and some constructs are measured better than others. Nevertheless, this strategy results in a number of methodological issues associated with the reliability and validity of the measure of constructs, particularly when those constructs are multidimensional or have a very broad range of indicators. However, the potential problems associated with the use of such limited measures, even when the construct is not highly complex, may be exacerbated when the research focuses on selected ethnic or economic groups. Hence, national sample designs can easily lead to comparisons of particular constructs based on measures that are both inadequate within a particular group and not equivalent among diverse groups.

Inadvertently Diverse Designs

Inadvertently diverse designs are those in which the research team was originally interested in examining the relations among some set of constructs but ends up sampling the broader population in a way that leads them to a somewhat ethnically and/or economically diverse sample. These are designs in which the sample became ethnically and/or economically diverse by happenstance rather than because of a plan to purposefully select a diverse sample. Although the research team did not originally intend to use this data set to make group comparisons, the data derived from these types of designs are sometimes subsequently used to make group comparisons or to examine within-group relations among constructs. When this happens, the credibility of the scientific inferences based on these comparisons is limited by the potential confounds and alternative explanations described previously. However, the severity of these threats is even greater in inadvertently diverse designs because there is no way of knowing exactly how the samples are biased and how they are less than equally representative of their respective ethnic minority or economic groups. Indeed, lack of knowledge regarding the ways in which bias may have entered into the sampling in inadvertently diverse designs may be serious enough to preclude even a qualified inference about cross-group comparisons and within-group relations among constructs in contrast to what is possible with cross-group comparison designs.

For example, a research team may be interested in examining a research question focused on the development of self-esteem that leads them to sample children of different ages in a school setting. The research team may have developed a cross-sectional design to examine age differences in self-esteem by collaborating with a public school system to sample child participants and may have viewed sampling from public schools desirable in part because they would be likely to produce a reasonably representative sample. However, if the developmental theory is grounded completely in a research literature based on studies of European Americans, then the research team may not consider the potential sampling and measurement issues associated with participants from another ethnic–racial group. If the research team group-administers a self-esteem measure to children in classrooms that include a relatively small proportion of African Americans, and if the African American children are from highly select segments of the African American population (e.g., all from high-income families or all from low-income families), then comparisons of the age differences in self-esteem among these African American children and the European American children may not reflect the differences or similarities that may have been found if one had sampled a more representative population of African Americans. Furthermore, because the research team probably did not consider the ethnic diversity in the schools participating in the research (because it was not an original goal of the study), the data necessary to identify or understand the selectivity of the African American children included in the sample are probably not available if one wanted to try to characterize the selectivity and make qualified scientific inferences.

The lack of focus on the ethnic or racial composition of the public schools being sampled may also lead to measurement issues that could limit the credibility of the scientific inferences when one is comparing the African American and European American children. For example, the research literature comparing the self-esteem of African Americans and European Americans has produced findings that are difficult to reconcile given the broader understanding of these groups. One possibility is based on the evidence that some measures of self-esteem may not be equivalently assessing the self-esteem construct among African American and European American adolescents (Michaels, Barr, Roosa, & Knight, 2007). That is, it is very possible that African American and European American adolescents interpret the meaning of the items in a typical measure of self-esteem differently, and hence their responses to the items are reflecting different constructs. Of course, if the measure of self-esteem being used does not equivalently measure self-esteem among the African American and European American participants, then the interpretation of the comparisons of these two groups is compromised. Furthermore, given the original scope of the study, the research team probably spent little time considering the measurement equivalence issues associated with sampling schools that include ethnically diverse students, and they probably can do little after the fact to try to improve the measurement equivalence of their self-esteem assessments.

MEETING THE CHALLENGES

We believe that a better scientific understanding of the psychological or social science issues associated with being a member of an ethnic minority or economically disadvantaged group in the United States is critical to the way researchers will deal with the social and psychological service needs of the future. This is not to say that these needs are identical for individuals and families in ethnic minority and economically disadvantaged populations—or, for that matter, for individuals in ethnic minority groups from different cultural backgrounds and countries of origin. This is also not to say that these social and psychological service needs will be greater in the future than they are now or have been in the past. However, these needs may well be different because of the nature of the specific population changes that are occurring. We also believe that a better scientific understanding of the psychological or social science issues associated with ethnic minority or economic status and the huge diversity that exists within these groups require that greater attention be paid to the methodological challenges discussed in this volume. We hope that researchers find this discussion and the best practice recommendations helpful in leading us to that better scientific understanding.

As noted earlier, in this book we describe a number of methodological issues that complicate the research focused on ethnic minority and economically disadvantaged populations. These challenges may initially appear overwhelming to some, but they come with the territory, so to speak; that is, if one wishes to conduct research on ethnic minority and economically disadvantaged populations, and to make scientifically credible inferences, then one will eventually have to address some of these methodological challenges. Some readers may look at these issues, and the best practice recommendations for addressing them, and conclude that these challenges are too great and that they are better off pursuing a different research agenda. However, we hope that our best practice suggestions will alleviate this concern and help researchers see new avenues for their endeavors. We also hope that most researchers recognize the importance of research on ethnic minority and economically disadvantaged populations and agree that conducting the research necessary to understand the impact of the sampling, measurement, translation, and ethics issues with these populations is essential to enhancing our understanding of the social and psychological impact of ethnicity and/or economic disadvantage as well as for providing effective interventions and services for these populations. We hope that many researchers will understand that the recommendations we provide are based on what we know from the research literature and, to a great extent, our own experience. We also hope that readers understand that we are describing our attempts to address the challenges associated with studying ethnic minority and economically disadvantaged populations and that we hope readers can use these best practice suggestions as a starting point on which they can build in their own research. We hope that many understand that, over time, some of these recommendations may become more important, whereas others will wane in importance. Finally, although we have used most of the recommendations we make in this book in our recent joint research, we got to this point only after years of approximations, during which time we and many others tried a variety of ways of addressing these issues. We assume that most individuals entering this research area will take successive steps toward addressing these issues, just as we did.

2

Sampling, Recruiting, and Retaining Diverse Samples

Sampling and recruiting participants are basic steps in almost every research enterprise and are fundamental to determining the quality of the resulting research. In this chapter, we describe how commonly used sampling, recruitment, and retention strategies are not always the best choices when conducting research that includes or focuses on ethnic minority or economically disadvantaged populations, and we introduce alternative strategies that are likely to be more successful with these populations. We begin the chapter with a brief review of the basics of sampling, recruitment, and retention along with a review of the most common sampling strategies used in quantitative research in the social sciences. We then discuss several reasons why the most common recruitment and retention strategies often are not very attractive to, or successful with, ethnic minority and economically disadvantaged populations. This discussion is followed by recommendations for alternative strategies that appear to be more successful with these populations on the basis of the relatively scant research literature or our experiences. Next, we discuss the much-overlooked topic of how to retain participants in longitudinal studies. Finally, we look at the implications of the lessons learned in this chapter for the four common research designs introduced in chapter 1.

INTRODUCTION

Sampling is the process of selecting members of a population of interest to a researcher. In quantitative research, the ideal goal of sampling is to select members of the targeted population who are representative of, or very similar to, that population so that the results can be generalized or applied to the larger population. *Recruitment* is the process of trying to get the individuals selected during sampling to participate in a study. Together, sampling and recruitment determine the initial quality of the sample studied—that is, the degree to which the sample is representative of the population of interest and, therefore, the confidence with which researchers can say that results obtained are the same as would have been obtained if the entire population had been studied (i.e., the results can be generalized from the sample to the population). The degree to which sampling and recruitment processes result in samples that truly represent a population of interest determines the degree to which the study results can be confidently interpreted. Similarly, retaining participants in longitudinal studies is critical for maintaining the quality of a sample. When researchers have managed the difficult task of obtaining a representative sample of a population, the quality of the sample—and of the ongoing study—will deteriorate over time if a significant portion of the sample, or of a particular subgroup within the sample (e.g., recent immigrants in a study of the general Mexican American population), does not participate in later stages of the study.

The ability to generalize findings based on a sample depends on two factors: (a) the sampling context (i.e., the degree of similarity of the *accessible population,* those who can be located and contacted, to the target population) and (b) the results of recruitment (i.e., the degree of similarity of the sample to the accessible population). The more difficult it is to identify (e.g., illegal immigrants, homeless individuals) or gain access to (e.g., people without a permanent residence, those who speak rare dialects) members of a target population, the less likely the findings from the sample obtained will be highly descriptive of the target population. Under the best of circumstances, we can realistically generalize only to the accessible population, and we should be cautious and concerned about how well we succeeded in gaining access to the target population.

Although many researchers generally think of sampling and recruitment as affecting only the external validity of a study (i.e., the ability to generalize findings from a sample to a population), in many studies of ethnically diverse or economically disadvantaged populations sampling and recruitment are used to operationally define the independent variable. For instance, in studies that focus on the effects of culturally related processes associated with ethnicity or economic disadvantage (e.g., *fatalism*, the belief that a person cannot control what will happen to him or her), sampling ethnically or economically diverse populations becomes the mechanism that determines the nature of the independent variable. In such cases, sampling and recruitment may affect the internal validity (i.e., the accuracy of causal inferences) of the study as well. This is most easily understood in the context of comparative studies (e.g., comparing Mexican Americans with European Americans, comparing U.S.-born Mexican Americans with immigrants from Mexico). For example, if one believed that greater connection to the culture of origin causes greater adherence to familism values (e.g., beliefs that the family comes first, that the family is the primary source of support), then one might test this causal hypothesis by comparing the familism of immigrants from Mexico with the familism of U.S.-born Mexican Americans. Sampling only English-speaking participants of Mexican heritage would likely mean that the immigrant sample would poorly represent the targeted immigrant population, whereas the U.S.-born sample would be relatively more representative of the targeted U.S.-born population. This differential representativeness will likely be observed because immigrants from Mexico are much more likely to be either monolingual Spanish speaking or to have limited English fluency than U.S.-born individuals of Mexican heritage. Furthermore, immigrants who most desire to maintain contact with the culture of origin may be more likely to decide to live in border towns and ethnic enclaves in major cities in the southwestern United States and therefore be more likely to maintain their Spanish language use and less likely to become fluent in English. If this holds true, then becoming sufficiently comfortable with the use of the English language among immigrants may represent a selection threat to the internal validity of any causal inferences. If the exclusion of individuals with limited English proficiency reduces the systematic variance in familism in the samples, then a statistical comparison may underestimate the differences between these populations and lead to inaccurate inferences regarding the degree to which a greater connection to the culture of origin (operationalized as being an immigrant vs. born in the United States) causes greater adherence to familism values.

However, sampling, recruitment, and retention can also threaten the internal validity of studies of ethnically or economically diverse populations when one is not conducting research with a comparative design. If one is interested in studying a process within an ethnic minority or economic group by examining the interrelations among measures of several constructs, and if the sampling, recruitment, or retention (in longitudinal studies) procedures result in a sample that is inadequately representative of the population of interest, then the observed relations among these constructs may be biased and lead to inaccurate scientific inferences. For example, if one is interested in how familism values are related to prosocial behaviors among Mexican Americans, then excluding individuals with limited English proficiency could restrict the range of observed familism scores and in turn substantially attenuate the observed relation between familism and prosocial behaviors. If familism and prosocial behaviors are strongly related in the population, but the attenuation created by an inadequately representative sample is sufficient to result in a nonsignificant correlation (i.e., a Type II error), then the resulting scientific inference is inaccurate. Hence, sampling, recruitment, and retention, in addition to being critical to the external validity of research designs focused on ethnically or economically diverse populations, are also critical in determining the internal validity of such designs.

It is surprising that researchers have paid relatively little attention to how best to apply recruitment and retention processes when working with ethnically diverse or economically disadvantaged populations; most, in fact, simply have applied the methods that were developed and have been successful with middle-class and European American samples. As more research includes or focuses on ethnic minority or economically disadvantaged populations, researchers often are confronted with complex issues about recruitment and retention for which they may not be completely prepared. For instance, what will motivate a member of an underrepre-

sented ethnic minority or economically disadvantaged group to participate in a study? How can a representative sample of members of an underrepresented ethnic minority or economically disadvantaged group be
obtained? Once recruited, what can a researcher do to convince participants from these populations to continue in a longitudinal study? The well-
established methods that have been developed and used successfully with
middle-class European American groups may not always work as well with
these populations.

The social science research literature is equivocal with regard to whether
members of ethnic minority groups are less likely in general to respond to
recruitment efforts than European Americans, primarily because so few
studies have reported race- or ethnic-specific recruitment rates (for a review,
see Cauce, Ryan, & Grove, 1998). However, much of what social scientists
have learned about the recruitment of individuals from specific ethnic
minority or economically disadvantaged groups comes primarily from
studies that make minimal demands on participants (e.g., telephone surveys, short face-to-face surveys). In contrast, biomedical and health promotion researchers who have conducted studies that make greater
demands on participants consistently have reported that recruitment rates
are lower for ethnic minority groups while also demonstrating that
recruitment rates for specific ethnic minority groups can be improved
with targeted efforts (e.g., Gallagher-Thompson et al., 2004; Gavaghan,
1995; Hussain-Gambles, Atkin, & Leese, 2004; Levkoff & Sanchez, 2003;
Picot et al., 2002; Yancey, Ortega, & Kumanyika, 2005). Some social
science research also indicates that recruitment rates are lower for
both low-income individuals and those living in urban areas—two
categories in which most ethnic minority groups are overrepresented
(e.g., Capaldi & Patterson, 1987; Cauce, Ryan, & Grove, 1998; Gallagher-
Thompson et al., 2004; Spoth, Goldberg, & Redmond, 1999). Finally,
members of some ethnic minority groups may refuse to participate if they
believe their group has been misrepresented or taken advantage of by
researchers in the past (e.g., African Americans, American Indians, Inuits;
see Manson, Garroutte, Goins, & Henderson, 2004; Norton & Manson,
1996; Picot et al., 2002) or if they feel that participation might cause them
negative consequences (e.g., the fear of discovery among undocumented

immigrants). Perhaps most important, as researchers have begun more systematically to study recruitment processes with ethnic minority populations, particularly in the biomedical or health fields, we are learning that certain recruitment methods are more effective with specific ethnic minority subgroups than European Americans, and vice versa (e.g., Gallagher-Thompson et al., 2006).

BASICS OF SAMPLING, RECRUITMENT, AND RETENTION

Quantitative research generally is based on the *inductive* system of logic, in which the results of a few cases are considered to apply, or generalize, to the whole group. Thus, across the social sciences almost all quantitative research is based on studying a relatively small group of individuals or families— a sample—with the objective of being able to generalize the results to all similar individuals or families (i.e., the population). The research process typically begins with an idea that the researcher believes applies to a *target population*, a group defined by some set of shared characteristics (e.g., all 14- to 18-year-olds from a particular ethnic minority group, all persons of working age living in government-subsidized housing).

Despite the interest in studying a particular target population, studies are limited to the *accessible population:* that portion of the target population that can be identified and reached by the researcher, given reasonable effort. Limits in access to the target population often are due to factors beyond the researcher's control. For instance, researchers interested in studying undocumented Mexican immigrants who entered the United States with the help of a "coyote" (i.e., a person who facilitates illegal transport of people across the U.S.–Mexican border), will have no *sampling frame* (i.e., no master list of names and contact information) for this population, and self-reports of such behavior that might be used to identify this population may be biased because of fears of legal ramifications. In fact, rarely does any study of a general population of an ethnic minority or economically disadvantaged group have access to a sampling frame for that group. On the other hand, a study of a specifically defined subpopulation, such as African American adolescents enrolled at a particular middle school, might be able to obtain a sampling frame (i.e., a list of all African American students at the school), increasing both accessibility and the opportunities to obtain a representative sample. In other cases, limitations in access to the target population are due to practical issues such as time, costs, geography, or convenience. That is, it is much easier to study Chinese Americans in a specific state, city, or neighborhood than it is to study them nationally. For instance, researchers might make the decision to study Chinese Americans in a specific city (e.g., San Francisco) because of the known concentration of this ethnic minority group in that setting and the relatively low costs involved in reaching this portion of the target population. In contrast, obtaining a sample of Chinese Americans from each of the 50 states would be a difficult and expensive undertaking. However, research on Chinese Americans from a single city is likely to produce a biased, or at least incomplete, picture of the Chinese American population, for a variety of reasons. For instance, local Chinese American populations may differ in various cities or regions of the United States because of differences in the geographic sources of these populations (e.g., north China vs. south China, Hong Kong, or Taiwan) and associated differences in cultural traditions or because of the length of time the local population has been in the community and the degree to which they have become integrated into the social, economic, and political fabric of their communities.

Once potential participants have been identified through some sampling strategy, researchers use a variety of techniques to attempt to recruit the individuals or group identified into the sample. After a sample has been obtained, a common task is to describe the sample and determine how similar it is to the target population. This often involves comparing common demographic characteristics (e.g., parent or adult education level, family income, immigrant status, language spoken at home) for the sample with similar data from the census for the local population sampled (see Exhibit 2.1). When presenting these results in publications, researchers also should provide methodological information to help others understand how likely the sample is to be representative of the population of interest. For instance, readers will want to know the details of the sampling and recruitment processes as well as the participation rate for the study (i.e., percentage of the identified sample who were successfully recruited,

Exhibit 2.1

Information to Help Researchers Judge the Representativeness of Ethnic Minority or Economically Disadvantaged Samples

Compare means or distribution data on the sample with relevant census data on variables such as the following:

- Adult or parent education level
- Family income
- Immigrant status or years in the United States, if relevant
- Family structure (e.g., marital status)
- Language spoken or preferred
- Language spoken at home
- Methodological data

Describe how individuals/families from the target population were identified, sampled, and recruited.

- Participation rate information[a]
- Percentage of individuals sampled who were locatable
- Percentage of the locatable sample who agreed to participate
- Percentage of the locatable sample who did participate
- For longitudinal studies and intervention studies, percentage of those who participated in the initial stage of the research who also participated in each subsequent stage

[a]This information should be reported separately for each ethnic group or each social class group for samples that are purposely ethnically or economically diverse.

who refused to participate, who were not locatable, and who were retained in longitudinal studies). If the sample includes participants from multiple ethnic minority or social class groups, then results of the recruitment process for each group will be useful to readers. Too few studies published in the social sciences report any of this information, making it difficult for fellow researchers to clearly understand the methods, the effectiveness of these methods, and the likelihood that the sample is representative of the population of interest. Failure to report details about the recruitment methods used, and their success, also means that researchers often are not able to build on the strengths, as well as avoid the mistakes, of previous research but must learn through their own trial and error.

For longitudinal studies, retention of a sample is just as important as successful sampling and recruitment. People drop out of studies for both apparently random (e.g., accidental deaths, employer relocation) and nonrandom (e.g., personality characteristics, dislike of the research experience) reasons. To the degree that attrition is nonrandom, the representativeness of a sample can steadily decline as a study continues. In attempting to prevent this, researchers conducting longitudinal studies use a variety of strategies to maintain contact with participants and keep them interested in the study. These strategies usually involve efforts such as recurrent communication with participants, attempting to build a sense of belonging or attachment to the study, providing incentives for the participants to remain in contact with researchers, and making plans for locating participants with whom contact is lost. Unfortunately, the specific retention strategies researchers use are rarely described in publications, so it often is difficult to identify those methods that are most, or least, successful in retaining a high percentage of participants across time. Furthermore, almost nothing is available on retention strategies specific to ethnic minority or economically disadvantaged populations.

SAMPLING STRATEGIES

There are no unique sampling strategies for studying ethnic minority or economically disadvantaged populations. However, researchers may want to pay close attention to the implications of using certain strategies that include these groups or the interpretation of results in such studies. In the following sections, we discuss three general sampling strategies that are common in social science research: (a) *random sampling,* (b) *stratified random sampling,* and (c) *convenience sampling.* Although these strategies are equally valid when used with ethnic minority or economically disadvantaged populations as when they are used with the general population, often they must be combined with tailored recruitment processes to be successful.

Random Sampling

Random sampling involves selecting potential research participants in such a manner that each member of the targeted population has an equal probability of being selected into the sample. Proper use of random sampling will generate a sample that is more likely to be representative of the targeted population than any other method, assuming reasonably high and similar rates of successful recruitment for all segments of the population. Random sampling is simply the best strategy for any researcher who wishes to generalize his or her results to the population being studied, whether it is the general population of a school, city, county, state, or nation, or a specific subpopulation, such as low-income families of a specific ethnic minority group. It is the ideal sampling plan for determining how many people in a given group have experienced a given event (i.e., incident rates). In general, when the sample is large enough, and recruitment is relatively successful, there is good reason to believe that the sample will represent the population and that the results from the sample will allow one to draw accurate scientific inferences regarding the population.

Theoretically speaking, in a very large sample of the general population one would expect to have substantial numbers of people from a variety of ethnic minority and economic subgroups that would make between-group comparisons possible. That is, in a well-executed random sampling design with relatively successful recruitment rates and a large sample size, each subgroup should be represented in numbers that are similar to their proportion of the general population. However, groups that constitute a very small portion of the general population (e.g., Sudanese immigrants) might not be represented, or they may be represented in such small numbers that meaningful comparisons are not possible. When subpopulations of specific economic, racial, or ethnic groups are large enough, random samples of the general population are good for making cross-group comparisons on both incidence rates and on the relationships between variables (i.e., comparisons of the fit of theoretical models). Similarly, when random sampling is applied exclusively to a single economic, racial, or ethnic group, the resulting sample should provide a strong foundation for studying within-group diversity on incidence rates (e.g., rates of depression for low-income vs. middle-income African American men) or the utility of theoretical models for that group (e.g., whether the experience of stressful life events is as strongly related to depression in a Chinese American sample as has been reported in research with European American samples).

Because of the difficulties in recruiting disadvantaged populations, urban dwellers, those who have been discriminated against, and those who think that participation might be harmful to their well-being, random sampling designs rarely represent all segments of the population equally well. Even a well-executed random sampling design might not be fully representative of the more marginalized ethnic minority or economically disadvantaged populations; therefore, research that uses random sampling may produce results with a somewhat biased perspective of these groups. For this reason, researchers using random sampling may want to use recruitment methods that are more attractive and effective with a broader audience than has often been the case in the past, or they may want to tailor recruitment methods for each targeted subgroup using procedures such as those described later in this chapter. Regardless of the recruitment strategy, researchers using random sampling should monitor recruitment rates for subgroups and use caution in interpreting and generalizing results to the degree that response rates are low or uneven among one or more subgroups.

Stratified Random Sampling

In the stratified random sampling strategy, the random sampling process is applied to specific, preidentified subgroups (i.e., *strata*) in the population to make sure that each selected subgroup is proportionally represented in the final sample. In a typical procedure, people are randomly sampled from the general population until the quota for each stratum is filled. This process is used to make sure that groups that represent small portions of the population are represented in the final sample. When applied successfully, these are the strongest sampling designs for studies that want to make comparisons across groups on incident rates, means, or relations between variables. Because researchers decide in advance exactly what subgroups will be included in the final sample, these designs can be implemented readily with group-specific recruitment strategies to achieve the highest possible recruitment rates within each group, an option that is more difficult to implement in other sampling methods. Stratified random sampling strategies can also be used for studying diversity within an ethnic minority or economic group by using preidentified characteristics (e.g., family income, family structure, acculturation level, language use) on which there is substantial diversity within the group as the stratifying variable.

Researchers sometimes use a modification of the stratified random sampling strategy and oversample strata, thereby overrepresenting groups that make up only a small portion of the general population. This approach is used when group comparisons are planned and one or more subgroups represent such small portions of the general population that comparisons with these groups would have little statistical power to identify differences when they exist. For instance, if ethnicity were the stratifying variable of interest, then smaller subpopulations that are of interest to the study but that comprise only a small portion of the general population (e.g., Cambodian Americans) would have to be oversampled.

Convenience Sampling

Convenience sampling refers to any nonrandom method of obtaining a sample. This might include studying volunteers from a college student population (e.g., students in a psychology undergraduate research pool), developing a partnership with a school district and studying members of selected grades in that district, or studying individuals who use a particular service (e.g., shop at a particular store, use a particular medical facility, attend a particular church). In addition, convenience sampling includes systematic approaches, such as *snowball sampling.* In this approach, after identifying a few cases of a rare or difficult-to-identify population (e.g., persons in the country illegally, persons working in the cash economy), the researcher asks participants to refer him or her to other members of the group or to refer other members of the group to the researcher. Each new participant is requested to do the same until a large enough sample is obtained. Most studies in the social sciences rely on convenience samples because these samples are obtained more easily, inexpensively, and quickly than is possible with any other sampling method. Such samples rarely, if ever, are representative of the population, and in general, important subgroups of the population may be represented poorly or not at all. For example, ethnic minority and economically disadvantaged populations are generally poorly represented among college student samples, yet such samples are popular because they are comparatively inexpensive and relatively quick and easy to obtain. Therefore, generalizations based on convenience samples need to be very limited and made with considerable caution.

PROBLEMS WITH COMMON SAMPLING AND RECRUITMENT METHODS

Why is it that common sampling and recruitment methods may not always work well with ethnically diverse or economically disadvantaged populations? What is it about these populations that might require different approaches? In this section, we examine the assumptions and common practices behind the most popular sampling and recruitment methods.

Assumptions Underlying Common Methods May Not Apply

At least three assumptions behind most common sampling and recruitment procedures bear examination before those processes are applied to ethnic minority or economically disadvantaged populations. First is the assumption that research is conducted for the common good and that when asked, potential participants should be willing to participate to contribute to the common good. The catch is that "the common good" usually refers to that which benefits most of society, and this generally means those who are mainstream and middle class. Ethnic minorities and economically disadvantaged groups often do not consider themselves as part of mainstream society. Thus, altruism toward research likely is a much stronger motivation for middle-class individuals to participate than it is for those more on the fringes of mainstream society (e.g., Word, 1992; Yancey et al., 2005).

A second assumption is that universities and other research institutions are well known, universally trusted, and deserving of our support. Members of the middle class are much more likely than members of economically disadvantaged groups to have attended college or to be aware of these research institutions. Similarly, European Americans attend college at much higher rates than most other ethnic groups (U.S. Census Bureau, 2004c). Those who attend college are introduced to research in their classes and often learn that research is one of the major activities of university faculty. In fact, a substantial proportion of college students are required to participate in research (e.g., those who take a course in introductory psychology), usually as study participants, which contributes to their familiarity with research. At a minimum, these experiences would make individuals who attend college more comfortable about participating in research and less fearful of possible harm from participating. Members of ethnic minority and economically disadvantaged populations, however, may be less likely to understand the purposes of research or to be connected to or familiar with institutions that conduct research.

The third assumption is that most White, middle-class persons probably think of participation in social science research as quite benign and that they give little, if any, thought to the possibility that participation could harm them in some way. This assumption of lack of harm does not necessarily apply to ethnic minority and economically disadvantaged groups (Word, 1992; Yancey et al., 2005). Members of these groups often have experienced various forms of discrimination in society, and at times this has carried over to research. For example, it is difficult to imagine that studies such as the Tuskegee study of syphilis in the Black male (Jones, 1981) could have been conducted with any group other than a disenfranchised ethnic minority group, in this, case low-income African Americans in the rural South during the Depression. Recruitment methods that used misleading information, medical tests conducted for research purposes but described as treatment, and efforts to prevent participants from quitting the study or seeking outside medical care, just a few of the unacceptable methods used in the Tuskegee study, are procedures that would not likely occur in a study of middle-class European Americans. The legacy of the Tuskegee study is well remembered in certain communities, and this memory can hinder recruitment efforts, particularly for health-related research (Word, 1992; Yancey et al., 2005).

Unfortunately, more recent events have reinforced the concerns initially raised by the Tuskegee study. For instance, the Environmental Protection Agency sponsored the "Lead-Based Paint Abatement and Repair and Maintenance Study" from 1993 to 1995 (Maloney, 2006; Nelson, 2001), which may have enhanced the salience of the potential harm associated with participating in scientific research for African Americans. The study was designed to evaluate the relative cost-effectiveness of various approaches to reducing or preventing child poisoning from lead-based paint in low-income housing. However, the study researchers did not inform residents of the potential harmful conditions that lead-based paint in their homes posed for their children, nor were parents told about the primary purpose of the study or about the methods of lead abatement used. Furthermore, the researchers required that all children submit to blood tests on a regular basis as a condition for having access to the housing, yet they provided no explanations for these tests. This study was limited to housing for low-income families, and most families in the study were African American. Because of these and other incidents, one should not be surprised if or when members of ethnic minority and economically disadvantaged groups are skeptical about researchers' intentions and suspicious or cautious when asked to participate in research.

Misrepresentation in Research

To make accurate scientific inferences regarding the ways in which being a member of an ethnic minority or economically disadvantaged group influences individuals, samples that are adequately representative of the population are necessary so that empirical findings are adequately generalizable to the population. Unfortunately, studies too often have failed the basic goal of sampling and recruitment: to represent the target population (L. Case & Smith, 2000; Cauce, Ryan, & Grove, 1998; Flaskerud & Nyamathi, 2000). For instance, research on African American families, children, or adolescents typically overrepresents those who are living below the poverty level. Although it is true that African Americans, and most other ethnic minority groups, are more likely to be living in poverty than European Americans, the majority of African Americans and of most other ethnic minority groups are not living in poverty (U.S. Census Bureau, 2004c). Even so, middle-class African Americans are rarely represented in studies of African Americans. Furthermore, even research on low-income African Americans usually focuses on a particular subgroup rather than representing the diversity within this subpopulation. Most research on economically disadvantaged African American families is limited to inner-city families, although there are significant numbers of rural poor African Americans. Certainly, some of the bias in deciding to study this particular subgroup of low-income African Americans is driven by legitimate public policy and service issues, given the well-known problems this population faces with housing, crime, education, discrimination, and other issues. However, African Americans living in rural poverty, who are rarely included in research, face many of the problems that stimulate research on inner-city, low-income African Americans.

Several other factors not linked to public policy, service needs, or scientific processes probably contribute to this bias toward research on inner-city African Americans. Urban poverty is more visible to the rest of the population than rural poverty, in part because problems faced by the urban poor or problems in the broader community attributed to the urban poor often are the topic of popular stories in major news and entertainment media, which themselves are concentrated in urban areas. Urban poverty also is generally more accessible to researchers; a large portion of the urban poor are concentrated in relatively small areas, whereas the rural poor are much more broadly distributed. Thus, it is less expensive on a per-participant basis to sample, recruit, and study the urban poor than the rural poor. In any event, researchers, primarily for reasons not associated with theory, scientific methods, or policy issues, have helped create a literature on low-income African American families and children that is biased heavily toward a subgroup within the population. Research on many other ethnic minority populations (e.g., Mexican Americans, Puerto Ricans, Hmong, and other immigrants) is similarly biased.

Studies of ethnically diverse populations often use designs that compare group means, or the slopes of the relations between variables, for the ethnic minority group with the means or slopes of one or more other groups, most commonly a middle-class European American group, which is often considered to be the normative comparison group (Cauce, Coronado, & Watson, 1998; Cauce, Ryan, & Grove, 1998; Safren et al., 2000). Because the sample of the ethnic minority group studied is very often also economically disadvantaged, the results of such comparisons often contribute to a "deficit model" of the ethnic minority group. Comparative research designs that confound social class and ethnicity in this way have produced a literature that depicts ethnic minority individuals as commonly pathological, involved in drug use and sales or other criminal activity, with unhealthy home and community environments. This biased perspective has provided little insight into the lives of successful members of these groups, and it may be a great disservice to the majority of the members of most ethnic minority groups whose personal and family lives are not pathological or who do not live in poverty. This body of research too often provides relatively little useful information about the subpopulation studied because the research is also decontextualized. For instance, one concern raised by these types of comparative studies is that low-income African American parents may be more likely than European American parents to be authoritarian in their approach to parenting (i.e., high on parental control, low on communication and negotiation), in contrast to the middle-class ideal of parenting (i.e., high on control, high on communication and negotiation). Research that has taken into consideration the context of the low-income African American families studied has suggested that when parents are raising children in unsafe inner-city communities, greater parental control, including more severe discipline, may be associated with better outcomes for the children (e.g., Baldwin, Baldwin, & Cole, 1990; Baldwin et al., 1993). Parents who use authoritative parenting in such environments by encouraging children's autonomy and participation in decision making instead of obedience might be risking the safety of their children in that they are neglecting to consider the threatening circumstances.

Another contributor to misrepresentation of ethnic minority groups in research is the practice of *pan-ethnic research,* in which researchers ignore distinctions between ethnic minority subgroups by treating groups of people as though they were very similar simply because they come from the same continent (i.e., Africans, Asians) or a more general geographic area (i.e., Latinos) or share a label developed by the U.S. Census Bureau for convenience in sorting and counting people (e.g., *Hispanics, Asians and Pacific*

Islanders). This is particularly troublesome in studies that are either testing for differences between Latinos or Asians and another ethnic group or those testing the effects of cultural variables on behavior. There is a long tradition of treating mixed samples of Latinos as though they represent a homogeneous group while ignoring differences in history, culture, immigration experiences (e.g., Puerto Ricans are U.S. citizens; also, for decades, Cubans were automatically granted special immigrant status on arrival, whereas all other individuals from Latin American countries face serious restrictions), variations in race or skin color that influence how immigrants are treated in the United States, and even variations in the use of Spanish among Latino subgroups. In addition, the majorities of people in some Latin American countries speak French or Portuguese and have historical experiences different from those of individuals from Spanish-speaking countries. Although there are some important background similarities among most Latino groups (e.g., most Latinos or their ancestors came from Spanish-speaking areas, the majority share a religion, and large portions of the population in most Latin American countries are economically disadvantaged), research has shown the importance of acknowledging differences among Latino nationalities (Marín & Marín, 1991; Umaña-Taylor & Fine, 2001). Rational arguments can be made for conducting studies of several research questions with samples of Latinos from multiple countries of origin, such as Mexico and other Spanish-speaking countries in Central America, because of relatively similar uses of Spanish, economic circumstances, and political histories. On the other hand, it is more difficult to justify research that contains significant numbers of Cuban Americans, Puerto Ricans, and Mexican Americans in a single sample referred to as *Latino,* unless the study is specifically designed to make comparisons among these groups, because of their linguistic, cultural, racial, ethnic, and historical differences. Similarly, research on Latinos that includes people with origins in Brazil, Haiti, or Trinidad (i.e., countries where Spanish is not the dominant language), along with others with origins from Cuba, Mexico, and/or other Spanish-speaking countries, are extremely difficult to justify because of the linguistic and cultural distinctiveness of these groups.

In contrast to Latinos, most Asian nationalities have distinctly different languages. The religious differences between some countries are quite dramatic, and education and economic well-being also vary dramatically across the continent. When the target group is described using the census category "Asian and Pacific Islander," the within-group diversity becomes much greater, and the ability to interpret results as applying to all (or any) of the subpopulations involved becomes impossible for most research questions. However, studies of pan-Asian immigrants and pan-Asian Americans are not uncommon, often with little or no attention given to subgroup differences. Thoughtful combinations of Asian American subgroups (e.g., East Asians, including Japanese, South Koreans, and Chinese) may be justifiable for some research questions, but numerous other combinations (e.g., Chinese Americans and Indian Americans, Pakistani Americans and people from the Solomon Islands) would be difficult to justify because of the large differences and few commonalities among these groups. Similarly, African immigrants probably should not be included in most studies of African Americans, and researchers should be very thoughtful about when research with American Indians should be executed at the tribal level or when it is acceptable conceptually to conduct research across tribal groups.

There probably are very few research questions that are best addressed by studying broadly mixed groups of Latinos or Asians, for instance, while ignoring the differences among subgroups. Worse, research based on such mixed groups may give some people the mistaken impression that the results can be used to guide intervention or public policy for any or all subpopulations within the sample studied. Interpretation of research with pan-ethnic samples that are treated as a homogeneous group should be done with a great deal of caution. More so than in most other studies, researchers who are tempted to use pan-ethnic samples should carefully define which subpopulations should be included in the study on the basis of the nature of their research question.

Finally, ethnic minority groups historically have been underrepresented in psychosocial intervention studies as well as biomedical and health services studies, research from which they potentially could benefit (e.g., L. Case & Smith, 2000; Gallagher-Thompson et al., 2006; Gavaghan, 1995; Valle, 2005). Some of this underrepresentation may be due to minority group members' fears because of echoes from the Tuskegee syphilis study and other studies in which minority groups were mistreated, combined with experiences of discrimination from the larger society. However, minority groups often simply were not recruited for some types of research, particularly medical and health studies, until the National Institutes of Health changed the regulations for studies they funded. Beginning in 1994, researchers either had to provide a convincing scientific argument for excluding ethnic minorities from biomedical research or make active efforts to include them in these studies. Despite this mandate, medical studies often are not very successful at recruiting ethnic minorities, particularly African Americans (e.g., Corbie-Smith, Thomas, Williams, & Moody-Ayers, 1999; Hinton, Guo, Hillygus, & Levkoff, 2000; Maxwell, Bastani, Vida, & Warda, 2005; Nagayama Hall & Maramba, 2001; Safren et al., 2000). It is clear that researchers need to improve rates of ethnic minority participation, both in sheer numbers and in representativeness, in social science, biomedical, and health research, so that we can be sure which results apply to the entire population.

Defining *Ethnic Minority* and *Economic Disadvantage*

One possible key to improving research with ethnic minority and economically disadvantaged populations is having researchers more closely examine who really should be included in their research. Ignoring or dealing simplistically with this task also contributes to the misrepresentation of these populations. In most studies, researchers rely on participants' self-reports to determine whether they are members of specific ethnic minority or economic groups. For many studies, however, researchers might need to give more attention to how group membership is defined and how best to assess it before beginning the sampling process.

For example, there are several ways of defining *economic disadvantage* (for a review, see Roosa, Deng, Nair, & Burrell, 2005). The most common of these is the federally computed poverty thresholds, which vary by household size. Despite widespread criticisms of this measure, which is based on a formula developed in the 1950s, it remains popular. Although separate thresholds are computed for Alaska and Hawaii, a single set of thresholds applies to all areas in the remaining 48 states. Thus, although the cost of living in Los Angeles or New York City may be several times the cost of living in the Mississippi Delta, the same poverty thresholds apply. Alternatively, federal poverty guidelines or levels take local costs of living into account to determine eligibility for a variety of state and federal poverty programs. The use of these guidelines or whether families participate in poverty programs may be a better barometer of economic disadvantage than federal poverty thresholds. Poverty thresholds, poverty guidelines, and eligibility for or participation in poverty programs are government-determined indicators that might be useful for identifying economically disadvantaged participants for many studies. These indicators can be attractive to researchers because of their apparent objectivity, the fact that they are defined by government entities and not the researcher, and their ease of use. However, numerous other indicators of economic disadvantage are available (Roosa et al., 2005), and researchers should carefully determine which indicator best fits their research questions or hypotheses before defining group membership and using this definition to develop a sampling plan.

The issue of how to define membership in an ethnic minority group rarely receives much attention in social science research. Although issues of group membership may not be important to all studies, studies that focus on some research questions or on certain groups might be improved if more attention were paid to the issue of membership. For instance, for some groups, such as American Indians and Alaska Natives, there are legal definitions that vary across groups that determine formal tribal membership (Norton & Manson, 1996). Researchers conducting research on a specific tribe will need to know the legal definition for membership in that group and define processes for determining membership. Similarly, studies of other ethnic minority groups can present complications because of interethnic marriages that sometimes blur the ethnic membership of families and children. Studies focusing on questions about discrimination or the cultural influences on family or child adjustment in ethnic minority groups might want to consider whether families with parents from different ethnic backgrounds should be included at all, included if the mother is a member of the targeted ethnic minority group, included if the father is a member of the targeted group, or included if either parent is a member of the targeted group (e.g., Roosa et al., 2008). For example, how might the results, or the interpretation of those results, differ if a study of the influence of Japanese cultural traditions on children's success in school sampled 30 Japanese American families with 6 having a European American father, 2 having an African American father, and 3 having a Cuban mother? The decision of how to define group membership should be determined for each study and be based on consideration of how the various options might affect study results, the ability to interpret results, and the ability to generalize these results.

Practical Issues Hindering Recruitment of Ethnic Minority or Economically Disadvantaged Individuals

We have observed at least five challenges associated with recruiting representative samples of economically disadvantaged or ethnic minority individuals or families.

First, low-income families and individuals often are more mobile than the general population. Some of the poorest families rent their living quarters on a weekly or month-to-month basis. Any disruption in income or spike in expenses due to illness, loss of a job, need for car repairs, or other issues can mean eviction or moving to reduce costs. When short-term rentals are involved, such moves are relatively easy and quick to make. At the extreme are seasonal farm workers who travel much of the year according to the season to tend to or harvest crops, sometimes living in quarters provided by the farming operation only while this work is being completed. Although most of these farm workers are males, many travel with their families and, as a result, mothers and children also are not available for research in their home communities for much of the year. High mobility makes it more difficult to locate some families for research purposes or to track them and retain them in longitudinal studies. It also is likely that less mobile low-income families are different on some important personal or family characteristics than their more mobile peers.

Second, low-income families are less likely than the general population to have access to working telephones or to be listed in telephone directories. Low-income adults may not have home telephones, and if they are highly mobile, any residential telephones they do have may not be functioning for long. In our experiences with primarily Mexican American families, some low-income families use telephones in their apartments that are listed under a previous tenant's name, and others rely on neighbors for access to telephones. Although relatively low-cost cell phones technically make it possible for resourceful low-income families to have access to telephone service even with poor credit or high mobility, it is our experience that these often are an unreliable means of communication for many. The services may expire; families may stop buying service as soon as there is a financial pinch; and telephones are easily damaged, lost, or stolen. Those who use pay-as-you-go cell phone services periodically may not be able to keep their telephone service active. Some purchase prepaid cell phones that can be thrown away after the minutes are depleted, and regardless of the nature of the cell phone service they have, some carefully control the incoming calls they answer because of the cost associated with answering them. Telephone surveys or other studies that attempt to contact potential low-income participants via telephone must expect a certain portion of this population to be inaccessible at any given time.

Third, low-income members of ethnic minority groups often live in high-density inner-city communities. Higher income members of ethnic minority groups often are widely scattered throughout urban and suburban areas. Thus, it usually is more cost-effective to recruit ethnic minority populations in inner-city neighborhoods, but this produces biased samples that are less representative of the target population than is desirable (i.e., middle-class members of the group are underrepresented or not represented). Relatively few studies tackle the more difficult task of seeking out the middle- and upper income members of ethnic minority groups.

Fourth, researchers working with members of ethnic minority groups who are recent immigrants need to be prepared to work with such individuals in their native language (e.g., Flaskerud & Nyamathi, 2000; Lau & Gallagher-Thompson, 2002; Levkoff & Sanchez, 2003; Taylor-Piliae & Froelicher, 2007). This is a considerable undertaking that has important implications for measurement (discussed in chap. 4, this volume) and translation processes (discussed in chap. 5, this volume). When engaged in research with populations that include significant numbers of immigrants, research team members need to be prepared to speak in either English or the participants' native tongue, and rarely will they know which is required until the moment of contact over the telephone or face to face. Thus, the individuals involved in recruiting these populations need to be fluently bilingual, understand the cultural perspective of potential participants (i.e., be bicultural), and be flexible. Even so, our experiences in research with Mexican Americans indicate that being English–Spanish bilingual will not be sufficient in some cases; indigenous languages, with which the researchers might be unfamiliar, can result in a failure to communicate with some members of immigrant populations (Roosa et al., 2008).

Fifth and last, experiences of discrimination from the larger society and the sometimes distrusting, skeptical, or adversarial relationships between some ethnic minorities and economically disadvantaged groups and authority figures may impede the recruitment of members of these groups. African Americans and indigenous Americans (e.g., American Indians, Native Hawaiians) in particular have been the focus of many types of discrimination (Katz et al., 2006; Norton & Manson, 1996). These groups have numerous reasons to believe that researchers may not always have their best interests in mind. Furthermore, when a professionally dressed individual approaches the apartment of a low-income family in an urban area to recruit them for a study, he or she should not be surprised if the family at least initially acts defensively because of assumptions that the recruiter is an authority figure from the police or a social service agency, who too often represents a threat for many low-income families. Middle-income and more highly educated ethnic minority group members are likely to be aware of the biased perspective that society has of their ethnic group, a perspective that has evolved from the misrepresentation of this population in research, so they too may be reluctant to participate in some forms of research.

Latinos also have experiences with discrimination that may make them more hesitant to trust authority figures whom they perceive to be associated with the government. For instance, the first decade of the 21st century saw a reemergence of anti-immigrant feeling in the United States, particularly toward Latino groups, with public demonstrations; anti-immigrant legislation at local, state, and federal levels; and increased visibility of immigration enforcement efforts. Because many Latinos residing in the United States came into the country illegally (U.S. Census Bureau, 2001b), they and many of their documented Latino counterparts may be wary of coming into contact with authority figures either because of the legal ramifications or because of the potential for stigma by association. We expect that immigrants of other nationalities who entered the country without visas or who overstayed their officially sanctioned visits share some of the same concerns in their contacts with researchers who have the appearance of authority figures. Furthermore, anti–illegal immigrant efforts sometimes have targeted individuals who are U.S. citizens and legal residents because of racial profiling practices (Bernstein, 2007; Macfarquhar, 2007). The more that politicians, legal authorities, and activist groups are focused on illegal immigrants, and the more the ensuing discrimination against immigrants grows, the more likely it is that members of populations with significant numbers of immigrants are to react defensively when approached by researchers. Thus, researchers face a serious challenge to establish trust and reduce feelings of threat when interacting with potential research participants who are members of ethnic minority groups, particularly if they are undocumented immigrants.

OVERCOMING CHALLENGES TO RECRUITMENT

Research on recruitment practices and their outcomes with ethnic minority and economically disadvantaged populations tend to be descriptive and informally comparative at best. Relatively few researchers describe their recruitment processes in the type of detail that would allow replication. Similarly, relatively few researchers report the response rates to recruitment processes for specific ethnic minority or economically disadvantaged groups. Moreover, we know of only one modern study in which one research project has systematically used two or more competing recruitment processes, randomly assigned to each potential participant, and determined which is most effective with which type of potential participant (Sue, Fujino, Takeuchi, & Zane, 1991). Journal articles describing new recruitment processes typically describe a modification of commonly used practices and compare their response rates with those of a few other similar studies. Although this descriptive and incremental process has contributed to improvements in recruitment techniques used with ethnic minority and economically disadvantaged populations, it also leaves much to be desired. The results of recruitment efforts probably vary to some degree by the reputation of the institution or investigators (e.g., a history of cooperation, or friction, between the sponsoring institution or researchers and the ethnic minority or economically disadvantaged community), the location of the study (e.g., in the community, in a hospital, in a campus laboratory, in participants' homes), the demands of participation (e.g., completing a short questionnaire while the investigator waits vs. a 2-hour interview vs. participation in a 10-week intervention), political history in the targeted community (e.g., highly publicized disclosure of discriminatory practices), and numerous other factors that rarely are discussed in research on recruitment. Thus, a simple comparison of recruitment rates between one institution or investigator using a common method and rates reported by another institution or investigator using a modification to common practices does not necessarily provide clear evidence that one method is superior to the other; too many uncontrolled variables make simple comparisons across studies questionable.

Two other issues make the existing literature on recruitment processes difficult to interpret and evaluate. First, although many of the articles written about recruitment processes focus on the response rates for a particular racial or ethnic group, in most cases race or ethnicity is confounded with other important demographic factors (e.g., social class, immigrant status, acculturation level, inner-city residence). In these cases, it is unclear whether the recruitment method used applies to the racial or ethnic group, the social class group, or the immigrant portion of the group studied. Second, many recruitment studies use pan-ethnic designs, such as comparing recruitment rates of Asian Americans with rates for European Americans, even though it is likely that participation rates also vary widely between Asian subgroups (e.g., Hmong Americans vs. Chinese Americans).

For these reasons, it is not possible to reach simple conclusions regarding the relative utility of various recruitment methods in research involving ethnic minority or economically disadvantaged populations. Instead, in the section that follows we outline the lessons learned from studies that have tried innovative approaches and described their results in enough detail to suggest the value of their methods. We report the specific groups used in these studies and, when appropriate, comment when we believe the methods used might apply to other ethnic minority or immigrant groups or other groups of the same social class. However, because of the state of the literature on recruitment, these comments and recommendations are based on our best judgment rather than on solid empirical evidence.

Understanding and Acknowledging Participants' Values

One of the most fundamental aspects of successful recruitment (and retention) processes, as well as the ethical treatment of study participants, is to treat all potential participants respectfully. This is usually not an issue when one is working with middle-class groups, because researchers (virtually all of whom are of middle- and upper class socioeconomic status) know the rules of social interactions of their own social class group and take these rules for granted. When dealing with ethnic minority or economically disadvantaged populations, however, many researchers need to become familiar with the rules of social interaction, with attitudes toward authority figures, and with the values and belief systems of the targeted group before trying to engage members of the group in research (e.g., Dumka, Lopez, & Carter, 2002; Flaskerud & Nyamathi, 2000; Miranda, Azocar, Organista, Munoz, & Lieberman, 1996; Picot et al., 2002; Sue et al., 1991; Valle, 2005). Without adequate familiarity with the target group, researchers may inadvertently violate social norms that keep them from engaging potential participants. With some groups (e.g., Spanish-speaking Latinos), this means using particular pronouns to show respect, taking time to ask questions about the children in the family—and to listen to the answers—or taking time to share a cup of coffee or tea, or otherwise having warm and personal interactions before getting down to business (Miranda et al., 1996; Sanchez-Burks, Nisbett, & Ybarra, 2000).

Personal contact may be particularly effective for recruiting ethnic minority or economically disadvantaged populations (Cauce, Ryan, & Grove, 1998; Dumka, Garza, Roosa, & Stoerzinger, 1997; Gilliss et al., 2001;

Maxwell et al., 2005). Personal contact and showing signs of respect are consistent with the traditional value orientations of several ethnic minority groups, particularly those that include significant numbers of immigrants who emphasize the importance of personal relationships and showing deference toward family leaders, the elderly, or those in authority (Marín & Marín, 1991; Skaff, Chesla, Mycue, & Fisher, 2002). Negotiating these relationships in a professional capacity requires an understanding of a group's value systems and adjusting recruitment strategies accordingly. For instance, in some immigrant groups that have rigid hierarchical lines of authority, attempting to recruit a family member into a study by talking with the mother while the father is not at home might be seen as threatening the father's position of authority. Even if a researcher believes strongly in gender equality, acting on or expressing such beliefs to those with very different value systems might lead to selective nonparticipation and thereby reduce the representativeness of the final sample. Miranda et al. (1996) recommended incorporating the family into recruitment processes for Latinos; we suspect that this strategy would also be helpful with other groups that are high on familistic values. Because the decision of whether a particular family member participates in a study will be a family decision in many cases, recruiters may want to explain the study to other family members, particularly the head of the family, in addition to the family member targeted for recruitment. Showing respect for more collectivistic decision-making styles rather than making recruitment an individual experience that shuts out other family members may help the researcher overcome barriers to participation in some ethnic minority families. Of course, this approach is not appropriate if the topic of the study is highly sensitive (e.g., HIV status, drug use), such that involving the family in the recruitment process could result in the disclosure of information that had not been shared with the family or, if known, has created bad feelings among family members.

Personal experience, such as being a member of the target ethnic minority group or having experienced poverty earlier in life, also may prepare a researcher for successful recruitment with ethnic minorities or economically disadvantaged populations. However, personal experience can also be misleading. The process of completing multiple college degrees and becoming a researcher can change people in critical ways and alter memories of their early life experiences; it is easy to overestimate how easily one can reconnect with or be accepted by members of an ethnic minority or economically disadvantaged community of which one was once a member (Gone, 2006). Even for those researchers who share an identity with members of the ethnic minority or economically disadvantaged group targeted for research, we recommend using one or more of the partnership approaches described later in this chapter to ensure that personal perspectives and memories are accurate and that recruitment methods will be acceptable, attractive, and effective.

Finally, researchers who have acquired extensive experience working with members of ethnic minority or economically disadvantaged populations in service or research capacities, who have built a strong positive reputation within these communities, or who are affiliated with research institutions that have positive reputations within these communities are likely to find fewer barriers to recruitment and retention than those who are strangers to the community or who are affiliated with institutions that have negative reputations within the targeted communities (Levkoff & Sanchez, 2003; Manson et al., 2004; Roosa et al., 2008). The former are more likely than most to understand the values, goals, and lifestyles of the targeted communities. Even so, reputations are fragile and need constant efforts to be maintained.

Matching Participants and Research Personnel on Demographic Characteristics

Much has been written about the need for demographic matching of research participants and front-line research personnel (e.g., recruiters, interviewers), particularly with regard to race, ethnicity, language, and gender (e.g., Gallagher-Thompson et al., 2006; Picot et al., 2002). However, at least one systematic study of what is called the *cultural responsiveness hypothesis* (i.e., demographic matching) reported no significant benefit to recruitment success from demographic matching (Sue et al., 1991). Ultimately, the answer to this question is probably complex and dependent on a variety of factors, such as the particular ethnic group being recruited, their history of discrimination or exploitation by the larger society, and the topic under investigation. For example, an African American adult living in a racially polarized community may be more likely to agree to participate in a study about racially sensitive topics, such as discrimination experiences, if the recruiters and interviewers with whom they interact are themselves African Americans rather than European Americans. On the other hand, racial or ethnic matching of interviewers and participants might contribute to less honest responses if participants are concerned about looking bad or losing face in front of someone from their group. Given the complexity of this issue, a potential strategy is to carefully document the demographic characteristics of interviewers and participants and test for potential interviewer effects (i.e., whether there are systematic differences in responses given by participants on the basis of whether the interviewer was of the same or different ethnic background as the participant). If interviewer effects are found, this knowledge would be valuable for the research community. Future research will benefit if researchers are conscientious in describing the approach they used and reporting the results of tests for potential interviewer effects.

Unlike other aspects of demographic matching, being able to conduct recruitment and research processes (e.g., instructions, assessments) in the language of potential participants is absolutely essential for studies of populations that include significant numbers of people who do not speak English (e.g., L. Case & Smith, 2000; Flaskerud & Nyamathi, 2000; Gallagher-Thompson et al., 2006; Valle, 2005). This usually means that recruiters and interviewers need to be fluently bilingual because many members of the targeted group may not be monolingual English speakers. As we discuss in chapters 4 and 5 of this volume, conducting research in a second language is more challenging than simply finding enough bilingual staff to conduct the study: All written and orally communicated materials must be translated into the second language, which is a major undertaking. Our subjective evaluation of a few decades of cumulative experience interviewing Mexican Americans suggests that having recruiters and interviewers who are bilingual and bicultural (i.e., respect and understand the cultural values, beliefs, lifestyles, and practices of the traditional culture as well as the U.S. mainstream culture) is more important to recruitment and retention than the ethnic background of recruiters and interviewers. Being familiar with the target population, comfortable interacting with members of the population, and capable of communicating easily with members of the group are strong assets for anyone on a research team studying an ethnic minority or economically disadvantaged population (Arean & Gallagher-Thompson, 1996; Miranda et al., 1996; Norton & Manson, 1996).

Members of Targeted Group as Advisors or Collaborators

Another way of designing recruitment processes that are attractive and not insulting to a targeted group is to get members of that group to serve as collaborators with, or as advisors or partners to, the researchers (e.g., Arean & Gallagher-Thompson, 1996; Dumka et al., 2002; Manson et al., 2004; Valle, 2005; Wallerstein & Duran, 2006). *Collaborative models,* sometimes referred to as *university–community partnerships* or *community-based participatory research,* can take on several forms. At one level, researchers ask members of the targeted group to serve in advisory roles, which can involve activities such as answering direct questions about the population or community, reviewing and critiquing research plans, or assisting in training research personnel. At the other extreme, these partnerships can involve representatives of the targeted group as equal partners throughout the research process, from deciding which research questions to pursue through interpreting the results (Beals et al., 2005; Levkoff & Sanchez, 2003; Manson et al., 2004; Valle, 2005; Wallerstein & Duran, 2006). Because of historical problems with researchers and the resulting mistrust of the research community, much research on American Indian reservations at this time requires high levels of consultation and collaboration as equals, from the research question generation point onward (Manson et al., 2004; Wallerstein & Duran, 2006). Projects using a collaboration-as-equals approach usually require more time to develop and implement because of the time spent building social and political ties and trust between partners. These types of projects also require researchers to give up their usual levels of autonomy in deciding on research questions and processes. These more intimate partnerships are most likely to happen in local, somewhat geographically restricted areas, whereas statewide or national studies are more likely to benefit from more limited-partnership models. In both cases, the partnerships help prepare researchers and their staffs to interact more successfully with the targeted group, which can lead to improved participant recruitment and retention. These types of partnerships likely are most important when researchers want to conduct research with groups that have the greatest levels of distrust of research and researchers, such as American Indians and African Americans, although this issue has not been directly tested in research.

A related strategy for improving recruitment and other interactions with ethnic minority or economically disadvantaged populations is to partner with well-known organizations that represent or serve the interests of the targeted group (Cauce, Ryan, & Grove, 1998; Roosa et al., 2008; Umaña-Taylor & Bámaca, 2004). These organizations could include national or local advocacy groups or social service organizations (e.g., civil rights groups, immigrant rights groups, public schools, tribal councils). In any event, the relationship between the organization and most members of the targeted group should be positive before a researcher tries to implement this strategy. Members of such organizations may serve in an advisory capacity or in a more equal and active partnership. They also may actively recruit or refer people into the study (e.g., Gallagher-Thompson et al., 2006). The research team benefits from the "reflected glory" of the partner organization, which helps remove barriers and suspicions when researchers approach members of the targeted group. In partnerships of this type there may be some costs as well as benefits. The more equal the partnership, the more researchers must be willing to allow for a shared research agenda in order to integrate their agenda and that of the partner organization. Also, in almost all cases some portion of the target population will have political disagreements with the organization representing the population and, therefore, may be more difficult to recruit than they might have been if approached by researchers without the organizational partner. For instance, recruiting ethnic minority children or families through public schools with the assistance (e.g., a letter to parents) of a principal or superintendent may be helpful in most cases (e.g., Roosa et al., 2008), but it can backfire in cases in which the school official has had bad relations with the targeted population. Similarly, recruiting participants with the assistance of a social service agency that targets a particular ethnic minority group may be very successful in most cases, but this partnership also may be the reason why other families who have been denied services or who have had negative interactions with agency personnel do not participate. Thus, this strategy should be used in combination with other recruitment strategies so as not to limit the sample being recruited to members of the target population who have political views similar to those of the partnering organization.

Method of Contact and Communication

A common way of recruiting people into research is through the use of written materials, such as letters, Internet postings, or advertisements in newspapers. In general, these methods are likely to be more effective with middle-class samples than with economically disadvantaged groups. Compared with low-income individuals, middle-class individuals from almost any ethnic group are likely to have higher levels of literacy, making written communication more effective. Furthermore, middle-class persons probably are more likely to consider formal, written communication from a well-known institution as a positive thing. Individuals in economically disadvantaged communities may be less likely to have had the direct experiences that provide knowledge of the reputation of research institutions. Thus, impersonal communication in writing, even when literacy is not an issue, is less likely to be effective with low-income individuals. We also suspect that, for some low-income persons, formal written communication may be associated with official notices from authority figures and therefore associated with bad news.

On the other hand, in-person referrals (i.e., face-to-face contact with respected members of community) have been shown to be more effective with Chinese Americans than with European Americans (Gallagher-Thompson et al., 2006). Media sources (e.g., radio announcements) also were more effective with Chinese Americans, whereas nonprofessional referral sources, such as health fairs, were more attractive to European Americans. Miranda et al. (1996) recommended recruiting Latinos through medical centers and churches. Gallagher-Thompson et al. (2004) also recommended partnerships with agencies as effective methods of recruiting Latinos into health care studies. Finally, Dumka et al. (1997) reported that face-to-face recruitment at one's home by members of the local community was particularly effective across racial or ethnic groups in a low-income inner-city community. Although much of the research on the effectiveness of contact methods conducted with specific ethnic minority groups has focused on health care issues, we believe there may be a more general lesson to be learned. It may be that personal contact with a respected member of the community, whether a resident or someone with a positive reputation for providing services to the community or individual, can be a particularly effective recruitment tool for many individuals from ethnic minority or economically disadvantaged groups. Whether that tool is more effective with members of ethnic minority groups versus European Americans or whether the important demographic characteristic is social class instead of ethnicity cannot be determined from these studies. For low-income and ethnic minority individuals, the little research literature available suggests that personal contact with respected professionals from well-regarded local agencies or neighbors may be necessary to gain trust and contribute to more effective recruitment outcomes. Thus, partnerships with members of the targeted community or the professionals who serve them, as described earlier, may be critical aspects of the recruitment process with these populations. We hope that researchers will address many of these recruitment issues more systematically and in greater detail in the near future.

Benefits and Incentives

As mentioned earlier, members of low-income groups may be less motivated than members of higher income groups to participate in research. Instead, research that has immediate personal benefits (e.g., receiving treatment, incentives) or clearly articulated longer term benefits for the individual or the targeted ethnic minority or economically disadvantaged group may be more attractive and more likely to elicit participation (Roosa et al., 2008). Paying participants a reasonable amount to reward them for their time will reduce, at least partially, other barriers to participation. Financial incentives in studies with significant numbers of low-income participants should be commensurate with the time and stress demands of participating in research; of course, incentives should not be large enough to be coercive and make it difficult for low-income individuals to refuse to participate. It is important that financial incentives in studies of economically disadvantaged populations be in the most accessible form possible (e.g., cash, cash card, gift card, coupon) rather than in the form of a check because of the costs involved in cashing checks for individuals without bank accounts or appropriate identification (e.g., undocumented immigrants). However, research that has broader benefits (e.g., intervention programs) or that will lead to the development of intervention programs to benefit the larger group also are expected to be attractive to many people in low-income and ethnic minority groups. In particular, interventions that are aimed at helping children in low-income and ethnic minority families be more successful or that ultimately help the larger ethnic or geographic community are likely to be highly attractive (Dumka et al., 1997; Lengua et al., 1992). Participating in research that gives back in this way is consistent with the cultural values of collectivism or familism, which place the emphasis on what is good for the group or family more so than for the individual and are shared by many ethnic minority groups.

Obviously, not all research can be linked to intervention programs, but studies that are might find a very receptive audience in otherwise hard-to-recruit populations. It is also true that not all researchers can afford to pay participant fees. In those cases, researchers should seriously consider why members of ethnic minority or low-income populations would want to participate. This would be a time when partnerships with members of the targeted group might be particularly helpful. Consultations with the target population, perhaps in the form of focus groups (e.g., Lengua et al., 1992), can help generate a recruitment strategy that is consistent with the values, goals, and life experiences of the group.

Obtaining Diversity in Samples of Ethnic Minority Populations

Much of what has been written about the recruitment of ethnic minority or economically disadvantaged populations has focused on increasing the participation of these groups in research, not necessarily on obtaining samples that represent the diversity within a population. All ethnic groups are diverse with respect to educational or income level, family structures and living arrangements, and mental or physical health problems, to name a few. Given the hundreds of studies of ethnic minority or economically disadvantaged populations, relatively few have represented the diversity within these groups well. Of critical importance is that very little has been written about how to obtain samples that are representative of ethnic minority or economically disadvantaged populations. Although increased participation rates should improve the representativeness of samples, some additional steps may be necessary to obtain samples that represent the diversity within ethnic minority or economically disadvantaged populations. The strategies described previously are intended to improve researchers' ability to obtain representative samples of these groups. Later in this chapter, we present an example of a study in which the researchers used many of these strategies to obtain a diverse sample of an ethnic minority group that was quite representative of that group.

RETENTION

For longitudinal studies, successful sampling and recruiting are just the beginning. Researchers conducting longitudinal studies also need a plan for retaining as many as possible of the individuals who initially enrolled in the study (i.e., a retention plan). Failure to retain participants creates problems in data analysis in longitudinal studies and in researchers' ability to interpret their results as well as their ability to generalize those results to the target population. Again, there has been little systematic research into the effectiveness of retention techniques or strategies and less still that has focused on the ethnically diverse or economically disadvantaged populations. Indeed, relatively few researchers report the retention techniques used in longitudinal studies (Scott, 2004).

Retention in Intervention Studies

By design, most intervention studies involve more than one contact with participants and, therefore, are longitudinal in nature. In intervention studies, using culturally attractive and effective recruitment techniques seems to make a significant contribution to retaining participants in multiple-session interventions across multiple ethnic minority groups (Arean & Gallagher-Thompson, 1996; Coen, Patrick, & Shern, 1996; Keller, Gonzales, & Fleuriet, 2005; Lau & Gallagher-Thompson, 2002; Taylor-Piliae & Froelicher, 2007; Warren-Findlow, Prohaska, & Freedman, 2003). For instance, employing a bilingual and bicultural staff, developing a program focused on the perceived needs of the individuals recruited, having the program cosponsored by well-known and respected community agencies, locating the intervention in the community so it is readily accessible to the target population, building social relationships between staff and participants as well as among participants, and making sure the program does not interfere with family obligations appear to be related to high recruitment and retention rates. Using culturally specific elements or symbols may increase retention rates as well (Dumka et al., 2002). For instance, a strategy used in a health promotion intervention specifically for Latinos was the use of *promotoras,* lay workers who provided social support and encouragement to participants (Koch, 1996). The role of the *promotora* probably has both practical and symbolic value to participants in that it not only offers a supporter–cheerleader–coach to help a person stick with the intervention but also shows that the intervention was designed specifically for the participant's ethnic group. Once again, these strategies have been described as part of the overall process of interventions that have been deemed successful and have had acceptable recruitment and retention rates. However, none of these strategies has been scientifically evaluated (i.e., included in the processes for one group, left out of the processes with another, and then subjected to a comparison of retention levels) to determine whether they contribute to higher retention. Finally, intervention programs rarely describe retention efforts beyond the recruitment and program development processes.

Retention in Longitudinal Panel Studies

In panel studies, researchers typically begin by recruiting a certain number of participants and conducting interviews or administering questionnaires almost immediately after successful recruitment. Then, depending on the specifics of the research design, the researchers want to reinterview the original participants at specific intervals (e.g., 3 months, 1 year) or ages after the initial interviews. These repeated assessments may conclude after one follow-up or after many follow-ups. In panel studies it is critical to be able to locate the original participants at the predetermined follow-up periods and to maintain positive relations with previous participants so that they are motivated to continue. The good news is that retention rates of 90% or greater between assessments are not unusual, even with high-risk populations (e.g., substance abusers; Scott, 2004). The bad news is that relatively few studies have described recruitment processes specifically designed to maximize the retention of ethnically diverse or economically disadvantaged populations.

The challenges associated with retaining ethnic minority and econom-ically disadvantaged samples in longitudinal studies are often the same challenges associated with recruiting representative samples of these pop-ulations. Retaining participants in research involves, among many other things, keeping the lines of communication open. With a sample that con-tains relatively recent immigrants, this often means maintaining the capa-bility of communicating in the participant's native language as well as in English according to his or her preference as well as communicating in cul-turally respectful ways. For the portion of a sample that is low income there are likely to be more problems with mobility and literacy than with middle-class samples. Mobility issues are particularly challenging in longitudinal studies with certain groups (e.g., Puerto Ricans who can freely move between the mainland United States and Puerto Rico; Mexican or Central Americans in the southwestern United States who may leave the United States and return to their country of origin because of its proximity to the United States). In such populations, some may move back and forth between countries as family needs or economics dictate. In addition, stepped-up enforcement of immigration laws and resulting deportations is a relatively new complication for longitudinal studies of populations con-taining significant numbers of undocumented immigrants.

Just like intervention studies, longitudinal panel studies that use cul-turally sensitive recruitment and assessment methods like those described previously are taking an important first step toward retaining participants in research. It makes logical sense that if participants find the objectives of the research attractive, are treated with respect, do not find the research process threatening, and develop rapport with research staff during interviews or other assessments, they are likely to be more receptive to requests for continued participation in the research than if their initial experiences were negative. During the recruitment and initial assessment stages of the study researchers would do well to emphasize the importance of two things: (a) the research project's goals, particularly if the research might ultimately benefit the participant's family or the larger ethnic minority or economically disadvantaged population (i.e., not just the participant) and (b) the importance of the participant's contributions to the study. These strategies can serve as tools to develop the participant's commitment to the study and thus aid the retention process. Engaging other members of participants' families during the recruitment process, when possible, may be particularly helpful in gaining their support later when one is trying to locate participants who have changed addresses. Still, to retain participants in research over the long term is a labor-intensive process that requires a well-developed multidimensional plan and careful coordination that builds on the use of positive and effective methods at the recruitment stage but cannot depend on success at that stage alone.

Most longitudinal studies use a subset of five commonly recommended strategies to maintain contact with study participants for future follow-ups (e.g., Coen et al., 1996; Hampson et al., 2001; Scott, 2004; Stephens, Thibodeaux, Sloboda, & Tonkin, 2007).

First, obtain tracing information either at first contact or during the assessment process. This means getting the names, addresses, and telephone numbers of several people (we recommend at least three) who will always know the participant's location. These tracers can include family, neighbors, friends, employers, and children's schools. Scott (2004) recommended verifying the names and addresses of all tracers within 7 to 10 days after the information is obtained. When working with relatively new immigrants, we recommend not relying exclusively on family members as tracers because of the possibility that the extended family will move at the same time, even when they live independently of one another. In addition to gathering tracer information, it is incumbent on the researcher to obtain permission to contact these individuals in the event he or she loses contact with the study participant. To overcome fears among the tracers about your intentions when you contact them for information about the participant, we recommend having the participant sign a letter addressed to the tracer that states that the participant is in a study and that the participant requests the tracer to provide contact information to the researcher. In our experience, such letters can be quite helpful in gaining the confidence of tracers if participants are of low income, have had problems with authority figures, or if they are undocumented immigrants. Letters such as these are a legal requirement if school officials or employers are going to release information about the participant or the family of former students; even with these letters, schools and employers may not always provide the requested information.

Second, if the interval between interviews or assessments is more than a few weeks, systematically make contact in the interim to determine whether the participant has changed addresses. We recommend more frequent contact attempts (i.e., at least once every 4 months) with low-income participants or others who have a history of mobility (note that this requires asking about the number of residences in the past few years during the initial assessment). All contacts with study participants should be done in ways that indicate how important they are to the study's success and should attempt to strengthen the participant's commitment to continuing in the study. For instance, researchers can send out personalized birthday cards to participants and to participants' spouse or parents. A card or flier can be included in this mailing to remind the participant of the study and upcoming interviews/assessments and to keep him or her engaged in the study (Scott, 2004). A toll-free telephone number and/or a postage-paid envelope will allow participants to respond with address changes almost painlessly; the Internet also can provide a useful means by which participants can contact researchers, but low-income individuals are less likely to use this method than are middle-class participants. As motivation, researchers can offer an incentive (e.g., cash, coupon, gift card) to participants for contacting the research team regardless of whether there has been a change in address. The same request for updating their address can be included in a mailing containing a short newsletter with information about the study, a calendar of local low-cost events, or coupons for fast food items. Well-designed newsletters can keep participants interested in the study and open to future participation.

Third, it is important to follow up on mailings that do not generate a response. If there is no response 2 to 4 weeks after a mailing, use other means (telephone, e-mail, home visits) to make contact. If the study participant has relocated and these processes are not successful in locating his or her new address, begin contacting tracers. It is important to follow up on study participants as soon as you discover that they have changed addresses because the longer they are in a new location, the more likely it is that tracers also will lose contact with them. It is not unusual for dozens of contact attempts to be necessary before successfully recontacting a participant who has moved (Scott, 2004); therefore, this stage of the process requires organization, persistence, and resources.

Fourth, when tracers are not able, or willing, to help you contact participants who have moved, consider using the Internet to search various public records. Potentially useful sources include municipal water customer records, electronic white pages directories, property tax records, police and court records, and drivers license records (Hampson et al., 2001; Stephens et al., 2007). There are commercial companies that will conduct such searches for researchers. Unfortunately, Internet sources are most likely to be successful with middle-class participants and probably least likely to be useful for recently immigrated or low-income participants.

Fifth, prepare participants for the timing of upcoming assessments via mailings and direct contacts, and schedule their continued participation well in advance of the targeted assessment date. Then remind them of the upcoming assessment a week in advance and again 24 hours before the assessment.

These retention strategies were not specifically designed for ethnic minority or economically disadvantaged populations but were collected from a wide variety of studies with various populations. For studies examining ethnic minority populations, the only adaptations required probably involve the adaptations described earlier in the recruitment process: being able to communicate in the participant's preferred language and being sensitive to cultural values and taboos, for example. For low-income participants, whether they are the target of the study or a subpart of a larger ethnic minority population, adaptations might include more frequent contacts, more personal contact, more tracers, or larger incentives to remain in contact. It is our hope that in the future more researchers will report successful retention strategies used specifically with low-income or ethnic minority populations. Because there have been so few longitudinal studies of ethnic minority and economically disadvantaged populations, it is important that researchers give more attention to the challenges these types of studies represent in order to obtain the highest quality information from future longitudinal studies with these populations.

RECRUITMENT AND RETENTION CASE STUDY

For a study of cultural and contextual influences on child adjustment in Mexican American families, Roosa et al. (2008) designed a multistep sampling and recruitment process with the goal of obtaining a sample that represented as much of the diversity within this population as possible on several indicators of social class and cultural orientation. They recruited a sample that was highly diverse and relatively representative of the local Mexican American population in a major metropolitan area by relying on 10 important elements.

First, Roosa et al. (2008) began with many years of active contact with the target population through basic research and intervention studies. Their knowledge of this part of the community, as well as the positive reputation they had developed within this community over the years, improved their access to the population. For instance, when they decided to create a community advisory board to assist them with various aspects of the research design and implementation, they already had a list of contacts and, when asked, almost all volunteered to join the board and gave generously of their time, expertise, and experience.

Second, they created a community advisory board composed of highly respected leaders in the educational and Latino communities who advised the research team on all facets of the research process. The names of the members of the advisory board were prominently featured on the letterhead used by the team and on their Web site, providing instant recognition of their connection to the project to anyone who received mailings from the team or who searched the Web site for more information about the project.

Third, the project's purpose was to obtain information that would help guide the development of programs to help Mexican American children who have difficulties at home, school, or in the community (e.g., appealing to the collectivistic orientation of much of the population). The research team also used a culturally attractive label as shorthand for the project ("La Familia").

Fourth, they identified the communities in which Mexican Americans lived and then sampled these to represent the diversity in community contexts for this population. They argued that it was not possible to represent the diversity within an ethnic minority group unless steps were taken to ensure that the diversity in living conditions was represented in the sample. Samples of an ethnic minority group that come exclusively from urban ethnic enclaves are likely to differ dramatically on some theoretically important characteristics (e.g., portion of population that speaks English, degree of commitment to the traditions of the culture of origin, degree of commitment to mainstream U.S. traditions, social class) from samples of the same ethnic group that come from more integrated suburban or rural communities. Thus, they used a multistage sampling plan that began with systematically sampling of communities that varied in important cultural and economic dimensions.

Fifth, they developed partnerships with elementary schools to assist in the process of sampling children and their families. Note that using school partnerships to recruit a representative sample of Mexican Americans becomes less viable at the junior high and high school levels because of the cumulative dropout rate for this population (U.S. Department of Education, 2000). These school partnerships were an asset to the recruitment process in probably 80% of participating schools, but because of friction with the Mexican American community partnerships with a few schools made recruiting more difficult.

Sixth, families were initially contacted by letters and fliers sent home with every child in the targeted grade regardless of ethnicity. These letters and brochures, like all recruitment and research materials, were written in both English and Spanish. These letters asked Latino parents to indicate whether they wanted to be considered for a research study and, if so, to provide contact information. To encourage the return of these letters, regardless of parents' ethnicity or willingness to participate, classrooms received an incentive (i.e., pizza party) if at least 80% of children returned a form. In addition, teachers received a gift certificate if their classroom had the highest return rate in their school. The average return rate across 47 schools was more than 86%.

Seventh, Latino parents who returned forms indicating interest and providing contact information were contacted by bilingual and bicultural recruiters, screened for Mexican cultural background and family characteristics for eligibility and, if eligible, asked to participate in the study. Although most of these contacts were made using telephones, families without telephones, or whose telephones were never answered, were contacted through visits to their homes. Whenever possible, fathers were included in discussions about the study and recruitment. More than 70% of those families who were eligible expressed interest in the study, were locatable, and completed interviews.

Eighth, interviews were scheduled with eligible and interested families at a time of their convenience (e.g., evenings or weekends). Although most interviews took place in families' homes, eliminating problems with transportation or unfamiliarity with the local university, in a few cases in which the home did not provide sufficient privacy (i.e., it was shared with others), interviews took place in the evening at the child's school.

Ninth, all interviewers were bicultural, and most were bilingual and Latino. Monolingual English-speaking interviewers were assigned to only those cases in which researchers were certain that no Spanish would be spoken.

Tenth, and finally, participating family members received $45 each in cash (as soon as consent and assent forms were signed) for participating in the study.

The resulting sample was very similar to the local Mexican-origin community on most demographic characteristics according to comparisons with census data (Roosa et al., 2008). The only differences were that the sample included a higher portion of adults born in Mexico and who preferred speaking Spanish than one would expect from the census. Most important, the resulting sample was much more diverse than most prior studies of Mexican Americans in terms of social class indicators, place of birth (United States or Mexico), language preference, and personal cultural orientation. Although the methods used were intense, rigorous, and costly, this study demonstrated that it is possible to obtain more diverse and representative samples of ethnic minority populations than has been common in the literature.

To maintain participant retention, Roosa et al. (2008) began by obtaining families' permission to maintain contact with them between interviews, which were 2 years apart. Then parents were asked to provide names and contact information for at least 3 people who would always know where they lived even if they moved (i.e., tracers). Parents then addressed and signed form letters to each of these tracers that stated that they were involved in a study and asking the tracers to provide help to the researchers if ever contacted about the participant. On the basis of responses during the interviews to questions about family income and the number of homes people had lived in during the previous 3 years, families were divided into a "high risk to move" category and a low-risk group; the former were contacted every 3 months between interviews and the latter were contacted every 6 months. Initial contacts involved sending letters asking participants to contact the research team to report either that they were living at the same address or to provide their new address. Participants could respond by completing a brief form and returning it in a postage-paid envelope, calling the research team, or contacting them by e-mail. Participants were promised a $5 incentive for contacting the research team. If no response was received within 4 weeks of mailing, researchers tried to make contact by telephone, and if that was not successful, someone would visit the home. In addition, participating family members were sent birthday cards, and twice each year families received a two-page (one-sheet) newsletter with information about local activities that might be of interest to families with children in the targeted age group. These mailings also included forms for updating addresses if families had moved. Attrition for this study was less than 5% across a 2-year period.

Roosa et al.'s (2008) study demonstrated that by using the best practices recommended in this chapter, including addressing cultural issues and being aware of the challenges involved in research with ethnic minority and low-income populations, researchers can obtain and retain diverse and reasonably representative samples of these groups. These strategies were informed considerably by the advice of a highly committed advisory committee. Application of these processes required thoughtful training of members of the research team. Relatively few studies can afford to include all the steps used in Roosa et al.'s study, but several of the steps are relatively inexpensive and can be included in most studies with a similar population. As more researchers attempt to develop successful recruitment and retention strategies with ethnic minority or economically disadvantaged populations, we hope that even more effective and less expensive strategies will become common.

IMPLICATIONS FOR THE FOUR COMMON RESEARCH DESIGNS

Cross-Group Comparative Designs

Studies that are explicitly interested in making comparisons between groups would, in most cases, best be served by using stratified random sampling and using recruitment methods designed specifically for each defined subgroup. By developing recruitment processes that are designed to be culturally attractive to each specific group, including having recruitment and research materials available in languages other than English if this is necessary to reach all members of a group, researchers improve the likelihood that they will achieve reasonably similar and high recruitment rates for each group. In most cases, it also would be important to pay attention to how group membership is defined and operationalized. A well-designed and well-executed study using these processes would contribute to both the internal (depending on the research question) and external validity of the study.

Within-Group Designs

For studies interested in the diversity or variation within ethnic minority or economically disadvantaged populations, the definition and operationalization of group membership is of primary concern. Will including individuals or families of mixed racial or ethnic background affect tests of the hypothesis? For instance, if a researcher is interested in the relationship of ethnic pride to Navajo adolescents' persistence in school, does it matter if some children come from homes that in addition to having a Navajo parent have an African American parent, or a European American parent, or a parent from another American Indian tribe?

Most within-group research designs would be well served by a random sampling design. Properly executed, a random sampling design would represent all segments of the targeted population and demonstrate the diversity of members of this group on a number of important variables. With a focus on a single ethnic minority group, researchers would be able to develop recruitment processes that are broadly attractive to members of that group. Still, they might want to target some techniques specifically for individuals at the low and high economic strata within the group, perhaps more personal or face-to-face recruitment at the lower income level and more formal and written recruitment processes at the upper income level. If the target group involves an ethnically diverse sample of individuals, many or all of whom are also part of an economically disadvantaged group (e.g., members of families participating in one or more federal or state assistance program), then recruitment methods become immensely complicated. In addition to using methods that are known to be attractive to low-income groups, the researchers would need to develop culturally attractive methods specific to each ethnic minority group likely to be included in the study—potentially an immense undertaking depending on the size and population diversity in the area being studied.

National Sample Designs

National sample designs generally are used to determine population-level incident rates, means, or relations among variables. As such, these designs often explicitly attempt to have participants from each ethnic minority and economic group in the population, although not necessarily in numbers large enough for separate analyses by ethnic or economic group or for comparisons between groups. Because of the complexity and costs of sampling and recruiting participants in multiple states, these studies typically use a single recruitment process with no explicit attempt to increase recruitment rates among ethnic minority or economically disadvantaged groups or to include more marginalized members of these groups (i.e., recent immigrants, limited English speakers, undocumented). In some of these studies, the sampling designs deliberately oversample participants who are economically disadvantaged or members of select ethnic minority groups, to improve the likelihood that generalizations made can apply to these groups or so that some cross-group comparisons will be possible. Oversampling in most cases is achieved simply by repeated effort and rarely, if ever, by using recruitment methods designed specifically for targeted groups. To more broadly represent the diversity within the various groups included in most national sample designs, researchers would need to translate all recruitment and assessment materials into a variety of languages; develop multiple recruitment processes specific to the ethnic minority groups; and hire much more diverse, bilingual, and bicultural staff than is commonly the case. Needless to say, achieving such diversity within economically disadvantaged and ethnic minority groups within national data sets would be enormously demanding and expensive. With the exception of the national census, we are not sure that any study has attempted to capture the true ethnic and economic diversity of the U.S. population.

Perhaps the most important point about national sample designs for researchers who are interested in ethnically diverse or economically disadvantaged groups is that these data sets rarely represent the full diversity within minority groups or economically disadvantaged groups. Although the data sets generated by these studies are excellent for their intended purposes (i.e., identifying national-level incidence rates, means, or relations between variables at the national level), when researchers use these data sets to make cross-group comparisons or to make estimates of the incident rates, means, or intervariable relations for specific ethnic minority or economically disadvantaged groups, the results can be at least somewhat misleading. To the degree that members of the ethnic minority or economically disadvantaged group were not recruited (i.e., did not speak English, were not locatable) or did not respond as well to recruitment as the overall sample, the results will not accurately reflect the true incidence rate, mean, or relationship for that group—or for the nation.

Inadvertently Diverse Designs

Inadvertently diverse designs generally are based on convenience samples. No attempt is made in these designs to accommodate the special needs (e.g., language) of any particular group, and no special effort is made to reach out to any subgroup of the readily accessible population to ensure that members of that group participate in reasonable numbers. As a result, these samples almost always are limited to English speakers and made up of the most highly motivated or readily accessible portion of the population. Generalizations from such studies to ethnically diverse or economically disadvantaged populations should be made in the context of their limitations and with caution.

Convenience samples can be used for all research purposes: estimating incidence rates, comparing the strength of relationships across groups, and studying within group diversity. However, because convenience samples rarely represent any population or subpopulation well, results of these studies should be generalized with caution. In fact, because convenience samples tend to select the most accessible portions of each subpopulation, from the perspective of any individual study this is the worst sampling strategy for most types of research questions; the results of any single study must be interpreted with caution. However, because of the relatively low costs associated with studying convenience samples, these studies can be replicated more easily than studies that use more expensive random or stratified designs. When studies are replicated several times, with each study representing different cross-sections of the targeted population, it may become possible to create a composite generalization by applying the results of these multiple studies using meta-analytic techniques that better represent the target population. However, there are limits to our ability to generalize from multiple replications. For instance, replicated studies of relationships between variables focused exclusively on samples of college students can rarely be safely generalized to the population of individuals living in poverty or to a specific ethnic minority group because these groups will be, at best, poorly represented in all repetitions of the study. Similarly, replicated studies, each of which includes very small numbers of people from an ethnic minority or economically disadvantaged group, can never safely be used to generalize to other members of the group. In an ideal situation, researchers would use convenience samples primarily for pilot studies that test recruitment and retention methods, develop measures, and generate hypotheses prior to using one of the stronger sampling designs in a study designed to produce more generalizable findings.

SUMMARY

Research studies on ethnically diverse or economically disadvantaged populations continue to increase in number and sophistication. Much of the research to date has been conducted with convenience samples and using recruitment methods that are more appropriate for middle-class and European American populations. Numerous studies, often in the biomedical and health fields, have demonstrated that recruitment efforts tailored to the language needs of specific ethnic minority groups and sensitive to cultural and lifestyle issues specific to those groups can achieve reasonable response rates and obtain samples that represent at least some of the diversity within the targeted population. As more researchers who focus on ethnically diverse or economically disadvantaged populations adapt methods similar to those discussed in this chapter, we expect to see more representative samples throughout a wide range of social science literatures. All researchers can contribute to improvements in recruitment and retention in the social sciences by systematically describing their recruitment and retention processes as well as reporting the results of these procedures and breaking down these rates by ethnic minority or economic subgroups when appropriate. There is much room for improvement in current recruitment and retention processes but the foundation exists for stronger efforts in the future.

3

Ethical Issues

When we discuss ethics in research, we actually are referring to the moral code one assumes and practices when conducting research: How do you treat people and the information they share with you? Everyone in the United States involved in research with human participants should have received training in the basic moral code (reviewed in The Belmont Report from the National Commission for the Protection of Human Subjects of Biomedical and Behavioral Research [National Commission], 1979), as well as the federal regulations designed to codify this moral code, which guides the way researchers should treat individuals who are kind and generous enough to participate in research. For readers who have not yet participated in this basic training, we note that often there are short courses in research with human participants offered on university campuses. There also are online courses (e.g., the "Protecting Human Research Participants" course [http://phrp.nihtraining.com/users/login.php], offered through the National Institutes of Health [NIH], which takes 1 to 2 hours to complete). We recommend that readers complete one of these training options before continuing with this chapter.

In addition, most social science professional organizations have developed and published ethics guidelines for their members. Many of these ethics guidelines cover all aspects of the research and publication processes; many also cover professional ethics for clinical practitioners. If you are not already familiar with the ethics guidelines for your professional organizations, we recommend looking them up and becoming familiar with them. Ethics guidelines for two of the largest professional organizations for social scientists, the American Psychological Association (http://www.apa.org/ethics/code2002.html) and the American Sociological Association (http://www.asanet.org/cs/root/leftnav/ethics/code_of_ethics_table_of_contents), for example, are available on these organizations' Web sites. Each provides detailed guidance on the research and publication processes as well as for professional practices. Many other social science organizations provide similar guidelines.

The same moral code, and professional ethical standards, should guide research with human participants of all races, ethnicities or social classes. However, because ethnic minority and economically disadvantaged persons have occasionally been exploited by researchers, many believe that extra emphasis on how to ethically conduct research with these groups is warranted (e.g., Fisher et al., 2002). We already have described the well-known case of the mistreatment of low-income African American men in the Tuskegee study, which involved lies, deception, and active efforts to prevent participants from leaving the study and seeking proper medical treatment over several decades (Jones, 1981). In addition, we have mentioned the lead-based paint abatement study that failed to inform low-income, mostly African American participants of the purpose of the study and the risks their children faced (Nelson, 2001; see chap. 2, this volume). Another study, conducted with an economically disadvantaged population of orphans, experimentally induced stuttering in children with normal speech (Ambrose & Yairi, 2002). In each of these cases, researchers recruited relatively powerless, disenfranchised groups to participate in research that probably never would have been possible with middle-class, educated, more empowered groups. It is important to note, however, that most forms of research misconduct, including most of those discussed in this chapter, are not this dramatic or obvious. We hope that reminding researchers about some of the most egregious cases of ethical problems in research will encourage social scientists to be diligent about ethical issues in their own research.

In this chapter, after briefly reviewing general ethical principles that can be used to guide research decisions, we analyze ethics problems that occur too frequently in research with economically disadvantaged and ethnic minority populations as well as solutions to these problems. We do not attempt to provide a comprehensive overview of ethical issues in research; the focus of this chapter is on those issues that are specific to, or need emphasis for, ethnic minority and economically disadvantaged populations.

BASIC ETHICAL PRINCIPLES FOR RESEARCH

The Belmont Report (National Commission, 1979) provided the philosophical underpinnings for the subsequent federal regulations regarding research with human participants (Protection of Human Subjects, 2005). This document identified three basic ethical principles that are useful guides to all research actions involving humans as participants: (a) respect for persons, (b) beneficence, and (c) justice.

Respect for Persons

Respect for persons means that one assumes that each individual is an autonomous being, capable of rational thought and decision making. Under this principle, researchers should respect people's actions and opinions and consider them capable of deciding on their own whether to participate in research if given enough appropriate information. This also means that researchers should ask people to participate or continue in a study rather than convincing or coercing them. Certain individuals are considered to have diminished decision-making capacity (e.g., children, individuals with diminished mental capacity), and in those cases, researchers should look to their caretakers or guardians to make rational decisions for those individuals or exclude them from research. However, individuals' capacities to make decisions for themselves should be based on clearly accepted indicators of capacity (e.g., persons defined as minors by state laws, those deemed as dependents because of limited intellectual capacity regardless of age, those labeled emancipated minors by state law) and not on race, ethnicity, social class, gender, or other characteristics not related to maturity or mental capacity.

Beneficence

Beneficence generally refers to acts of charity or kindness. This means that research with human participants is conducted for the general good and that researchers are obligated to conduct research in ways that "maximize possible benefits and minimize possible harms" (National Commission, 1979, p. 4). At a minimum, this means avoiding doing anything that one knows will bring harm to study participants whenever possible and accepting the possibility of serious risk only in those very rare cases in which the potential value of the research results to participants and/or society are extremely high and there is no other way to conduct the research. For instance, it is ethical to test drugs with known dangerous side effects as potential treatments for diseases such as cancer or AIDS if the alternative is no treatment and a high likelihood of death for the participant. On the other hand, conducting drug trials with similarly dangerous side effects as potentially improved treatments for common headaches is not acceptable. Beneficence is also one of the key principles of the American Psychological Association Code of Ethics (see http://www.apa.org/ethics/code2002.html).

Ethical risks that must be considered range from the disclosure of sensitive personal information that could embarrass participants or result in their loss of income, employment, health insurance coverage, rights enjoyed by their peers, or their freedom (i.e., incarceration) to direct damage to their physical or mental health. Researchers are required to think carefully about each step of the research process, from sampling and data collection to data analysis and storage, to determine whether their actions could reasonably result in harm to participants. Identification and evaluation of potential risks is one part of the research process in which consulting with members of the target population should be considered. Researchers may have blind spots about potential risks or how serious known risks would appear to study participants. Thus, consultation with representatives of the individuals who would be affected by study risks, but who have no stake in the research itself, can be very informative.

If a study has the potential to harm participants, researchers must communicate this risk to potential participants as part of the recruitment and informed-consent processes. In addition, researchers must design protections to eliminate or mitigate potential harms or to respond appropriately if harm occurs despite efforts to prevent it. Similarly, if unanticipated or unforeseeable risks become evident once a study has begun, researchers are required to halt the study until these risks can be removed.

In such circumstances, informed-consent procedures must be modified to acknowledge the new risks and inform all new potential participants and all participants in longitudinal studies. If the potential for harm cannot be eliminated or minimized, only research with a very high likelihood for considerable positive benefits for participants and/or the larger society should go forward and, even then, only if individuals volunteer to participate after being fully informed about the risks.

Sometimes risks are not so obvious. For instance, questions that seem innocent and standard in research with most families (e.g., employment information, other sources of income, household composition) can, if obtained by government officials, threaten the income of individuals receiving government benefits. Similarly, problems can occur in research with populations that include significant numbers of people who are in the United States illegally because such persons usually cannot work in the country legally, may not pay taxes because of their legal status, or may pay taxes in someone else's name because they are using a false Social Security number. These persons could be arrested, incarcerated, fined, and/or deported as a result of participating in research if seemingly innocent information they supplied to researchers became known to others. As a private citizen, you may inform local, state, or federal authorities if you have evidence that someone is committing fraud by falsely receiving government benefits, is in the country illegally, or is involved in other illegal activity (e.g., drug use or sales, prostitution). As a researcher who has given participants assurances that their responses to questions will be confidential, ethically you cannot use any information obtained as part of the research process to report illegal activity to authorities, except when there is a possibility that a participant may harm others or is a threat to harm him- or herself. In studies in which the disclosure of responses to research questions could be harmful to participants and these responses can be linked to the respondent (e.g., there is a master list that connects participants' names with identification numbers used to code the data), researchers need to obtain Certificates of Confidentiality before beginning the recruitment and data collection processes. These certificates are provided by various branches of NIH to researchers conducting studies that pose these kinds of risks to participants; the certificates also provide researchers with a legal tool to use to refuse requests from legal authorities, including those accompanied by subpoenas, to view participants' data. Studies that focus on sensitive populations, such as undocumented immigrants, persons who work in a cash economy (and therefore often do not report income or pay taxes), drug users or dealers, children who are homeless or living on the streets, and prostitutes, all of which are more common among low-income populations, often require Certificates of Confidentiality to protect participants. One also could argue that a rational person from these kinds of groups would not volunteer to be in such studies without this form of protection. (Studies of such sensitive populations also can be conducted without certificates if data are collected anonymously, often including waiver of signed consent forms.) Details about the criteria for Certificates of Confidentiality and the application process are available at the Certificates of Confidentiality Kiosk on the NIH Web site (http://grants.nih.gov/grants/policy/coc/index.htm).

Justice

Justice is the principle of fairness in the research process and refers particularly to fairness in sharing both the burden of participating in research and the benefits, if any, that accrue from research. In practice, this means that researchers are expected to exhibit fairness in allowing persons to participate (e.g., minorities have equal access to participation in research; no groups are arbitrarily excluded from research); fairness in exposure to and protection from harm if harm is unavoidable (e.g., research with the potential for harm is not restricted to minorities or low-income individuals); and fairness in access to benefits of research, including programs, processes, or products developed from the research process. The principle of justice is the main reason that NIH formally requires researchers to open their studies to all populations and make an effort to more broadly represent the general population unless researchers provide convincing theoretical or scientific arguments for why research samples need to be more restricted for a particular study. The principle of justice does not exclude research limited to a single ethnic minority or socioeconomic group or research limited to the White European American middle-class majority. However, this principle does mean that there must be clear scientific justification for limiting the breadth of samples. In addition, whenever possible and scientifically feasible, research must be conducted in such a way that any benefits will eventually be applicable to the whole population. Conducting research on a new drug to treat diabetes or cardiovascular problems, for instance, with exclusively White European American samples most likely is not justifiable given the high incidence of these diseases among ethnic minority groups and therefore is not ethical. However, research with more representative samples, or a series of studies, each using an ethnic homogeneous design focusing on a different ethnic group, would be acceptable ways of determining whether the treatment was effective with multiple groups. Justice is also one of the key principles of the American Psychological Association Code of Ethics.

Although these principles may seem abstract, they can be boiled down to a few simple questions: How would you like to be treated if you were a potential participant in a research project? How would you like a member of your family to be treated in a research study? How would you like to be treated, or would like a member of your family to be treated, in a study that presented the possibility of harm? Honest answers to these questions would prevent most ethical violations in the treatment of human research participants. These principles apply to all potential research participants, not just members of ethnic minority and economically disadvantaged groups; however, documented evidence indicates that they have been overlooked, applied loosely, or violated most often or most egregiously in research with these populations (e.g., Ambrose & Yairi, 2002; Fisher et al., 2002; Jones, 1981; Nelson, 2001).

COMMON ETHICAL PROBLEMS IN RESEARCH WITH ETHNIC MINORITY OR ECONOMICALLY DISADVANTAGED POPULATIONS

Participation

Despite decades of calls for more developmental and family research on minority groups, the majority of articles published in the major journals in these fields continue to be based on samples that are all White, or overwhelmingly White, and usually middle class (McLoyd, 1990; McLoyd,

Cauce, Takeuchi, & Wilson, 2000; Quintana et al., 2006). Although we do not think this practice is a result of purposefully biased practices or racist beliefs, we believe that there are limits to the credibility of continued reliance on arguments that these practices are solely the result of the use of convenience samples (i.e., much developmental research is conducted in university child laboratories that serve overwhelmingly White faculty and student bodies; much family research is conducted with students or families living near major universities). For instance, we have seen letters from editors of some of the leading journals in these areas chastising authors for submitting articles on research that has used an ethnically homogeneous research design with ethnic minority participants rather than requesting a scientific justification for such a design. At the same time, the editors' journals were overwhelmingly dominated by ethnically homogeneous studies with White and usually middle-class samples.

There is a growing body of literature documenting that parenting goals and practices, for instance, sometimes differ between racial, ethnic, or social class groups and that the impact of parenting practices also may differ across racial, ethnic, or social class groups (e.g., Baldwin, Baldwin, & Cole 1990; Halgunseth, Ispa, & Rudy, 2006). Because of these and similar findings, one would expect the scientific community—particularly editors and reviewers, who serve as gatekeepers—to demand scientific justifications for studies that continue to use ethnic homogeneous White samples and/or support research that attempts to extend established psychological or social science principles to ethnic minority and economic subgroups that were not represented in the literature that developed these principles (Adamopoulos & Lonner, 2001). Similarly, one would think that researchers would either take steps (e.g., recruitment and scholarship plans for their child or family laboratories, child care scholarships, community partnerships, moving facilities off campus) to integrate their laboratories across racial, ethnic, or social class lines or to obtain samples in other ways. Until a larger percentage of studies in the social sciences fairly represent the behaviors, beliefs, and attitudes of ethnic minority or economically disadvantaged populations through either representative samples or ethnic homogeneous samples that examine the diversity within ethnic minority or social class groups, we will lack the information needed to design effective child care programs, prevention programs, or policies that meet the needs of these populations. There are too many cases documenting differences in basic psychological or sociological processes between ethnic minority or economically disadvantaged groups and the middle-class White majority to justify generalizations from studies based on predominantly White middle-class samples to the whole population (e.g., Baldwin et al., 1990; Broman, Reckase, & Freedman-Doan, 2006; Bryant, Schulenberg, O'Malley, Bachman, & Johnston, 2003; Guerra & Knox, 2008; Halgunseth et al., 2006). Significant changes are needed before we can begin to claim that social science research in general meets the principle of justice.

Informed Consent

In addition to assuming that individual adults have the capacity to make decisions on their own, the process of *informed consent* requires that individuals be given sufficient information in a form they understand in order to have a basis for making a decision about whether to participate in a given study. Researchers may be challenged by the relatively limited education of many potential participants in low-income populations. The situation is exacerbated by the too-common practice of consent form content being presented in legal jargon that is better designed to protect researchers or research institutions from lawsuits (i.e., exculpatory language) than to meet federal requirements of informing potential participants. In addition, consent forms often include technical or academic jargon (e.g., *skin conductance, control group, randomized trial*) that raises reading levels to undergraduate or graduate student levels. Such complex language may limit the comprehension of the information presented in consent forms by members of the general population (e.g., Breese, Burman, Goldberg, & Weis, 2007), thus reducing the utility of these documents to inform potential participants about the study. The problem is greater in the low-income portion of the population because of reduced levels of education and lower reading levels. Researchers should place at least as much importance on the wording and clarity of consent forms as they do with the wording and clarity of survey or interview questions. Consent forms should be as short as possible and written in the simplest language possible; we recommend writing forms for the general public at fifth- to eighth-grade reading levels. (One example of the types of formulas or programs available online to help compute approximate reading grade levels of documents can be found at http://en.wikipedia.org/wiki/Automated_Readability_Index.) New consent forms should be tested in pilot studies with the target population in much the same way that new measures are tested to be sure they are easily understood or to identify potential barriers to understanding that need to be removed before a study begins. Consultation with representatives from the target population may be an important part of this process.

Informed consent does not depend completely on the qualities of a written consent form; it also is a process. In studies conducted with ethnic minority and economically disadvantaged populations, researchers often need to consider the challenges posed by the power differential between research staff and potential participants. The research team members who interact with participants and conduct the informed-consent process often are college educated or current college students. As representatives of a university or other research institution, these individuals, who usually come predominantly from White middle-class backgrounds, may have few life experiences in common with potential study participants from low-income or ethnic minority communities. Potential participants might be overwhelmed when research staff members approach them with well-rehearsed recruitment scripts, pages of brochures or other project descriptions, and pages of consent documents. At least some potential participants may be confused by the abundance of information, the common demand that a decision about participation be made immediately, and the feeling that they may not really have a choice regarding their participation. This experience may be much more intense if the potential participant is someone who recently immigrated to the United States and whose native language is not English. Immigrants may have more difficulty understanding consent documents, particularly if the documents are not available in their native languages. For immigrants from many Latin American countries, cultural concepts such as *respeto,* which requires that one maintain pleasant relations and avoid conflict (Marín &

Marín, 1991), may further erode beliefs that the potential participant may decline the invitation without insulting the person asking. In addition, many immigrants come from countries where governments were more authoritarian and where freedom of choice was less common than in the United States. It may take extra effort to convince such individuals that they really do have the freedom to choose to participate and that no harm will come to them for exercising their choice. When dealing with populations who are unlikely to be familiar with the research process and who may have difficulty understanding that they really do have an option to say no, the consent process should include educational elements to familiarize potential participants with the meaning of research and the purposes and possible benefits of the study and should emphasize repeatedly the voluntariness provisions of consent.

Researchers should think through each step of the consent process and how it will appear from the perspective of the target population. The use of an advisory board (see chap. 2, this volume), conducting research in partnerships with the targeted community, or conducting focus groups with the target population in advance of the study can be helpful in designing a consent process that shows respect for potential participants. This can in turn result in consent processes that succeed in informing potential participants adequately, reducing perceptions of pressure, and increasing the likelihood that participants understand both what the study is about and that participation is voluntary. Such processes might include consent forms available in languages other than English, careful training of research staff in the cultural beliefs and practices of the target populations as well as in the philosophy of informed consent, and a strong emphasis on voluntariness (e.g., Fisher et al., 2002).

Poor Research Methods and Designs

If research should be conducted only when there is a chance that it will contribute to the general good (e.g., contribute to general knowledge, contribute to the solution of practical problems), or at least benefit those who participate in it (interventions), then research that is flawed in design or method and therefore has no chance to produce benefits should not be conducted (e.g., Fisher et al., 2002). Studies that rely on measures that are not at the appropriate reading level for participants, that are not available in participants' language, or that are not equivalent across language or culture are highly likely to produce biased results. Most important, consumers (i.e., readers) of this research may never know of these flaws or, if they are aware of them, be unable to determine the direction or magnitude of any biases.

Another common problem in research with ethnic minority and economically disadvantaged populations occurs with the simplistic use of *comparative research designs*. Too often, comparative research designs select a sample of an ethnic minority group or people living in poverty and compare them with a group assumed to be normative: usually White, middleclass individuals (Cauce, Coronado, & Watson, 1998; Fisher et al., 2002; Gonzales, Knight, Morgan-Lopez, Saenz, & Sirolli, 2002). With few exceptions, these studies confound race or ethnicity, culture, and social class; that is, there often are multiple explanations for any group differences found. Another unfortunate aspect of these designs is that they often are intended to identify how cultural differences between groups contribute to different behaviors, attitudes, beliefs, or practices between groups. However, relatively few of these studies include measures of anything cultural (e.g., beliefs or adherence to traditional cultural values such as familism, degree of adherence or belief in mainstream U.S. values, degree of adherence to mainstream U.S. beliefs such as the value of autonomy, degree of involvement in traditional religion or lifestyles) that could be used to see if any differences found were related to culture (e.g., Quintana et al., 2006). Most unfortunate is that because the comparative group is assumed to be normative in many of these studies, researchers or consumers of research often inadvertently interpret group differences as evidence of the inferiority of the minority or lower social class group (i.e., their results are considered "not normative"), even though the research design rarely lends itself to this sort of interpretation (e.g., Cauce, Coronado, & Watson, 1998; Fisher et al., 2002; Gonzales et al., 2002).

Comparative designs can be quite useful in providing answers to many important research questions. To have a reasonable chance to contribute to the common good, however, studies using comparative research designs must be very carefully planned. Members of each group to be compared should be selected to generate a sample that is reasonably representative of each ethnic or socioeconomic group (see chap. 2, this volume) and to eliminate as many confounds as possible (e.g., comparing groups from different social classes within a single racial or ethnic group; comparing members of different racial or ethnic groups from the same social class; comparing persons of different racial groups within the same ethnic group, e.g., comparing Black and White Puerto Ricans), and the measures used must meet the criteria for cross-group and/or language equivalence (see chap. 5, this volume). If variations in cultural beliefs or practices are to be used to explain any group differences found, then these cultural variables need to be measured and appropriate statistical tests conducted to determine whether the cultural hypothesis is supported. Given that it will take many years of concentrated effort to determine whether the most common measures in the social sciences are in fact equivalent across groups, we think that comparative research designs should be used extremely carefully, and perhaps less frequently, until measurement practices make these designs more practical.

Cultural Competence

Perhaps the biggest barrier to a researcher's ability to conduct studies in an ethical manner with diverse populations is a lack of understanding of the values, beliefs, and lifestyles of the ethnic minority or economically disadvantaged groups he or she wants to study. We emphasize throughout this book that researchers need to understand targeted study participants in order to design effective recruitment strategies, to identify or develop measures that are effective with a particular group, or to design effective interventions. Understanding the values, needs, worldviews, challenges, feelings of empowerment or disempowerment, and discrimination experiences of targeted populations makes it easier for researchers to anticipate potential ethical problems in the conduct of their research and to avoid these problems. Knowing, for instance, that some immigrant populations may have difficulty saying "no" directly to research staff in response to a request to participate in research may lead to a recruitment process that would allow potential participants a chance to think over their options and contact the researcher if they decide they are interested in the study. Knowing that a minority group has been the target of virulent discrimination may lead to the hiring of members of that ethnic group exclusively as research staff. Knowing that most members of a minority group have conservative views of sex roles and restrictive views of when or how women may interact with men other than their husbands might lead to rules within the research team to match participants and recruiters/ interviewers on gender. Knowing the importance of power hierarchies, and the perspective on children's roles, in a particular immigrant group might mean that a research team would change their previous practice of using children of immigrants as translators for their parents during recruitment, the consent process, or interviews (Fisher et al., 2002).

Although researchers can acquire the in-depth knowledge they need about an ethnic or economic group after years of conducting research with the group, this knowledge may come at a cost to the targeted group in the form of violations of their values or belief system or unintended violations of their rights as research participants (e.g., voluntariness). Partnerships with members of the targeted population or with institutions that serve or represent that population can help researchers design culturally sensitive and ethical methods of conducting research. Studies that emerge from community-based participatory research are most likely to be sensitive to community values and norms because of the input from members of the community at each step of the process (e.g., Wallerstein & Duran, 2006). Hiring key research staff from the targeted population, as long as these individuals are clearly empowered to participate in decision making about research procedures, also can help researchers begin the research process in synchrony with the values, beliefs, and lifestyles of minority and economically disadvantaged groups. Equally important, all members of the research team, including those who are members of the targeted population, should receive training about the culture of the targeted population and the culturally sensitive methods that were developed for working with this population. Such training should improve both the ethical practices involved in all aspects of the study and the quality of all other aspects of the research project. Training in cultural competence can include numerous methods of learning, such as reading anthropological or descriptive information about the targeted group; training in cultural practices and traditions led by members of the target group or by bicultural persons familiar with the target group; participation of members of the target group, perhaps as research partners, in training of recruiters, interviewers, and other staff; and role-playing aspects of the research processes (e.g., going through the consenting procedures) with members of the target population.

APPLICATION TO THE FOUR TYPES OF RESEARCH

The four types of research designs introduced in chapter 1 represent different challenges to the ethical treatment of ethnic minority and economically disadvantaged populations. In this section we highlight the implications of ethical practices for each of these designs.

Cross-Group Comparative Designs

Cross-group comparative designs need to be carefully planned so that the results are interpretable and have the potential to add to scientific understanding of important psychological or social science constructs or theory. When these studies do not adequately represent the two (or more) populations of interest; do not remove common confounds, such as social class, through appropriate designs and sampling; do not use measures that are equivalent across ethnicity, race, culture, language, or social class; and, if they are hypothesizing that some aspect of culture will explain any differences found, do not measure the hypothesized cultural construct of interest, then the resulting study may not be capable of making a contribution to scientific understanding. In that case, asking people to participate in the research would be considered an unethical use of their time, an invasion of their privacy, or both.

In well-designed cross-group comparative studies, researchers need to plan carefully to create consent processes that meet the needs of each targeted group. In most cases, this would mean designing a consent form whose wording meets the literacy limits of the lowest income target group, then using this document with all participants. If there is reason to expect cultural differences between targeted groups, then researchers may need to develop different consent processes to enhance understanding in each group. In some cases, researchers may need to develop consent forms specific to the cultural needs of each group. Pilot-testing consent forms and processes may be required to determine whether more than one version is needed.

Within-Group Designs

Studies that are examining variations within an ethnic minority group or within an economically disadvantaged group may face challenges similar to those described for cross-group comparative designs. Studies that target a specific ethnic minority group should design the consent process to fit the cultural beliefs and practices, and the historical discrimination experiences, of that group. If a significant portion of the targeted population is composed of low-income individuals and/or people who do not speak English, then consent forms need to be designed to meet the literacy and language needs of this part of the sample as well as the rest of the sample. Studies that target an economically disadvantaged population that also is ethnically diverse need to consider, when designing consent forms and processes, the literacy, language, and cultural needs of each ethnic minority population that will be included in the study. Although this could be a daunting task, anything less potentially compromises the rights of one or more subgroups in the targeted population. Of course, most of these same concerns (i.e., literacy, understanding the content and intent of written materials) apply to the measures used in a within-group design to ensure that research results can be interpreted and have the potential to contribute to scientific understanding of the phenomenon being studied.

National Sample Designs

Because national sample designs attempt to represent the general population, they come closer than any other design to fulfilling the principle of justice despite their common limitation of samples to English speakers. However, they probably do relatively little to adapt their processes to fit the cultural needs of ethnic minority groups in the population or the literacy needs of low-income populations, which would be huge tasks. For instance, to meet the ethical standards discussed in this chapter, national sample designs would need to develop consent forms in multiple languages, train their interviewers in the cultural values and practices of numerous ethnic minority groups, and design consent processes that conformed to the needs of multiple cultural and social class groups. Because national sample designs typically study only those individuals who are reasonably fluent in English, they rarely, if ever, deal with the challenges of developing consent forms in multiple languages. Although it is common in these studies to develop measures and consent forms that meet the needs of people with a modest literacy level, researchers conducting these studies rarely invest the time to train their recruiters and interviewers in the cultural beliefs and practices of all the ethnic minority populations that will be included in their study or in the use of consent processes that respect the cultural differences among these groups and ensure equivalent understanding of the research process and the rights of participants across groups.

Inadvertently Diverse Samples

Because studies of samples that are inadvertently diverse do not plan in advance which ethnic or economic groups will be included in their samples, they do not, and cannot, prepare consent forms or processes that meet the needs of diverse segments of the population. Much like national sample designs, these studies are very likely to exclude people who do not speak English and to risk failing to fully inform potential participants with limited English ability or with cultural histories that do not prepare them to exercise their rights as research participants. In addition, because studies using inadvertently diverse samples typically use convenience samples, there is little likelihood that all ethnic minority groups in the larger community will have the opportunity to participate in the research (i.e., the justice principle is not usually fulfilled). Similarly, these research designs fail to meet the principle of beneficence because it is very unlikely that the results generated will apply to all ethnic minority and economic groups, and therefore, these groups are unlikely to benefit from the research results.

SUMMARY

With the dramatic demographic shift now occurring in the United States, research on ethnic minority populations is bound to grow in the coming decades. We certainly hope that the research that appears in social science journals rapidly comes to better represent the general population than is currently the case (i.e., fulfills the ethical standard of justice). It also is time that researchers conducting research with ethnic minority and economically disadvantaged individuals or families give more thought to the rights of research participants. Following the guidelines provided by the three concepts of (a) respect for persons, (b) beneficence, and (c) justice, and training new researchers in the meaning and application of these concepts, will provide a foundation for more respectful and ethical treatment of these populations. Being cognizant of the challenges of communicating with persons who feel disempowered or who come from cultural backgrounds that did not prepare them for exercising their right to refuse to participate in research also will contribute to better practices in social science research. Conducting research in partnership with community groups or consulting with community advisory boards or other representatives of targeted minority groups or economically disadvantaged populations can provide researchers with both needed insights into the targeted group that may help identify ethical concerns as well as insiders' perspectives on other potential ethical concerns.

4

Measurement and Measurement Equivalence Issues

Measurement is a basic process in every research enterprise and is fundamental to determining the internal and external validity of the findings. When a researcher measures something, he or she assesses the degree to which participants possess the target constructs and assigns numerical values to represent each participant's status on those constructs. In the social sciences, researchers have usually developed measures of constructs with the aid of predominantly White and middle-class samples. Also, there is often little, if any, thought given to whether measures that are reliable and valid with this particular population are appropriate for use with ethnic minority and economically disadvantaged samples. For example, researchers in general have rarely asked whether a measure of self-esteem yields scores with similar meanings for members of populations that are very individualistic and for members of populations that are very collectivistic, or whether certain indexes of socioeconomic status (e.g., parents' education, particularly among immigrants) are as useful for differentiating groups within families living in poverty as they are for differentiating among middle-income families. Researchers who study ethnic minority and economically disadvantaged populations have often adopted measures developed with White middle-class populations without questioning whether scores on these measures convey the same meaning in the different populations. In addition, researchers rarely have considered that some populations might have response tendencies that may bias cross-group comparisons and make results difficult or impossible to interpret.

Researchers who plan to study ethnic minority or economically disadvantaged populations need to consider these measurement issues when creating new measures or deciding which measures to adopt for their studies. These measurement issues are of particular importance when making group comparisons either among pan-ethnic groups (e.g., Latinos vs. Asian Americans vs. African Americans vs. European Americans), among more narrowly defined ethnic groups (e.g., Mexican Americans vs. Cuban Americans or Chinese Americans vs. Japanese Americans), or between socioeconomic status groups (e.g., middle income vs. low income). Measurement equivalence is also critical in any research endeavor that includes an ethnically or economically diverse sample, even when the research is not focused on group comparisons.

Hence, measurement issues, particularly *measurement equivalence* (the degree to which a measure assesses the same construct in the same way across groups), are important for studying ethnic minority or economically disadvantaged individuals. Recent significant advances in the methods can be used to assess *factorial invariance* (the similarity of the factor structure of a measure across groups) and measurement equivalence as well as a burgeoning understanding of the importance of these issues with respect to making accurate scientific inferences regarding processes within and across ethnic and economic groups. In this chapter, we describe these measurement issues, discuss how these issues are critical in determining the quality of research involving ethnic minority and economically disadvantaged populations, and provide some guidance for how to use recently developed analytical methods to evaluate and improve the equivalence of measures. We provide a brief overview of these analytical methods; readers interested in a more detailed description are directed to Camilli and Shepard (1994); Hines (1993); Knight and Hill (1998); Labouvie and Ruetsch (1995); Malpass and Poortinga (1986); McDonald (1995); Reise, Widaman, and Pugh (1993); Rudner, Getson, and Knight (1980); Widaman (1995); and Widaman and Reise (1997).

THE BASICS OF MEASUREMENT

The creation of a reliable and valid measure of any construct requires a relatively well-known set of methodological procedures (cf. Cronbach, 1970; McDonald, 1999; Nunnally, 1967). Although much of the subsequent discussion is more clearly relevant to self-report questionnaire and survey-type measures, the principles and practices are also relevant to other forms of measurement systems (i.e., observational measures) that may require some adaptation of the analytical approaches discussed. This process ideally starts with a theory that specifies critical features of the underlying construct. This theory defines the nature of, or the elements of, the underlying construct in the population of individuals to which the measure will be administered, and it provides the basis for the generation of items or observations that reflect the construct. Furthermore, it is essential that the theory be informed by an understanding of the groups to which the measure is to be administered. That is, the theory describing the nature of the construct must be specific to the ethnic or economic populations being sampled. A theoretical understanding of the basic nature of, or the elements of, the underlying construct in the population of interest is critical because this provides the basis for the generation of items or observations that reflect that particular construct in that particular population. This *item identification* is the first step in the process of developing a measure. For example, when developing a measure of depression, it would be reasonable to include items reflecting, among other things, suicidal ideation because this is a known indicator of depression. To provide an unbiased assessment, the developed measure should include a set of items that is a representative subset of the potential population of items that represent depression in the group of interest. In this case, if depression is reflected by suicidal ideation, crying, sadness, and so on, then the measure should include items regarding these thoughts and behaviors. As the set of items becomes less representative (i.e., becomes a select subset) of the population of depression items in the ethnic or economic group of interest, it becomes less likely that those items accurately assess depression in that group, a concern that we discuss in greater detail later in this chapter.

In addition, theory also defines how the construct of interest relates to other constructs or how it fits within the nomological net of construct validity relations. The presumption here is that we know what any particular measuring system is truly measuring primarily by examining the degree to which the numerical scores produced by that system covary with scores produced by theoretically related measures. For example, it is reasonable to expect harsh parenting to lead an adolescent toward negative mental health outcomes, low self-esteem, and a poor relationship with parents but not toward any specific intelligence level or toward androgynous gender roles. To the degree that these kinds of observed relations conform to expectations, we begin to believe that we are indeed measuring the construct we intended to measure on the basis of our understanding of the theoretically driven nomological net of relation expectations. Again, it is essential that the theory be informed by an understanding of the ethnic/economic groups to which the measure will be administered. A theoretical understanding of the basic nature of the construct validity relation expectations for the underlying construct in the population of interest is critical because this provides the basis for evaluating the degree to which the measure is assessing the construct one wishes to assess. In an ideal case, one would examine the construct validity relationship of a measure of harsh parenting with a representative set of constructs for which one would expect convergent validity (i.e., either positive or negative correlations) and a representative set of constructs for which one would expect discriminant validity (i.e., zero correlations) on the basis of theory informed by the nature of the ethnic or economic group to which the measure is to be administered.

Measurement Error

An important premise of the psychometric conceptualization of measurement is that any measurement system includes inaccuracies; that is, measures of constructs produce numerical values that are designed to reflect the degree, intensity, or magnitude of the construct in the individual. However, these numerical representations are not perfect reflections, because all measures are subject to inaccuracies. To the extent that these inaccuracies are random, they are considered measurement error. In the ideal case, these inaccuracies are random and relatively small. It is important to note that the variance in a measure of a construct that is attributable to measurement error cannot be related to any measure of another construct because this variance is created randomly. Therefore, these random errors limit the degree to which the scores on a target measure can be correlated with scores on other measures, including the same measure administered at another time. Thus, the degree of unreliability associated with a target measure influences the validity coefficients (i.e., the correlations with scores on measures of other theoretically related constructs) associated with a measure. Random measurement errors result in attenuation of the validity coefficients by means of a reduction in the proportion of systematic variance. Therefore, if a measure includes substantial random measurement error (i.e., the scores are not highly reliable), then the validity coefficients will be a substantial underestimate of the degree of covariation between the two constructs in the population. However, knowledge of the degree of measurement error that exists (i.e., knowledge of the reliability of the measure in the population of individuals being studied) allows one to determine the degree to which covariation among constructs observed in the sample data underestimates the covariation among the underlying constructs in the population of interest.

Hence, measurement error can create substantial difficulties in a researcher's ability to make accurate scientific inferences from comparisons across ethnic or economic groups, or within ethnic or economic group examinations of the relations among constructs. When comparing ethnic or economic groups, differences in the degree of measurement error across groups may, under some circumstances, lead to misleading interpretations of the mean differences or similarities across those groups. However, measurement error becomes an even more important concern in comparative designs that are examining the relations among constructs, because any observed relations may be differentially attenuated by differences in the amount of measurement error across groups. That is, if there is more measurement error in an assessment of a construct in one group than in another, then the observed relations of that construct to other constructs will be attenuated more in one group than in another group. This differential attenuation may look very much like a difference in the magnitude of the relation among the underlying constructs in the ethnic or economic group populations when it is indeed nothing more than a measurement artifact.

Similarly, when examining the relations among constructs within an ethnic or economic group, differences in the degree of measurement error across the diversity within that group (e.g., across immigrant status, acculturation level, ethnic identity, etc.) also may lead to misleading interpretations of observed relations among constructs. That is, differences in the degree of measurement error across the diverse individuals in the sample lead to considerable difficulty in determining the degree to which the observed relations are attenuated. Furthermore, to the degree to which the sampling strategy produces a less than perfectly representative sample, differences in the degree of attenuation associated with observed relations among constructs across the diversity in the population of interest may lead to inaccurate inferences regarding the magnitude of the covariation of constructs.

Measurement Bias

Unfortunately, the variance in a set of scores produced by a measure often is influenced by more than one construct as well as by random measurement errors. That is, there are often inaccuracies in the numerical representation of a construct because the responses on that measure are influenced by secondary constructs other than the target construct of interest. These secondary constructs add systematic variance in the scores (in contrast to the random variance contributed by measurement error) that are attributable to the secondary constructs that create measurement bias. These secondary constructs often are response biases or other methodological artifacts that are undesirable but often unavoidable. For example, there is evidence that Latinos more frequently have an extreme-alternative response bias on Likert-type response scales (i.e., *strongly agree/disagree* vs. *agree/disagree somewhat*) compared with non-Latino Whites (Hui & Triandis, 1989; Marín, Gamba, & Marín, 1992) and that less acculturated Latinos more often have an extreme-alternative response bias than more highly acculturated Latinos (Marín et al., 1992). The impact of these secondary constructs may be quite important, largely because the variance they add to the scores is not random and yet not the result of the target construct one is trying to measure. Furthermore, because this added variance is not random it can be systematically related to other constructs even if the target construct is not related to those particular constructs.

The systematic variance contributed by a secondary construct increases the variance in the scores derived from a measure and can lead the validity coefficients to be either upwardly or downwardly biased. If the target measure and the measure of the validity construct both introduce variance from the same (or very similar) secondary constructs (i.e., both measures have the same or similar measurement bias), then the correlation between the two sets of scores may overestimate the degree of covariation between the target construct and the validity construct in the population. In other words, because the squared validity coefficient (i.e., squared correlation) is an estimate of the proportion of shared variance between the two sets of scores, increasing the variance of each set of scores with similar (i.e., highly correlated) systematic secondary influences increases the correlation between the two sets of scores by increasing the proportion of shared variance between the scores. For example, when one is examining the relation between the scores on a measure of familism and the scores on a measure of ethnic socialization in a diverse Latino sample, and each measure uses a 5-point Likert-type response scale, the observed correlation between familism and ethnic socialization may be upwardly biased (i.e., be an overestimate) because of the extreme-alternative response bias of less acculturated Latinos (Marín et al., 1992). In this case, the response bias adds systematic variance in each set of scores that represents additional shared variance beyond the shared variance between the underlying familism and ethnic socialization constructs in the population. This in turn inflates the observed correlation by increasing the proportion of shared variance between the scores on these two measures in the sample. This can be particularly problematic if the covariation among these constructs is being compared for immigrant Latinos and Latinos born in the United States, for example. The relationship between familism and ethnic socialization may be significantly stronger for immigrant Latinos, but this difference may be the result of the extreme-alternative response bias on both the familism measure and the ethnic socialization measure among immigrant Latinos rather than an actual group difference in the association between these constructs.

Another potential problem occurs when the target measure and the construct validity measure introduce very different systematic secondary constructs (i.e., the two measures have very different and unrelated measurement bias). In this situation, the sample correlation between the two sets of scores will underestimate the degree of covariation between the target constructs in the population. For example, when one is examining the relation between scores on a measure of familism that uses a 5-point Likert-type response scale and scores on a measure of ethnic socialization that are based on in-home observations made by a trained observer, the observed correlation between familism and ethnic socialization will likely be downwardly biased by the extreme-alternative response bias of less acculturated Latinos (Marín et al., 1992). Put differently, the score obtained from the self-report survey may add variance to the scores through the extreme-alternative response bias of Latinos, whereas the observational score provided by the trained observer may not. In this case, the extreme-alternative response bias adds systematic variance to the familism scores, but this additional variance does not constitute shared variance with the ethnic socialization scores. In essence, the proportion of shared variance between familism and ethnic socialization is decreased by the addition of measurement bias variance to the familism scores that is not also added to the ethnic socialization scores. Given that we usually have little knowledge of the specific secondary constructs being assessed by a measure, it is difficult to determine whether the observed relations are an overestimate or underestimate of the relations among the underlying constructs in the population.

Hence, measurement bias has the potential for dire consequences regarding the accuracy of the scientific inferences made from comparisons across ethnic or economic groups, or within ethnic or economic group examinations of the relations among constructs. When one is conducting mean-level comparisons across ethnic or economic groups, differences in the measurement biases across groups will contribute to misleading interpretations of the mean differences or similarities across those groups to the extent that these differential measurement biases increase or decrease the observed scores differentially across groups. Measurement bias is also an important concern in comparative designs that are being used to examine the relations among constructs, because any observed relations may be differentially biased (upward or downward) by different measurement biases across groups. That is, if there are different measurement biases in an assessment of a construct in one ethnic or economic group compared with another, then the observed relations of that construct to other constructs will be differentially biased across groups. This differential bias may look very much like a difference in the magnitude of the relation among the underlying constructs in the ethnic or economic group when it is indeed nothing more than a measurement artifact. Similarly, when one is examining the relation among constructs within an ethnic or economic group, differences in the measurement biases across the diversity within that group (i.e., country-of-origin differences or differences in connection to the mainstream culture) may lead to misleading interpretations of observed relations among constructs. Furthermore, the limited information usually available regarding the existence and nature of measurement biases makes it very difficult to detect or correct for such biases in either cross-group comparative research or within-group research. However, empirical information regarding the degree to which a measure of any construct is equivalent across groups in comparative research and across the diverse individuals in within-group research has the potential to make the difficulty of making accurate scientific inferences more manageable, even with measures that are subject to measurement error and measurement bias.

MEASUREMENT EQUIVALENCE

A number of different types of measurement equivalence, and the difficulties associated with assessing them, have been considered in the literature (Hines, 1993; Hughes, Seidman, & Williams, 1993; Hui & Triandis, 1985; Knight, Virdin, Ocampo, & Roosa, 1994; Knight, Virdin, & Roosa, 1994; Little, Preacher, Selig, & Card, 2007; Malpass & Poortinga, 1986; Vandenberg & Lance, 2000). Hui and Triandis (1985) organized these notions of equivalence into several categories, including *item equivalence, functional equivalence,* and *scalar equivalence.* Item equivalence exists when the items on a measure have the same meaning across different groups. Item equivalence is largely addressed during the examination of factorial invariance or the similarity of item functioning. For example, the assessment of the factorial invariance of a familism measure is generally based on either the correlations among the individual items in the familism measure or on the relation of each individual item to the total score or scale score generated from the total set of items. If the responses to the familism items are intercorrelated in a manner consistent with the culturally informed theory, and similarly across ethnic and economic groups when this theory proscribes similarity, then item equivalence is likely.

Whereas the empirical examinations of item equivalence are focused primarily on the functioning of individual items or observations in a measurement system, functional and scalar equivalence analyses are more focused on the functioning of the *total score* or *scale score* derived from the combination of multiple items or observations in a measurement system. For example, the assessment of the functional and scalar equivalence of a familism measure is generally based on the relations of the total score or scale score generated from the total set of familism items to the total score or scale score for measures of other constructs (e.g., ethnic socialization). If the familism total and scale scores are related to ethnic socialization scores (as well as many other construct validity variables) in a manner consistent with the culturally informed theory, and similarly across ethnic and economic groups when this theory proscribes similarity, then functional and scalar equivalence is likely. Functional equivalence exists when the total scores or scale scores generated by a measure have similar precursors, consequents, and correlates across groups (e.g., ethnic, language, or economic groups). That is, if the scores on a measure relate to scores on other measures in a manner consistent with culturally informed theory, and if these relations are similar across ethnic or economic groups when this theory proscribes similarity, then there is some evidence of functional equivalence. Scalar equivalence exists when a given score on a measure refers to the same degree, intensity, or magnitude of the construct across ethnic or economic groups. It is important to note that a measure could have similar precursors, consequents, and correlates (i.e., display functional equivalence) but that a given scale score can have quite different meanings in different ethnic or economic groups. For example, the appropriate diagnostic cutoff for inferring clinical depression from a standard survey measure may be different for the members of two different ethnic groups even though the measure is truly assessing depressive symptoms in each of these ethnic populations. Compared with the other forms of equivalence, scalar equivalence is the most important to achieve, because it is necessary to ensure the scientific credibility of the inferences researchers make from types of data analyses they most often conduct. Scalar equivalence is, in many ways, also the most evidentiary demanding form of equivalence to demonstrate. Furthermore, the assessment of the functional and scalar equivalence of a measure requires scale-level analyses in addition to the item-level analyses necessary for examining item equivalence.

Factorial Invariance

In general, empirical tests of factorial invariance (sometimes labeled *tests of measurement invariance*) across any two or more groups assess the degree to which the internal psychometric qualities of a measure are the same across groups and allow an evaluation of item equivalence. That is, factorial invariance tests are generally based on either the correlations among items or the relations between the individual items and the total scores for the measure. In the present context, we could empirically examine the factorial invariance of a measure across ethnic groups (e.g., between Asian Americans, Latinos, African Americans, and European Americans), across groups from different countries of origin but within a pan-ethnic group (e.g., between Chinese Americans and Japanese Americans, or between Mexican Americans and Cuban Americans), across groups within a specific country of origin but who primarily speak different languages (e.g., between English-speaking and Japanese-speaking Japanese Americans or between English-speaking and Spanish-speaking Cuban Americans), or across groups within a specific country of origin but with differing degrees of connection to the mainstream and ethnic cultures (e.g., Chinese Americans or Mexican Americans who are highly acculturated compared with counterparts who are not highly acculturated). In addition, we could empirically examine the factorial invariance of a measure across socioeconomic class groups (e.g., between middle-class families and families in poverty).

The analytic strategies used to examine factorial invariance allow for the systematic identification of specific items that are similarly interrelated or similarly related to the total scale score across groups as well as items that are not. The two most reasonable approaches to examining the equivalence of a measure's items rely on either *confirmatory factor analyses* (CFA) or *item response theory* (IRT) *analyses* (e.g., Camilli & Shepard, 1994; Hambleton, Swaminathan, & Rogers, 1991; Hines, 1993; Knight & Hill, 1998; Knight, Tein, Prost, & Gonzales, 2002; Labouvie & Ruetsch, 1995; Lord, 1980; Malpass & Poortinga, 1986; McDonald, 1995; Reise et al., 1993; Millsap & Kwok, 2004; Rudner et al., 1980; Widaman, 1995; Widaman & Reise, 1997). In essence, CFA uses the interrelations among the items on a measure or observational system in the evaluation of item equivalence. In IRT analysis, one uses the relationship of the responses on each individual item to the total scale score (without the inclusion of the specific item being evaluated) to examine item equivalence.

CFA is a structural modeling procedure in which each item is represented by a linear function of one or more factors (see Bollen, 1989). That is, the researcher specifies a theoretical model that identifies what factors or latent constructs are represented in each item in a measure. For example, Figure 4.1 represents a latent factor for a construct with six indicators or items in each of two groups. The latent construct represents each item as a linear combination of an item intercept (each α), an item slope or loading (each β), and a unique item error (each ε). The first subscript for each item parameter represents the item number, and the second subscript indicates group membership. Furthermore, the linear functions can be constrained such that each item parameter for the first group must be equal to the corresponding item parameter in the second group. If the fit indices for this constrained model indicate that the data fit the model, this provides evidence that the interitem relations and the factor structure are similar across the diverse groups. Although there has been considerable variability in the terminology used to describe the elements of factorial invariance, Widaman and Reise (1997) provided a useful description of the sequence of analyses necessary to examine the factorial invariance of a measure across diverse groups, and we adopt the use of their terminology.

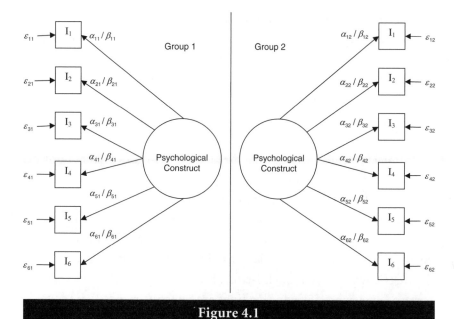

Figure 4.1

The measurement or factorial invariance model. The first subscript of each parameter refers to the item number, and the second refers to group membership.

A researcher can assess factorial invariance by using multigroup CFA to fit a series of hierarchically nested factor structures. The sequence of nested CFA models tested (configural invariance, metric factorial invariance, strong factorial invariance, and strict factorial invariance) progresses from the least restrictive (i.e., configural invariance) to the most restrictive model of invariance (i.e., strict factorial invariance). *Configural invariance* is established if a CFA model that allows the same set of items to form a factor in each group shows good model fit. This simply means that the items or observations from a measure must form a similar factor structure across diverse groups of individuals, but the specific factor loadings, item intercepts, and unique errors associated with each item may well differ across groups. For example, if configural invariance exists for a measure of familism, the individual familism items are a good representation of the construct in each group, and the items are all part of the familism factor in a CFA.

Metric invariance exists if the strength of the relationship (i.e., factor loading) between each item and the latent construct under consideration is invariant across groups. This is determined by examining the fit indices of a model that constrains the factor loadings to be identical across groups (i.e., $\beta_{11} = \beta_{12}$, $\beta_{21} = \beta_{22}$, $\beta_{31} = \beta_{32}$, $\beta_{41} = \beta_{42}$, $\beta_{51} = \beta_{52}$, and $\beta_{61} = \beta_{62}$) and comparing these fit indices with those from the configural model.

Strong invariance exists when the factor loadings and item intercepts are invariant across groups. This is determined by examining the fit indices of a model that constrains the factor loadings (i.e., $\beta_{11} = \beta_{12}$, $\beta_{21} = \beta_{22}$, $\beta_{31} = \beta_{32}$, $\beta_{41} = \beta_{42}$, $\beta_{51} = \beta_{52}$, and $\beta_{61} = \beta_{62}$) and the item intercepts (i.e., $\alpha_{11} = \alpha_{12}$, $\alpha_{21} = \alpha_{22}$, $\alpha_{31} = \alpha_{32}$, $\alpha_{41} = \alpha_{42}$, $\alpha_{51} = \alpha_{52}$, and $\alpha_{61} = \alpha_{62}$) to be identical across groups and comparing these fit indices to those from the metric invariance model. Items/observations that do not meet criteria for invariance in factor loadings are not constrained to be equal in the test of invariance in item intercepts (Millsap, 1997).

Strict invariance exists when the factor loadings (i.e., $\beta_{11} = \beta_{12}$, $\beta_{21} = \beta_{22}$, $\beta_{31} = \beta_{32}$, $\beta_{41} = \beta_{42}$, $\beta_{51} = \beta_{52}$, and $\beta_{61} = \beta_{62}$), item intercepts (i.e., $\alpha_{11} = \alpha_{12}$, $\alpha_{21} = \alpha_{22}$, $\alpha_{31} = \alpha_{32}$, $\alpha_{41} = \alpha_{42}$, $\alpha_{51} = \alpha_{52}$, and $\alpha_{61} = \alpha_{62}$), and unique error variances (i.e., $\varepsilon_{11} = \varepsilon_{12}$, $\varepsilon_{21} = \varepsilon_{22}$, $\varepsilon_{31} = \varepsilon_{32}$, $\varepsilon_{41} = \varepsilon_{42}$, $\varepsilon_{51} = \varepsilon_{52}$, and $\varepsilon_{61} = \varepsilon_{62}$) associated with each item are invariant across groups. This is determined by examining the fit indices of a model that constrains the factor loadings, item intercepts, and unique errors to be identical across groups and comparing these fit indices to those from the strong invariance model. As the name suggests, meeting the criteria for strict invariance is indeed challenging. At all levels of invariance, a partially invariant model may be obtained if some, but not all, items are invariant on each element of the factor structure across groups (Byrne, Shavelson, & Muthén, 1989).

IRT models are mathematical functions that describe the relationship between a particular item response and the individual trait (Camilli & Shepard, 1994; Hambleton et al., 1991). In IRT, the relationship between responses to a given item and the underlying construct measured by that item can be described by a monotonically increasing function called an *item characteristic curve* (ICC). These ICCs are defined by three parameters in

IRT models: (a) item difficulty, (b) item discrimination, and (c) the chance parameter (see Camilli & Shepard, 1994; Hambleton et al., 1991; and Reise et al., 1993, for more detail). *Item difficulty* is the point on the continuum of the trait being measured where the respondent has a probability of .5 of a particular response (e.g., the overall standardized achievement test score associated with a .5 probability of correctly answering a given test question). *Item discrimination* refers to the slope of the ICC at the point along the curve that defines item difficulty. The term *chance parameter* refers to the probability of respondents with low levels of the measured trait responding to the item in a manner compatible with the construct.

IRT has also been used to determine measurement invariance by comparing the ICCs for each item on the measure across groups (Camilli & Shepard, 1994; Hambleton et al., 1991; Lord, 1980; Rudner et al., 1980). If the ICCs are similar across groups, the item is considered invariant and not biased. Where ICCs are different, there is a chance that the item may be biased. Lord (1980) claimed that an item is biased only when individuals from different groups have the same ability or level of the measured trait but do not have the same probability of responding correctly to an item. A mean group difference in performance on an item is not relevant here, because the comparison is made only on individuals with the same level of the trait of interest and not on the basis of their respective groups. Camilli and Shepard (1994) and Hambleton et al. (1991) described several methods for assessing item bias by comparing the individual parameters and examining the area between the ICCs for each group. Unfortunately, IRT requires very large sample sizes to develop accurate ICCs, and few tests of model fit are currently available. Furthermore, those fit indices that are available are based on a chi-square statistic that is heavily influenced by sample size in a manner that creates a reasonably high probability that differences in the ICCs will result in a significant chi-square and an inference of noninvariance even when the ICC differences are relatively trivial (see Reise et al., 1993).

Indeed, one of the major advantages of the use of CFA rather than IRT is the availability of numerous indices of model fit. CFA also relies on the chi-square statistic, and the difference in chi-square values between nested models, even though there is evidence that the chi-square criteria are sensitive to trivial modifications of fit (see Browne & Cudeck, 1993; Cheung & Rensvold, 2002; Kline, 1998; Steiger, 1998). However, there are also a variety of *practical fit indices* (e.g., the comparative fit index, the root-mean-square error of approximation, the standardized root mean residual) that have been developed for CFA approaches. Hence, there is a stronger basis for evaluating model fit in CFA compared with IRT. In addition, some researchers think it is odd to consider the relations of individual items to the total scale score when the ultimate goal is to evaluate the utility of the total scale score; that is, some worry that a group difference in one or more ICCs could be a function of the scale score not being equivalent across groups instead of an item that is functioning differently across groups. Therefore, we generally prefer the use of CFA to examine factorial invariance across ethnic and economic groups.

For many measures of constructs, factorial invariance should be expected. That is, for many measures the items should function quite similarly across groups, and the demonstration that the factor loadings, item intercepts, and unique errors are identical across ethnically and economically diverse groups (i.e., strict factorial invariance) is to be expected for all items. Indeed, for these measures strict factorial invariance may be a requisite for measurement equivalence to exist. When factorial invariance does not hold, or ICCs are not similar, differences across ethnic and economic groups may reflect real differences in the construct or differential functioning of the measure (e.g., Millsap & Kwok, 2004; Vandenberg & Lance, 2000). Unfortunately, the literature discussing how to determine whether observed differences reflect real differences or differential functioning of measures when factorial invariance fails is very sparse, and there is very little empirically based guidance regarding how to proceed when partial factorial invariance exists. Indeed, the examination of ethnic or economic group differences when partial factorial invariance exists is very controversial. Millsap and Kwok (2004), in perhaps the only empirical work on this issue, described a useful strategy for examining the degree to which failure of factorial invariance influences the sensitivity and specificity of a measure used for selection purposes. They also provided a program for estimating how much selection error one should expect to occur given varying degrees of partial invariance. These authors suggested that in the end, the decision to interpret group comparisons as meaningful when a measure is only partially invariant depends on how one is going to use the measure and how much error one is willing to tolerate in that use. Hence, researchers have very few tools available to help them determine whether observed ethnic or economic group differences reflect true effects or measurement artifacts.

We suggest that sound reasoning and culturally informed theory are useful tools when one is considering the importance of failures of full factorial invariance. Often, informed theory may suggest that measurement equivalence requires CFA parameters (i.e., factor loadings, item intercepts, and unique errors) or IRT parameters (i.e., the ICCs created by the item difficulty, the item discrimination, and chance) to be identical across ethnic and economic groups. However, if informed theory suggests some subtly different features of the underlying construct across ethnic or economic groups, then one might well expect some items to function differently across groups and for partial factorial invariance to exist. Hence, the linkage between factorial invariance and measurement equivalence may sometimes be more complex than is typically assumed because the theoretical relevance to populations of interest must be considered. Remember, it is imperative that the items or observations included in a measure are a representative set of the population of items or observations that define that construct within the diverse ethnic or economic populations of interest. Furthermore, the population of items or observations must be defined by the theory about the construct that is informed by the nature of the population of individuals in which the items or observations are to be used. If our culturally informed theory suggests that there are some subtly different features of the construct across diverse groups, then one might well expect some items to function somewhat differently across groups and for partial factorial invariance to exist. In this case, partial invariance may be quite compatible with measurement equivalence, and informed theory may be a useful basis from which to evaluate the specific nature of that partial invariance. Sound reasoning and clearly informed theory and knowledge about the target construct in the populations in which one wishes to use a measure may be very useful in deciding whether a partial failure in factorial invariance poses a likely threat to the interpretation of observed ethnic and economic group differences. We suggest that when the specific nature of the observed partial factorial invariance conforms to the partial factorial invariance expectations based on informed theory, then proceeding to cautiously use the scores as if the measure were equivalent across groups may be warranted.

For example, an item assessing the frequency of suicidal thought may be quite appropriate on a scale measuring depression. However, there may be less variability in the responses to this item in one ethnic or economic group because of a religious prohibition against such behavior, and the corresponding thought, associated with that culture. In this case, this item may have a somewhat different factor loading or function across ethnic groups because of the difference in variance of the responses. One common strategy used in this situation is to restore factorial invariance by dropping the "offending" item or items from the measure. However, dropping such an item from the measure simply because of the noninvariance in item functioning (i.e., solely for empirical reasons) may produce a nonrandom and nonrepresentative selection of the population of items in either or both ethnic or economic groups. Once the measure contains a nonrandom selection of items from the population of items defining the underlying construct, it becomes possible that the measure may not be a representative assessment, or may not be an equally representative assessment, of the construct of interest in each ethnic or economic group. That is, if there is some culturally related phenomenon that explains the ethnic/economic group difference in the factor loading, item intercept, or unique variance on this item, then eliminating this item from the scale would threaten the representativeness of the sample of items within each ethnic group. Indeed, this reasoning can be extended to the case in which it might be necessary to administer some different items across groups in order to attain measurement equivalence, although it may be quite demanding to generate the empirical support necessary to do this. Fortunately, CFA is flexible enough to allow researchers to sequentially constrain most factor loadings, item intercepts, and unique variances while allowing selected item characteristics to vary across groups for those items that culturally informed theory suggests should function somewhat differently. In these types of cases, partial factorial invariance may be more compatible with measurement equivalence.

Construct Validity Equivalence

The assessment of functional and scalar equivalence requires a systematic examination of the similarity of the empirical and construct validity coefficients across ethnic and economic groups. These validity coefficients identify the relationship between the score produced by the target measure and either scores produced by other measures of the same construct (empirical validity) or scores produced by measures of theoretically related constructs (construct validity). For example, Figure 4.2 represents the relationship between the target construct as a predictor (e.g., a measure of harsh parenting) and a validity construct as an outcome (e.g., a measure of adolescent mental health) in two groups. This relationship is represented as a linear combination of an intercept (each α), a slope (each β), and a unique error variance (each ε) in each group, with group membership identified by the subscript. There are at least two reasonable procedures for examining the validity coefficients for a measure across ethnic and economic groups: (a) the comparison of regression coefficients and intercepts using multiple regression analyses and (b) the comparison of constrained and unconstrained models using structural equation modeling (SEM) analyses.

One way to compare validity coefficients across ethnic and economic groups is to test the moderating effects of group membership on the partial regression coefficients (i.e., slopes, or β_1 and β_2) and intercepts (i.e., α_1 and α_2) describing the relationships between measures of the target construct and theoretically related constructs. If the regression equation for such an analysis produces homogeneous slopes (i.e., $\beta_1 = \beta_2$) and intercepts (i.e., $\alpha_1 = \alpha_2$) across ethnic and economic groups, and if homogeneous slopes and intercepts are observed for numerous construct validity tests, then it is likely that the target measure exhibits scalar (as well as functional) equivalence. For example, if a given score on any particular harsh

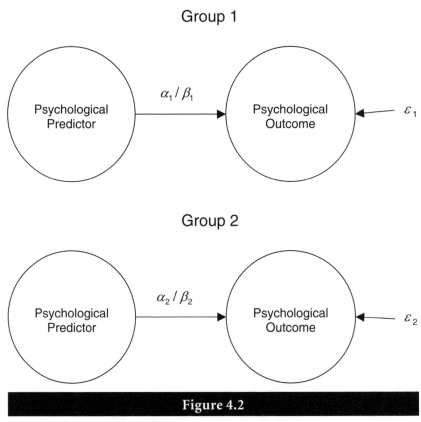

Figure 4.2

The construct validity invariance model. The subscripts refer to group membership.

parenting scale leads to the same expected score on a mental health indicator for adolescents from two different ethnic or economic groups, then it is somewhat likely that comparable scores on the harsh parenting and mental health measures refer to the same degree, intensity, or magnitude of harsh parenting and mental health across groups. As one provides additional evidence of invariant slopes and intercepts across ethnic or economic groups for more empirical and construct validity relations, it becomes increasingly likely that the target measure is scalar equivalent across ethnic/economic groups. One could enter a theoretically appropriate predictor (e.g., a vector of scores on a socialization or family interaction measure) and dummy vectors defining the ethnic or economic group memberships in the first block in a multiple regression analysis and then enter the cross-product (i.e., interaction) vectors in the second block. If the cross-product vector (or vectors) accounts for a significant proportion of the variance in the criterion, then the slope of the relation between the construct validity variable and target construct are different across groups. In this case, one could calculate the simple slopes for each ethnic or economic group and note the nonequivalence of the measures (for a detailed description of this procedure, including centering the predictor, see Aiken & West, 1991). If the cross-product vectors do not account for a significant proportion of the variance in the criterion, one can then test whether the intercepts are significantly different across ethnic and economic groups.

More specifically, suppose that you have a set of scores from a measure of harsh parenting, and culturally informed theory suggests that this construct is causally related to mental health similarly for two groups of adolescents. When you regress the scores from the mental health measure onto the scores from the harsh parenting measure using Aiken and West's (1991) procedures, several different outcomes can occur. One possibility is that the slopes and intercepts may not be significantly different across groups. In this case, any particular harsh parenting score leads to, or is associated with, a very similar predicted mental health score among the groups of adolescents. If this pattern occurs repeatedly for a number of different predictors of mental health, and if one assumes that the culturally informed theory suggests that these predictors should be similarly related to mental health among the groups of adolescents, then there is reason to believe that the mental health measure is scalar equivalent. That is, this pattern leads one to conclude that any given score on the mental health measure represents the same level of mental health regardless of group membership. Another possibility is that the slope may not be significantly different across groups, whereas the regression intercepts are significantly different. In this case, any particular harsh parenting score is associated with a higher mental health score in one group than in the other (i.e., the correlation between harsh parenting and mental health is the same in the two groups, but there is a mean difference in mental health scores that is not associated with a similar mean difference in harsh parenting).

If this pattern of findings occurs repeatedly for a number of different predictors of mental health, and if one assumes that the culturally informed theory does not suggest this observed pattern, then it appears as though the mental health measure may be functionally equivalent and measuring the same construct in each group but that it is probably not scalar equivalent.

A second way to examine the similarities and differences in validity coefficients across ethnic and economic groups is to examine the comparability of these relations using constrained and unconstrained SEM (see Bollen, 1989). This analytical strategy involves fitting a series of hierarchically nested models that systematically examine specific elements of the relationship between an exogenous (i.e., harsh parenting) and endogenous variable (i.e., mental health) across groups. The evaluation of the similarity of each element of the relationship between the target construct scores and the validity construct scores requires the comparison of a series of systematically computed SEM models. The first model is unconstrained and examines the degree to which harsh parenting is related to mental health regardless of group membership by allowing the slope and the intercept of the relations between harsh parenting and mental health to be different across groups. The second model examines the relation between harsh parenting and mental health while constraining the path coefficients or slopes between the two to be identical for the two groups of adolescents (i.e., $\beta_1 = \beta_2$). If the difference in chi-square between these two models is not significant, and the practical fit indices in the latter model are good and not substantially different from those produced by the unconstrained model, then the slope of the relation between harsh parenting and mental health is similar for these groups. The third and fourth models (respectively) sequentially constrain the intercept (i.e., $\alpha_1 = \alpha_2$), the variances of the exogenous variable, and the residual error variance in the exogenous variable (i.e., $\varepsilon_1 = \varepsilon_2$) in the model examining the relation between harsh parenting and mental health to be identical for the two groups of adolescents. If the difference in chi-square between each model and the preceding model is not significant, and if the practical fit indices for the model being considered are good and not substantially different from those produced by the previous model, then it appears as though the slope, intercept, and error variance (unexplained variance in mental health) are similar for these groups. If this pattern of findings occurs repeatedly for a number of different exogenous predictors of mental health, and if one assumes that the culturally informed theory suggests that these predictors should be similarly related to mental health among the two groups of adolescents, then there is reason to believe that the mental health measure is scalar equivalent. That is, this pattern of findings leads one to conclude that any given score on the mental health measure represents the same level of mental health regardless of group membership. If, however, the pattern of findings for multiple exogenous predictors of mental health indicates that only the slope of the relations between the exogenous variables and mental health are similar across these groups, then it appears as though the mental health measure may be functionally equivalent and measuring the same construct in each group, but it is probably not scalar equivalent.

As is the case with the consideration of factorial invariance, the demonstration that the slope and intercepts (as well as unexplained variance) are invariant across the diversity inherent to ethnic minority and economically disadvantaged groups may be expected for many constructs. However, our theory about the nature of the construct specifies how this construct should relate to other constructs (i.e., fits into the nomological net of constructs), and this theory must be informed by an understanding of the ethnic or economic groups to which the measure is to be administered. If our culturally informed theory suggests that there are some group differences in the way in which the construct of interest is related to other constructs, then one might expect differences in slopes or intercepts (or unexplained variance) for some analyses. Indeed, in this latter case, differences in construct validity coefficients that precisely mirror the theoretically prescribed differences in the associations of interest would indicate measurement equivalence.

For example, there is emerging evidence that harsh parenting and restrictive control, instead of representing an overcontrolling quality of parental behavior, may be an adaptive parenting strategy for ethnic and economically disadvantaged youth who live in a community that has high rates of violent behaviors (e.g., Gonzales, Cauce, Friedman, & Mason, 1996; Lamborn, Dornbusch, & Steinberg, 1996; Tolan, Gorman-Smith, Huesmann, & Zelli, 1997). Thus, this parental control may make the lives of children in these communities more predictable and safe and, in turn, have relatively positive, instead of negative, mental health outcomes. It has been argued that parents in these environments may rely on harsh, restrictive control strategies because the consequences of children's behavioral risk taking are severe (McLoyd, 1998). If this is the case, then one would expect parental control to relate differently to mental health outcomes in samples of children from relatively risky environments compared with those from safer environments. This differential expectation regarding the relationship between parental control and mental health would lead one to expect different slopes in the regression analyses or SEM analyses examining the relations between these constructs, if the measures of these constructs are indeed equivalent across these groups. Of course, parental control might be similarly related or differentially related to myriad other constructs across groups, depending on the breadth of the culturally informed theory. Hence, measurement equivalence exists to the degree that the functional relations between the construct of interest and theoretically related constructs conforms to the expectations derived from the culturally informed theory.

Complicating this even further is the impact of failures of factorial invariance on the examination of the equivalence of construct validity equivalence (see Millsap & Kwok, 2004). That is, if a measure is composed of items that do not equally represent the nature of the construct in two groups (i.e., there are some concerns regarding the equivalence of some items), these items will affect the scale score in ways that may bias the observed construct validity relations (i.e., the nonequivalence of some items will influence the functional and scalar equivalence of the measure). Although we know relatively little about these effects, factors that threaten the accuracy of the factor structure of a measure of a target construct in different ethnic and economic groups will have some impact on observed construct validity relations. Unfortunately, we do not know how much disturbance of factorial equivalence is necessary to produce artifactually significant differences in construct validity relations.

ROLE OF QUALITATIVE RESEARCH IN ESTABLISHING MEASUREMENT EQUIVALENCE

There are two ways qualitative research can be useful in addressing issues of measurement equivalence in ethnic minority and economically disadvantaged samples. First, qualitative research may help researchers in developing, as well as evaluating, the equivalence of measures for use with samples that are diverse in ethnicity and economic status. Qualitative research methods can be used to determine the breadth of the construct across the diverse individuals in ethnic and or economic groups and the accuracy of the operational definition of the constructs of interest within these groups. Second, qualitative methods may be instrumental in allowing one to determine whether there are variants of the construct or whether there are culturally specific forms of the construct in the different subsets of these diverse ethnic and economic groups. There has been substantial development of the methods available to generate this type of information (for descriptions of these methods, see, e.g., Berg, 1995; Bryman & Burgess, 1994; Feldman, 1995; Hines, 1993; Hughes et al., 1993).

As we noted earlier, the culturally informed theory describing the nature of the construct must be specific to the ethnic minority and economically disadvantaged populations being sampled. This information can only come from people with considerable knowledge of the cultures associated with those populations. Perhaps the best source of this knowledge is the people who live within each culture. For example, Gonzales, Gunnoe, Samaniego, and Jackson (1995) developed a stressful life events scale for adolescents living in multicultural urban environments. Separate focus groups were conducted with Mexican American, African American, and Anglo adolescents to generate items for the scale. Many similar items were identified across groups in the school, peer, family, and community domains. However, stressful events associated with discrimination experiences revolving around limited English-speaking abilities emerged specifically for the Mexican American adolescents, particularly in focus groups conducted in Spanish. Although these discrimination-related stressful events are not relevant to most Anglo and African American adolescents, they represent an important dimension of daily stress for many

Mexican Americans and other youths with a recent history of immigration. Individuals who have a history of studying these cultures, but who may not actually live within the culture, may also provide some useful but limited information about how the construct is represented in these populations. In this case, individuals who have a history of studying the respective populations may be better able to specify how the construct of interest should relate to other constructs but less able to adequately specify the nature of, or elements of, the construct of interest.

Focus group data can be examined for themes and important issues raised by the participants, and these themes can be compared and contrasted across the diverse elements of the ethnic and economic groups being studied. Often, focus groups provide enough information to develop a measure that is equivalent across various groups; however, issues may also be raised in focus groups that require a more detailed investigation in order to move toward the development of an equivalent measure. As a follow-up, researchers may want to conduct qualitative interviews with individuals from the diverse elements of the ethnic and economic groups to obtain clarification or more information about a theme identified in the focus group (for an introductory explanation of conducting qualitative interviews and ethnographic research in general, see Fetterman, 1989). The information gained from focus groups and interviews ultimately may be used to develop items or observations for a quantitative instrument assessing the target construct or constructs. The purpose of the focus groups and qualitative interviews, as well as a wide range of other qualitative techniques (e.g., Berg, 1995; Bryman & Burgess, 1994; Feldman, 1995; Hines, 1993; Hughes et al., 1993) in measurement development, is to determine whether the items or observations make sense to the members of the target ethnic or economic group and whether important content that represents the construct in the respective ethnic or economic group has been omitted from the measure.

In addition to their use for instrument development, qualitative research methods can be used to provide at least some of the critical culturally related information that will be used to explore measurement equivalence of measures. Gonzalez-Ramos, Zayas, and Cohen (1998) provided a good example of the use of these types of qualitative techniques to examine child-rearing goals in Puerto Rican mothers. These authors also described an example in which the assessment of a construct (e.g., autonomy or independence) may require quite different items or observations in different cultural groups. For example, when Puerto Rican mothers, in contrast to European American mothers, assert that they want their children to be more autonomous or independent, they likely do not mean that they want to encourage the type of physical separations associated with attending summer camps and sleepovers. Similarly, Puerto Rican children who display limited eye contact and a deferring style in school may be displaying complacent, obedient, and respectful behavior rather than inhibited, shy, and withdrawn behavior. Hence, in addition to being a good source for identifying the items or observations to be included in the measure of the construct, focus group findings may also provide important pieces of the culturally informed theory by which researchers may specify the nature of the construct validity relations to be expected in the diverse subsets of the ethnic and economic groups being studied.

The complementary use of qualitative and quantitative methodologies may lead to an understanding of the reason a measure is not equivalent across groups and provide guidance for revising a measure to achieve equivalence. Whether one is developing new measures or evaluating existing measures, qualitative methods may be used to determine which types of items or observations should be included to enhance the likelihood of achieving measures that are equivalent across groups. In contrast, quantitative methods are more useful for evaluating the degree of statistical success in creating measures that are equivalent. For established measures, quantitative and qualitative methods may be used in conjunction to ferret out sources of nonequivalence. Quantitative methods may be useful in identifying which measures or parts of measures are nonequivalent, whereas qualitative methods may be useful in the confirmation of nonequivalences and in modifying the measure, in particular when the nonequivalence is the result of the omission of relevant behavioral observations or items.

However, it is important to remember that informing our theories about the nature of the constructs of interest in the diverse ethnic and economic groups of interest is no small task. Although we may begin with relatively qualitative or subjective data, we must progress toward methods that are more standardized and quantitative. That is, the process of science often begins with relatively informal observation, much the way a member of a cultural group might observe the culture in his or her daily life. However, subsequent scientific observations must move toward meeting the more rigorous demands associated with being scientifically verifiable, much the way a social scientist might survey or conduct structured observations of members of the culture. As this process of science proceeds, we must continually reevaluate and revise the theory about the nature of the underlying construct of interest as it applies to the ethnic minority and economically disadvantaged population of interest. In turn, this changing understanding of the target population may lead to revisions in the measurement of the construct of interest and the need to repeatedly consider the equivalence of that measure.

IMPLICATIONS FOR RESEARCH PRACTICES

The perspective on measurement and measurement equivalence presented in this chapter has implications for resolving important methodological issues that occur in the process of studying ethnic minority and economically disadvantaged populations. There are several key presumptions and principals on which our perspective is based.

First, although we presume that there will be considerable commonality in the nature of most constructs across ethnic and economic groups, there may also be some ethnic or economic group specificity in the nature of many constructs. The implication is that although a measure of a target construct that is equivalent across ethnic or economic populations may have a set of common or core items or observations, such a measure may also have some items or observations that either function differently across ethnic and economic groups or items that are different in nature across ethnic and economic groups. For example, the focus group work of Gonzales et al. (1995) clearly suggests that a stressful life events scale should have different indicators among Mexican American adolescents, particularly those who speak Spanish, than among Anglo American and African American adolescents. In this case, items related to limited English capabilities would be part of the population of items defining stressful life events among Mexican American adolescents but not among Anglo American or African American adolescents. Indeed, such items may be part of the population of items defining stressful life events among more recent immigrants and less acculturated Mexican Americans, but not among very acculturated Mexican Americans whose families have been in the United States for several generations. A measure of stressful life events that included only items regarding school, peer, family, and community stressors might well indicate a highly similar factor structure across these groups. However, because this measure is not equally representative of the population of items defining stressful life events in these three ethnic groups, such similarity of factor structure would not indicate measurement equivalence.

Similarly, an item assessing the frequency of suicidal thoughts may be quite appropriate on a scale measuring depression. However, it is possible that this item may be a good indicator of depression in each of two ethnic groups but that there may be less variability in the responses to this item in one ethnic group because of the prohibition of such behavior, and corresponding thought, based on the religion more often associated with that ethnic group (e.g., the extremely devout Catholicism among some Latinos). In this case, this item may have a different factor loading or function somewhat differently across ethnic groups just because of the variance of the responses. Dropping such an item because it either appears not to be an indicator or to function differently in a second group (i.e., solely for empirical reasons) may yield a nonrandom and nonrepresentative selection of the population of items in either one or both ethnic groups. Furthermore, once the measure contains a nonrandom selection of items from the population of items defining the underlying construct, it becomes possible that the measure may not be a representative assessment, or may not be an equally representative assessment, of the target construct. Hence, keeping the item and accepting partial factorial invariance may be the best strategy for producing an equivalent measure.

The items defining a target construct may also produce evidence of differential item functioning or differences in confirmatory factor loadings because of the existence of a secondary construct, such as the response bias noted earlier (Hui & Triandis, 1989; Marín et al., 1992). Such a response bias could affect the variance of the responses to each item sufficiently to produce a failure of traditional tests of strict factorial invariance. Of course, knowledge that such a response bias is associated with the Latino culture would allow the researcher to address this issue and to conduct an appropriately fair test of the similarity of the item-level functioning either by correcting these factor loadings for attenuation or by accepting partial factorial invariance. Understanding the source of the factorial invariance may also allow the researcher to adjust his or her methodology to eliminate this issue. For example, Hui and Triandis (1989) found that Latinos endorsed more extreme responses on 5-point response scales but not on 10-point response scales, so a simple adjustment to the response alternative allowed in the research may eliminate this issue from concern.

Second, although we presume that there will be considerable commonality across ethnic and economic groups in the interrelations of the target construct and theoretically related constructs, there may also be some ethnic or economic group specificity in these interrelations that represent subtle differences in the nomological net of the target construct across diverse ethnic and economic populations. The implication is that although a measure of a target construct that is equivalent across ethnic and economic populations may have a set of common construct validity relations, a measure that assesses the target construct in a scalar equivalent way may have some relations to other constructs that are different across ethnic/economic groups. For example, Prelow, Tein, Roosa, and Wood (2000) found that coping styles such as restraint, acceptance, denial, venting of emotion, and humor have similar indicators across low-income Mexican American and middle-income Anglo American groups of mothers. However, for the Mexican American mothers the relations between denial and acceptance and between restraint and venting of emotions were positive, whereas these relations were negative for the Anglo mothers. These findings suggest that these coping styles do not function in the same manner in low-income Mexican American mothers as they do in middle-income Anglo mothers. One potential explanation for these differences revolves around the traditional Mexican cultural script *simpatia*. Low-income Mexican American mothers may rely more on coping styles that avoid conflict, such as denial, acceptance, and restraint, and thereby account for the positive relations between these coping styles. Another possibility is that low-income Mexican American mothers may initially use styles such as denial and venting of emotions to reduce negative emotions associated with stressors. This in turn may later facilitate the use of other coping styles, such as restraint and acceptance (Lazarus & Folkman, 1984). These measures of coping styles may well be equivalent, particularly regarding the degree to which these differences in the correlations among the different coping styles are consistent with expectations one might generate from any theory regarding the nature of coping styles and how these styles are utilized in these specific ethnic groups.

Third, the ultimate determination of the equivalence of a measure of a target construct depends on the degree to which the observed empirical psychometric findings correspond to the expectations based on the culturally informed theory. The implication is that appropriate factorial invariance exists to the degree that the items that comprise a measure of a target construct function similarly across diverse ethnic and economic groups for those items that the culturally informed theory suggests should function similarly. However, if there are items that should function somewhat differently, or that are fundamentally different in nature, across diverse ethnic and economic groups, then complete factorial invariance would ultimately be inconsistent with measurement equivalence. If the culturally informed theory suggests that there are ethnically or economically common and specific elements to the nature of the construct, then partial factorial invariance that corresponds closely with the expected similarities and differences described in the culturally informed theory would be more fully consistent with measurement equivalence. Similarly, if there are construct validity relations that should be somewhat different across diverse ethnic and economic groups, then complete similarity in the empirically observed relations among the constructs would ultimately be inconsistent with measurement equivalence. If the culturally informed theory suggests that there are ethnically and economically common and specific expected construct validity relations of the target construct to other constructs, then construct validity that corresponds closely with the expected similarities and differences described in the culturally informed theory would be more fully consistent with measurement equivalence.

IMPLICATIONS FOR THE FOUR COMMON RESEARCH DESIGNS

As we discussed in chapter 1, four basic research designs are commonly used to study ethnic minority and economically disadvantaged populations: (a) cross-group comparative designs, (b) within-group designs, (c) national sample designs, and (d) inadvertently diverse designs. Recall that these four designs are most often used to address one of two types of research goals regarding ethnic minority and economically disadvantaged populations. The first type of research goal is to compare two or more ethnic and economic groups. This may be a comparison of mean levels on some construct or a comparison of the relations between two or more constructs. The second type of research goal is to examine psychological or social science processes within a specific ethnic or economic group. This often leads to studies that are focused on examining the relations between two or more constructs or between some set of constructs and more demographic constructs (e.g., age or gender). The relevant question, then, is what are the implications of the measurement issues described in this chapter for the research designs that are most often used to address these two research goals?

Cross-Group Comparative Designs

As we noted in chapter 1, the research goal most often associated with the use of a cross-group comparative design is the comparison of mean levels or interrelations among constructs across ethnic and economic groups. If the goal is to determine whether the ethnic and economic groups are similar or different on a construct, then it is imperative that the measures of these constructs be scalar equivalent. That is, for a comparison of ethnic or economic group means to meaningfully reflect a group difference in the construct of interest, any given score on the measure of that construct must be indicative of an equivalent degree, intensity, or magnitude of that construct across ethnic and economic groups. Without clear evidence of scalar equivalence, any observed mean difference may be the result of an ethnic or economic group difference in the construct of interest or the result of bias in the observed scores introduced by the measurement process.

If the goal is to determine whether the relations among a set of constructs are similar or different across ethnic and economic groups, it is imperative that the measures of these constructs demonstrate at least functional equivalence, and they may require scalar equivalence. That is, for a comparison of the relations between constructs across ethnic and economic groups to meaningfully reflect a group difference in the psychological or social science processes driving the relations among these constructs, the scores produced by the measures of these constructs must have similar reliability and validity (i.e., have similar precursors, consequents, and correlates) across the groups of interest. Without clear evidence of functional equivalence, any group differences in the observed relations among constructs may be the result of an ethnic or economic group difference in processes, the result of differential attenuation of the observed relations among the constructs caused by differential reliability of the assessments, or the result of the assessment of either subtly different constructs or assessments that are differentially biased across groups.

Given that cross-group comparative designs are generally initiated for the purposes of group comparisons, the specific groups to be compared, and the constructs of interest, are generally known well in advance of the data collection. As long as the number of ethnic or economic groups of interest is not too large, it is possible to sample representatively and to address the cross-group, and within-group, measurement issues. That is, if the research was initially designed for the comparison of means or relations among constructs for Chinese Americans and European Americans, the research team will have opportunities to examine the equivalence of measures across these ethnic groups and within the diversity that exists within these groups (e.g., across levels of acculturation, immigrants vs. nonimmigrants, or levels of language fluency). As the number of groups increases (e.g., the study includes Mexican Americans, Chinese Americans, and African Americans from South Africa), or as the nature of the groups of interest becomes very broad (e.g., a comparison of pan-ethnic groups such as African Americans and Asian Americans), the demands associated with evaluating the equivalence of measures and the solutions one may engage to produce equivalent measures become more taxing.

Within-Group Designs

As we noted in chapter 1, the research goal most often associated with the use of a within-group design is the examination of psychological or social science processes within a specific ethnic or economic group. This examination is most often represented by a within-group examination of the relations among constructs, or between some set of constructs and some demographic constructs (e.g., age or gender), for which it is imperative that the measures of these constructs demonstrate scalar equivalence across the diversity that exists within that ethnic or economic group. In other words, for the relations between constructs within an ethnic or economic group to meaningfully reflect the processes driving the relations among these constructs, the scores produced by the measures of these constructs must indicate an equivalent degree, intensity, or magnitude of that construct across the diversity that exists within that ethnic group (e.g., across levels of acculturation, immigrants vs. nonimmigrants, or levels of language fluency). Without clear evidence of scalar equivalence, any observed relations among constructs may be the result of the process of interest, the differential bias in the observed relations among the constructs caused by differential reliability of the assessments across the diversity that exists within that ethnic or economic group, or the assessment of subtly different constructs across the diversity that exists within that group.

Given that within-group designs are generally initiated for the purposes of examining a process within an ethnic or economic group, the specific group to be examined and the constructs of interest are generally known well in advance of the data collection. As long as the number of relevant ways in which the members of the group are meaningfully diverse is not too large, it is possible to sample representatively and to address the within-group measurement issues. That is, if the research was initially designed to examine relations among a set of constructs among Japanese Americans, the research team will have opportunities to examine the equivalence of measures across the diversity that exists within these groups (e.g., across levels of acculturation, immigrants vs. non-immigrants, or levels of language fluency). As the number of ways in which the members of the group are meaningfully diverse increases, or as the nature of the group of interest becomes very broad (e.g., Asian Americans), the demands associated with evaluating the equivalence of measures and the solutions one may engage to produce equivalent measures becomes more taxing.

National Sample Designs

As we noted in chapter 1, the research goal most often associated with the use of a national sample design is to examine some psychological or social science process in a sample that is as representative as possible of the U.S. population to ensure that observed relations among constructs are generalizable to the broad national population. Such studies are rarely designed primarily to examine either ethnic or economic group differences or similarities in mean levels or relations among constructs. Neither are these studies designed primarily to examine a process and the relations among constructs within an ethnic or economic group. Unfortunately, the data from such studies are often used to address cross-ethnic or economic and within-ethnic or economic group research goals, even though the research plan was not designed specifically to do so.

The measurement problems, which are above and beyond the other potential methodological problems (e.g., sampling and translation demands), associated with the use of national sample designs to study ethnic and economic group diversity are twofold. First, these research designs often specifically attempt to sample many or all ethnic and economic groups within the United States. The sheer number of groups included in the research makes an a priori consideration of measurement equivalence across groups and across the diversity within groups virtually impossible. The task demands associated with acquiring or accessing the required culturally informed theory are themselves mind-boggling. That is, it is almost impossible to consider the possibility of culturally specific indicators of the key constructs, or any degree of cultural specificity of the process being investigated when there are more than a few groups in the sample. Second, perhaps in part because of the cost, these studies often try to measure as many constructs as possible while maintaining a reasonably manageable data collection plan. Because of this, there is sometimes an assumption that any construct can be measured with a few items. Although measurement issues and measurement equivalence can often be evaluated, and specific measurement problems can sometimes be addressed, after the data have been gathered this opportunity is much less likely to be useful in national sample designs. Because these designs often try to measure as many constructs as possible they often rely on a very small set of items, which limits the breadth of the construct being measured as well as the reliability of the measure. In turn, this limited breadth and reliability of the items may lead to the attenuation of observed empirical relations among constructs and may make it difficult to effectively evaluate the equivalence of the construct validity relations. Perhaps more important, if measurement equivalence analyses identify some specific item-level threats to the equivalence of the measure, the availability of very few items seriously restricts the ways in which measurement equivalence of the scale score may be improved. Hence, although there may be some situations in which data from national sample designs may be useful for studying ethnic and economic group diversity, the scientific inferences from such research should be interpreted with great caution.

Inadvertently Diverse Designs

As noted in chapter 1, the research goal most often associated with the use of an inadvertently diverse design is to examine some psychological or social science process and the relations among constructs. In these designs the sample is diverse in ethnic and economic groups by happenstance because it comprises a convenience sample. As in national sample designs, the studies that use these designs are rarely developed to examine either ethnic or economic group differences or similarities in mean levels or relations among constructs. Neither are these studies designed primarily to examine a process and the relations among constructs within an ethnic or economic group. Unfortunately, like national sample designs, the data from studies using inadvertently diverse designs are often used to address cross-ethnic/economic and within-ethnic/economic group research goals even though the research plan was not designed specifically to do so.

The measurement problems inherent to using inadvertently diverse designs to study ethnic and economic group diversity are largely associated with the absence of a priori thought about this diversity and an absence of culturally informed theory regarding the process and constructs to be investigated. Hence, the only means of addressing any nonequivalence of measures is to adjust the scoring of measures (e.g., dropping selected items or observations from scale scores, changing the factor calculations in multifactor constructs) after the data collection process is completed. Furthermore, because the degree of ethnic and economic diversity present in the sample is based solely on the happenstance associated with the use of a convenience sample, it is often the case that the sample sizes for some ethnic and economic groups are too small to conduct the types of analyses necessary to identify measurement nonequivalencies. Even when the sample size is sufficient, the potential for the ethnic and economic subsets of the convenience sample to be differentially representative of their respective populations make it difficult to know exactly how to interpret observed differences in item or scale functioning once they have been detected. Thus, the scientific inferences regarding ethnic and economic group differences and similarities, as well as those inferences regarding any process within an ethnic or economic group, are very likely to be compromised by the measurement issues described herein.

CONCLUSION

The quality of our measures of psychological and social science constructs is critical to the quality of the scientific inferences we can make from our research efforts. If we do not use measures of the constructs that are equivalent across the groups of interest, then the scientific inferences we make on the basis of either the comparison of these constructs or the relations among constructs across ethnic and economic groups will be inaccurate. Although it may seem from our discussion that these measurement issues are daunting, analytical techniques for addressing these issues have been developed and are continuing to be developed, and they will continue to become more accessible. The application of these analytical techniques in a manner consistent with culturally informed theory is also becoming more common. Furthermore, there has been a growing realization by editors and funding agencies that good science requires us to consider these issues. That is, there is a growing realization that "getting the measurements right" is key to good research and good scientific inferences. As complicated as this may appear to scholars who are new to the study of ethnic minority and economically disadvantaged populations, addressing these measurement issues represents an opportunity to enhance greatly our understanding of psychological and social science processes as they apply to the changing population of the United States.

5

Translation Processes Associated With Measurement in Linguistically Diverse Populations

Conducting research with ethnic minority populations often involves administering instruments or conducting interviews in multiple languages. Issues of translation arise regardless of whether researchers are using quantitative or qualitative methods. With both methods, inaccuracies and translation problems can lead to erroneous scientific inferences.

In terms of quantitative methods, issues of conceptual and semantic equivalence are especially critical, whether researchers are interested in making cross-group comparisons or combining data across languages for analyses. Furthermore, the quality of translation can interfere with scientific inferences because researchers may be drawing conclusions based on an instrument that is not validly assessing the construct of interest (Wang, Lee, & Fetzer, 2006). More specifically, inaccuracies in the translation of the measures used in a quantitative research design introduce variance in the scores derived from these measures, which in turn can influence the observed findings.[1] If the variance added by inaccuracies in translation is systematic in nature, then this measurement bias may either elevate or reduce the observed relations among variables relative to the true relations. For example, if two measures of different but theoretically related constructs are translated with the same inaccuracies, then the observed relation between the scores on these two translated measures will be

---

[1] When speaking about the translation process, we use the term *measure* to refer to all instructions, examples, items, response options and formats, and/or graphic materials that are included when assessing a particular construct.

higher than the underlying relation in the population because of the common measurement bias. If the inaccuracies exist in only one of the two translations, then the observed relation between the scores on the two translated measures will be lower than the underlying relation in the population. If the variance added by inaccuracies in translation is random in nature, then this measurement error will reduce the observed relations among observed variables relative to the true relations. Hence, the need to translate the measures into a second language represents not only additional task demands for the research team but also a potential methodological confound that poses a threat to the accuracy of the scientific inferences drawn from the findings.

If translations are done poorly, the measures are not likely to be comparable across multiple ethnic groups or across individuals within a particular ethnic population who differ in language preference or in their degree of acculturation and enculturation. For example, if one's goal is to measure familism in a diverse ethnic group, it is essential that the measures be equivalent in both English and the second language to ensure that any mean differences or similarities across diverse members of that ethnic group, or any observed differences or similarities in the relations of familism to other constructs, represent true differences in the nature of familism in this ethnic group. That is, noncomparability of the measures can lead to differences across groups that are a function of differences in the measures resulting from poor translation rather than true differences in the constructs of interest. Hence, the quality and accuracy of the translation of the measures are critical in quantitative research.

With regard to qualitative methods, the accuracy of the translation of both the measure and participants' responses also is critical because both directly contribute to the quality of the information gathered from participants in much the same way as for more quantitative approaches. However, any inaccuracies in translation may be even more detrimental in more qualitative-type methods because these inaccuracies may be repeated or increase during the analysis phase if researchers analyze the data in a language other than the one in which interviews were conducted.

Various translation approaches have been used in existing research, and each has advantages and limitations. In this chapter, we explain why translation is essential for much research with many ethnic minority or economically disadvantaged populations and why it is critical for researchers to pay attention to and take great care with translations when designing research with these groups. We also present different types of equivalence, and we discuss issues central to achieving equivalence across original and translated versions of measures. Next, we discuss multiple approaches to the translation of research materials (e.g., direct translation, back-translation, committee approach), with special attention to how each approach facilitates or poses additional challenges for the examination of cross-language equivalence. Finally, we review the advantages and limitations of each approach and offer recommendations regarding best practices.

QUANTITATIVE RESEARCH WITH ETHNIC MINORITY POPULATIONS: TRANSLATION OF MEASURES AS A NECESSARY STEP

The growing interest in research with ethnic and economically diverse populations in the United States makes a discussion of translation issues inevitable. Many researchers are interested in conducting comparative studies in which a major criterion for comparison is ethnic group membership. Other researchers are interested in either comparing different classes of individuals within a diverse ethnic population (e.g., immigrants vs. U.S.-born individuals) or examining the relations among constructs within a diverse ethnic population. Given that substantial portions of many ethnic minority populations in the United States speak a language other than English (e.g., Spanish, Chinese), measures often have to be translated into other languages in order for a representative sample of these populations to be included in research. However, to validly conduct comparisons across ethnic groups when different language versions of an instrument are administered it is necessary to ensure that the measures being used are comparable or equivalent to one another. A similar concern arises when researchers are conducting within-group comparisons or examining the relations among constructs within an ethnic or economic group that comprises a linguistically diverse sample. Here again, it is necessary to ascertain whether the different language versions of the measures being used are valid and reliable for all groups included in the sample. For instance, in an effort to balance research burdens and benefits across all groups, federal granting agencies such as the National Institutes of Health require that researchers include members of ethnic and racial minority groups in all clinical research or provide a compelling rationale and justification for their omission. Although researchers often comply by including such participants in their research, many limit participation to English speakers, and this compromises the representativeness of the sample. For instance, as described in chapter 1 of this volume, 40% of members of the largest ethnic minority group in the United States (i.e., Latinos) report that they speak English less than "very well," and a majority of the immigrant Latino population in the United States does not speak English (U.S. Census Bureau, 2003, 2004c). Thus, samples that include only English-speaking Latinos will not be truly representative of the Latino population. Researchers who do include non–English-speaking Latinos in their studies will inevitably need to translate their instruments and, in order to have confidence in their results, must evaluate the equivalence of any translated measures they administer to non–English speakers to those completed by English speakers in their study.

Conceptual Equivalence

When measures are administered in multiple languages, there are a number of outcomes researchers should aspire to achieve. The first involves establishing what is referred to as the *conceptual equivalence* of the construct that is being measured between the original and translated versions of a measure. This also has been referred to as *construct equivalence* (Hambleton, 2004; van de Vijver & Tanzer, 1997). Lack of conceptual equivalence is present when one language version of a measure taps a certain construct and a second version of the same measure taps a distinctly different construct when administered in the second language. This may happen when the concept being measured is quite meaningful in one language but not in the second language (Kristjannson, Desrochers, & Zumbo, 2003). One example of how reaching conceptual equivalence can be difficult is evident in the translation of common anchors used in Likert-type scales. The anchors *strongly agree* and *strongly disagree* are often used in English language measures. There are a number of possible literal Spanish translations for these anchors, such as *fuertemente concuerdo* and *fuertemente discuerdo* or *convengo fuertemente* and *discrepo fuertemente*. There are two problems with these literal translations. First, the verbs *concuerdo* and *discuerdo,* as well as the verbs *convengo* and *discrepo,* are used relatively infrequently among native Spanish speakers and then usually in a very formal context, such as a legal proceeding. Second, an adverb such as *fuertemente* is commonly used to indicate the strength of a physical event, such as a noise or the force of an impact between two objects (e.g., "El terremoto sacudió la ciudad fuertemente" ["The earthquake strongly shook the city"]), rather than the strength of a personal belief. An adverb such as *firmemente*—literally, "firmly"—may be more adequate (e.g., "Creo firmemente" ["I firmly believe"]). Hence, literal translations can often be inaccurate and problematic with regard to conveying the same information in Spanish and English. A more conceptual translation of these Likert-type scale anchors must consider how these evaluative anchors are expressed in Latino cultures. The most likely conceptually translated alternatives are *muy de acuerdo* and *muy en desacuerdo,* which, back-translated, literally correspond to "very much in agreement" and "very much in disagreement." This conceptual translation clearly is superior to the literal translations. However, it may not be adequate for all Latino populations. Some individuals, depending on their cultural orientation or their level of education, may find the *muy en desacuerdo* anchor relatively awkward or unnatural because they may not typically express disagreement. For instance, we observed some difficulty among participants in expressing disagreement in a sample of Mexican American mothers who were not very highly educated. These mothers preferred to indicate "No estoy de acuerdo para nada," which translates to "I am not in agreement at all." Of course, demonstrating the psychological equivalence of "strongly disagree" and "I am not in agreement at all" in this case represents a significant challenge. Educational and socioeconomic factors may influence the effectiveness of an anchor that uses a rarely used term in daily conversation (Knight, Roosa, Calderón, & Gonzales, in press).

Conceptual equivalence is necessary to conduct any type of comparisons across ethnic groups, to compare subsets of individuals (i.e., more vs.

less acculturated, immigrant vs. U.S. born), or to examine the relations among constructs within a linguistically diverse ethnic group. Developing a translated version of a measure when the concept is not relevant in the target language group would be nearly impossible as well as of little scientific value because the words necessary to describe the concept may not exist in the target language. In cases where the concept does exist, however, the items used in the source language to tap into the construct may have to be revised substantially for relevance in the target language. For example, the word *comadre* means *godmother.* In many Latino cultures, the qualitatively close relationship between a mother and the godmother of the mother's children, or *comadres,* has no equivalent word or phrase in the English language. Thus, if one wanted to study this relationship in an English-language survey, it would be impossible to use an English word, and although the word *godmother* exists in the English language, and it would be possible to create items that ask about the relationship between the godmother and the mother, the construct of *comadres* would be difficult to capture. Furthermore, the items would certainly vary across the two language versions because the English version would have to describe the unique closeness of the relationship, which could be confusing to people who have not been socialized to understand this relationship between *comadres.* We might refer to this process as *translation and adaptation* rather than as translation alone. Thus, it is possible that conceptually equivalent measures of a construct will not be composed of literally identical items across different language versions (van de Vijver & Tanzer, 1997). Considerable brainstorming by researchers and translators is required before such a bold step in measure development is taken, and extensive pilot testing and assessment of measurement equivalence are required to establish conceptual equivalence in these cases. The payoff, however, is that the resulting measure can be used for both cross-group and within-group comparisons.

Semantic Equivalence

A second and more common concern involves determining *semantic equivalence,* the mapping of meanings across languages (Kristjannson et al., 2003). This is achieved when ideas expressed in one language are accurately conveyed in a second language. Unlike conceptual equivalence, which is more focused on the measure as a whole (i.e., scale level), semantic equivalence is determined at the item level. First, researchers must examine whether each item in a measure can be translated into the target language. This is particularly relevant when items include phrases or sayings that are unique to the original language and culture in which the measure was initially developed. For example, the colloquialism "robbing the cradle" is commonly used in the United States to refer to dating or marrying someone who is significantly younger; in other languages, however, a literal translation of this item may be misinterpreted, and participants may believe researchers are asking about an act of theft or kidnapping. Lack of semantic equivalence also can occur if items are poorly translated (van de Vijver & Tanzer, 1997), which is likely when translators attempt a literal translation for a colloquialism, idiom, or expression rather than a semantically equivalent or meaningful translation. Of course, a lack of semantic equivalence for one or more items could contribute to a lack of conceptual equivalence.

Lack of conceptual and semantic equivalence can pose significant problems because researchers may be drawing conclusions on the basis of an instrument that is not validly assessing the construct of interest across language groups. If equivalence is assumed and differences emerge between participants who completed the measure in English and those who completed it in a second language, researchers will not know whether these are true differences between the two groups or whether the differences are an artifact of the translation of the instrument. Researchers may erroneously attribute group differences to potential differences in acculturation (e.g., participants who chose to complete the measure in English were perhaps more acculturated), when in fact the differences are due to different constructs being assessed.

APPROACHES TO TRANSLATION IN QUANTITATIVE RESEARCH

In an effort to produce equivalent versions of measures, researchers conducting quantitative research have used a variety of strategies in their translations to different languages (see Table 5.1). We review these strategies in

Table 5.1

Overview of Translation Approaches and Their Advantages and Limitations

Approach	Description	Advantages	Limitations
Back-translation	The measure is translated from the source language to the target language by a bilingual person; the translated version is then back-translated into the source language by a second bilingual person. The two source language versions are then compared with one another for equivalence.	■ Relatively quick and inexpensive. ■ If the researcher does not speak the target language, he or she is still able to compare the two source language versions and determine comparability.	■ A bilingual person is still needed to resolve any discrepancies that arise in the two source language versions. ■ Two language versions could be literally equivalent but not meaningfully equivalent, and this may not be discovered with the side-by-side comparisons of the back-translated versions.
Double translation/double back-translation	Two independent bilingual individuals each produce independent translated versions of a measure. A third bilingual person creates a revised translated version by comparing the two translated versions and	■ Multiple perspectives are considered, and the original translation is not dependent on one person. ■ The researcher is more likely to find and be able to resolve problems with	■ Costs and time constraints increase because multiple translators are involved in the process. ■ Only one person is producing the initial target-language version that will be

Process	Description		
	resolving any issues. Finally, two additional bilingual individuals produce independent back-translations of the revised translated version.	items that may be difficult to meaningfully translate into the target language.	back-translated; thus, the value of multiple perspectives may be minimized.
Forward-translation	The source language version is translated into the target language by a bilingual person, and a group of bilingual persons scrutinize the source and target language versions. The focus is on making the target language version meaningfully equivalent rather than on developing items that will translate exactly as written in the source language.	■ Judgments about equivalence are made directly about the equivalence of the source and target language versions, not by examining a back-translated version.	■ A high level of inference is being made by the translators and review team, all of whom are bilingual. ■ Translators could be more proficient in one language than another, which could limit their ability to determine whether the translation is accurate. ■ Ratings of equivalence may be biased because the translators know both languages and may be making insightful guesses based on their knowledge of both languages.

(continued)

Table 5.1

Overview of Translation Approaches and Their Advantages and Limitations (*Continued*)

Approach	Description	Advantages	Limitations
Review team/committee approach	A team of individuals can translate the source language version into the target language, evaluate the translated items to determine whether they are meaningful for the target population in the target language, and recommend changes to the original items and/or translated items. A team including experts in the content area, translators, and researchers work together to develop and evaluate the measure. Some researchers use a team for all aspects of the process; others use a team only at one or two phases.	■ Varied levels of expertise could potentially increase the quality of the translated measure by introducing multiple perspectives into the process. ■ Pooled translations may be more accurate than those provided by a single person.	■ Convening a group of experts can be difficult because of varying schedules, and the consulting costs can be high because of the level of expertise and time required. ■ There is also the possibility that groupthink could reduce the likelihood that members would identify and voice concerns.

the sections that follow. Although most researchers typically use only one or two of these strategies in a given research study, some suggest that the ideal approach is a multistrategy method that considers different kinds of equivalence because focusing on a single method may maximize one kind of equivalence but assume or ignore another (Erkut, Alarcón, Coll, Tropp, & García, 1999; Prieto, 1992).

Back-Translation

One of the most commonly used strategies among researchers is the *back-translation* approach, in which the measure is translated from the source language (e.g., English) into a target language (e.g., Spanish, Chinese) by one bilingual person and then back-translated into English by a second bilingual person. Then the two English versions are compared. Bradley (1994) recommended that the initial translation be done by a native speaker of the target language and that back-translation be done by a native speaker of the original source language. Some researchers recommend *blind back-translation*, in which the person translating from the target language back to the source language is not familiar with the original version of the measure (Wang et al., 2006). Another variation of this strategy is referred to as the *double translation/double back-translation approach*. This involves three steps: (a) having two translators each produce independently translated versions of a measure, (b) having a third person create a revised translated version by comparing the two translated versions and resolving any issues, and (c) having two additional translators do independent back-translations of the revised translated version (Kristjansson et al., 2003). The process of back-translation facilitates the evaluation of semantic equivalence because discrepancies between the two English versions would identify items that are perhaps not asking the same question in both languages, whereas items that are identical in the original version and the back-translation imply that semantic equivalence has been attained.

An advantage of double translation/double back-translation is that a researcher who does not speak the target language is able to evaluate the two English versions (i.e., original and back-translated) to evaluate equivalence. However, a bilingual person will still be needed to resolve any discrepancies between the two versions. A significant limitation of the back-translation approach is that a comparison of the original and the back-translation could suggest equivalence (i.e., the items read exactly identical), but it might not be clear whether this is the case because the translators used a shared set of adaptation rules that led to this (i.e., bilingualism) or because the adaptation may have retained inappropriate aspects of the source language measure, such as the same grammatical structure, which made it easy to translate word for word into the same item (Brislin, 1970; Hambleton, 2004). When this occurs, although the comparison of English versions would suggest equivalence, the translated version may be of little value for the purpose of asking questions of members of a target population who are solely or primarily monolingual. Monolingual individuals do not possess the adaptation rules (e.g., knowing that in English an adjective typically comes before the noun, as in "the red car," whereas in Spanish a noun is presented first, as in "el auto rojo") or understand the grammatical rules of the original language (Brislin, 1970) and thus likely will be confused by grammatical structures not used in their language. For example, the literal Spanish translation of "What is your marital status?" would be "¿Cual es su estado de matrimonio?" Thus, in the back-translation process this item would likely be back-translated to reflect the exact wording of the original English item. However, this would be confusing to monolingual Spanish speakers because this is not how you ask about marital status in Spanish; the correct translation would be "¿Cual es su estado civil?" Of interest is that some research suggests that translators who knew their work was going to be back-translated used wording that ensured that a second translation would reproduce the original version rather than simply a meaningful translation (Hambleton, 1993, cited in Geisinger, 1994), which would make it appear as if the original translator did an excellent job (i.e., because the back-translation is identical). Thus, researchers should carefully train translators to translate for meaning.

Forward-Translation

Another strategy for translation involves translating the source language version into the target language and having a group of bilingual individuals scrutinize the source and target language versions (Hambleton & Li, 2005). Some researchers argue that if time and resources permit, this strategy of *forward-translation* is preferable to the back-translation approach because the focus is on making the target language version meaningfully equivalent rather than on developing items that will translate exactly as written in the source language. A primary advantage of the forward-translation approach is that judgments are made directly about the equivalence of the source and target language versions, not by examining a back-translated version that is potentially flawed by characteristics of the translators, as described earlier. The main weakness, however, is that a high level of inference is being made by the translators and review team (Hambleton, 2004), all of whom are bilingual. It is possible that the translators are more proficient in one language than another, which could limit their ability to determine whether the translation is indeed accurate. Furthermore, ratings of equivalence may be biased because the translators know both languages, and they may be making insightful guesses based on their knowledge of those languages, an advantage that the monolingual persons for whom the translated versions are being developed do not have.

Review Team or Committee Approach

A variation of the back-translation and forward-translation approaches involves working with a team of individuals, referred to as a *review team* or *review committee,* to evaluate the translation at various steps of the process. The team can translate the source language version into the target language, evaluate the translated items to determine whether they are meaningful for the target population in the target language, and recommend changes to the original items and/or translated items in an effort to obtain semantic equivalence. For example, some researchers recommend a team approach for the initial translation because pooled translations may be more accurate than those provided by a single person (Hambleton & Li, 2005). Others recommend convening a team composed of experts in the content area, translators, and researchers to review the translated instrument after the preliminary version is developed (Geisinger, 1994; Kristjansson et al., 2003; Wang et al., 2006), and some use a review team throughout the translation process such that initial translation into the target language is conducted by a team and the multiple versions are compared, discussed, and revised (Brislin, 1970). The review team approach helps establish semantic equivalence because each translator may come up with a different translation of a particular expression and, as a team, the group can work together to determine the most appropriate meaningful translation. An advantage of a review team is that the translation is being evaluated by individuals with varied levels and types of expertise. The disadvantages of this approach are primarily the time and costs that it entails. Convening a group of experts can be difficult because of varying schedules, and the consulting costs can be high because of the level of expertise and time required. There is also the possibility that groupthink could reduce the likelihood that members would identify and voice concerns, although researchers could minimize this by emphasizing the importance of the unique perspective that each group member brings to the team and encouraging all team members to think critically about the items and voice any concerns, regardless of how minor they may perceive them to be.

Decentering

Finally, within these various strategies, some scholars follow the practice of *decentering* when conducting translations of quantitative measures. Decentering is the process whereby researchers make changes to both the source and target language versions of a measure until they are equivalent and relevant to the group or groups to which they will be administered. Because the items of either language version may change during the process of decentering, researchers who engage in this process view the source and target language versions of measures as equally important and equally open to modification (Prieto, 1992). Through the process of translation, both the source and target language versions of a measure contribute to the final measure that is accepted for use (Brislin, 1970). For instance, items from the source language version of a measure may be modified to make them semantically equivalent to items in the target language version. The goal of decentering is to reach two final versions that do not center on one of the languages (Prieto, 1992). An advantage of decentering is that equivalence may be easier to achieve once researchers are willing to accept changes in the original version, particularly the removal of colloquialisms, idioms, and culturally anchored items. Decentering might be disadvantageous if the original instrument has a history of use in the original language with accepted norms or cutoffs that can be used for comparative purposes. In addition, because of these changes, results gathered with the decentered measure in either language cannot safely be compared with published results based on the original measure. In some cases, decentering could alter the concept being assessed in the original language.

Cautions

Although the combined use of these translation methods, particularly with an emphasis on creating conceptually equivalent measures, is likely to produce reasonably equivalent measures in both English and the target language, there are ways in which these procedures can fail. Differences in both the content and the underlying structure of internalized cultural information between bilingual and monolingual individuals may result in translation failure in at least two ways. First, in terms of cultural content, bilingual translators are likely to have experienced more formal education than target participants, most of whom are likely monolingual. Thus, compared with target participants, bilingual translators may be more linguistically fluent in the ethnic language and have had more experience with complex constructs and terminology used in behavioral research. Furthermore, bilingual translators may be less aware of linguistic nuances of the ethnic language and of local usage of cultural constructs that pervade the daily lives of target participants. Indeed, the individuals involved in the translation processes in many cases may not be from the same country of origin as the target participants and therefore have little direct knowledge of common cultural referents shared by members of the target group.

Second, recent sociocognitive research suggests that some bilingual individuals may internalize information from two cultures in a manner that might interfere with a functional capacity to perform accurate conceptual translations. This evidence is derived from research focused on the phenomenon of *frame-switching* behavior among bicultural and/or bilingual persons (Benet-Martinez, Leu, Lee, & Morris, 2002; Hong, Morris, Chiu, & Benet-Martinez, 2000; Ramirez-Esparza, Gosling, Benet-Martinez, Potter, & Pennebaker, 2006; Verkuyten & Pouliasai, 2002). That is, a bicultural participant switches frames by responding in a manner consistent with the ethnic culture when exposed to external cues of that culture and in a manner consistent to the mainstream culture when exposed to mainstream cues. Furthermore, the language being spoken or written may well serve as a strong cultural prime. Cultural priming manipulations have been shown to influence expressions of values, causal attribution styles, and identity orientations among bicultural participants. In a theoretical sense, this evidence has been interpreted as supporting an associative network-based account of biculturalism that posits the existence of dual and somewhat independent networks of internalized cultural knowledge. Because cultural information is linked together in a cognitive network, it is suggested that exposure to external cultural cues selectively activates, or makes cognitively accessible, the system of knowledge that is associated with that specific culture. This selective activation of knowledge then leads to behavior aligned with the cultural system implied by the external cue.

To the extent that bilingual translators are also bicultural, this evidence for independent cultural knowledge networks implies that their ability to establish conceptual equivalence may be fundamentally limited. Establishing conceptual equivalence requires that the translator simultaneously consider both cultures, reflecting on key concepts for which clear and direct cross-cultural and cross-language analogs may not exist. If the bilingual translator possesses dual and somewhat independent networks of internalized cultural information, and if these networks become selectively active in response to cultural cues, then this process may interfere with the translator's ability to simultaneously consider both cultures. When the bilingual translator reviews a particular sentence or phrase in a given language, the language may itself serve as a cue that selectively activates a particular system of cultural knowledge. Therefore, when bilingual persons review the original measure and its translation, they may each make sense with the particular cultural meaning system that is active for them at the time. Thus, although selective rather than simultaneous activation of cultural knowledge systems might help a bilingual person avoid inner conflict when responding to specific cultural demands in everyday environments, this process may also interfere with his or her ability to notice and attend to problems with conceptual nonequivalence.

Unfortunately, the limited means of checking the equivalence of translations and back-translations provide little opportunity to search for problems that may result from the differences between the bilingual research team and the monolingual research participants. Too often, such errors, which can result in a loss of potentially useful data, are discovered only after the expense of gathering data from and conducting analyses with a complete sample. One recommendation that may help researchers avoid this problem is to include monolingual community members on the translation committee (Erkut et al., 1999) because these individuals may help identify translation failures prior to data collection. Monolingual individuals are more likely than bilingual individuals to notice when a technically correct translation does not make sense or will appear awkward or confusing to participants in the target population. However, this procedure is rarely used, and even when it is used it may not be sufficient by itself. Additional ways of examining the quality of the translated research protocols and measures are sorely needed to ensure that the scientific inferences are not simply a function of translation and measurement problems.

SELECTING TRANSLATORS

Aside from determining which strategy to use when translating measures, researchers must also spend considerable time selecting the individuals who will serve as translators. There are a number of factors to consider when selecting translators. First, national origin and geographic region must be considered because there is considerable variability in dialects within languages based on these factors. For example, Spanish spoken by Mexican individuals is not identical to Spanish spoken by people from Puerto Rico. Despite differences in accent and intonation, some words have different meanings for each of the groups. Also, some words may not exist for one cultural group, whereas they may be commonly used by another group. In addition to considering national origin differences in dialect it is important to consider differences in dialect based on geographic region. Within one country there will be variability in vocabulary and idioms based on the geographic region, and these regional dialect differences can introduce error into the translation process. Given the unique strengths and variability that individuals bring to the process of translation, it is ideal to have a team of translators, and it is important to consider potential within-group variability in the team of translators.

It is also important to carefully consider other demographic characteristics of the target population and select translators with those characteristics in mind. One demographic variable that often introduces important variability into the way in which languages are spoken is socioeconomic status (SES). For example, if the target population is a low-income Guatemalan immigrant community, researchers may want to select a translator who has familiarity with Guatemalan Spanish and has worked with low-income Guatemalan populations and thus has a more specific knowledge of the language needed for translation of an instrument. If translators and back-translators share the same SES background, and it is different from the target participants' SES, the back-translated version may be equivalent to the original, but the target language version that was back-translated may not be meaningful for members of the population who will complete the measure (Wang et al., 2006).

Finally, scholars also recommend considering the following characteristics when selecting translators: familiarity with both languages and both cultures, knowledge of the construct being assessed, and knowledge of test construction (Geisinger, 1994; Hambleton & Li, 2005). Specifically, translators who are familiar with both languages and both cultures as well as the construct that is being measured can assess conceptual and semantic equivalence while they are translating the items (Geisinger, 1994; Hambleton & Li, 2005). However, here we must bear in mind the potential limitations associated with the differences between these bilingual translators and monolingual research participants described earlier. Translators who have a basic understanding of test construction, such as knowing to avoid passive tense and minimizing the use of pronouns, can produce a better initial translation, which will make the translation process more efficient (Hambleton & Li, 2005). It is important to note, however, that translators with these characteristics (e.g., knowledge of test construction) are unlikely to share certain demographic characteristics with low-income participants, such as educational level and SES. Thus, for projects with a small staff of translators, researchers will inevitably need to make a choice regarding which characteristics of the target population they will mirror in their translation staff. In larger, well-funded projects it is ideal to have a translation team that is composed of multiple individuals, each of whom matches participants on specific demographic characteristics or possesses important knowledge regarding test construction and other skills necessary for translating instruments.

PILOT TESTING TRANSLATED MEASURES TO ASSESS EQUIVALENCE

Regardless of the specific approach that researchers follow in translating their instruments or how they go about selecting their translation team, there is a consensus that pilot testing is necessary in order to provide a more rigorous assessment of the equivalence of the two language versions (Geisinger, 1994; Kristjansson et al., 2003; Wang et al., 2006). Researchers, however, have differing opinions regarding whether pilot testing should involve bilingual or monolingual participants. In addition, researchers have described various analytic strategies that they use during pilot testing to assess the comparability of two language versions of a measure.

It is critical to consider the demographic characteristics of the samples that are being recruited for pilot testing because different cultural norms and experiences can introduce significant variability into analyses conducted during this phase (Kristjannson et al., 2003). If the groups on which the different language versions are tested are not matched on variables such as generational status, length of time in the United States, and other indices of acculturation and enculturation, then differences in the two language versions may actually be a reflection of different cultural norms and experiences between the groups (e.g., less acculturated individuals are less willing to divulge personal information, or they may have different norms for discussing certain topics, such as grief or infidelity; Kristjannson et al., 2003). One particularly important demographic factor to consider is the language ability of the participants involved in pilot testing. Some researchers recommend that pilot testing be conducted with bilingual participants, whereas others recommend that pilot testing be conducted with monolingual participants. We review the strengths and limitations of various strategies in the paragraphs that follow.

One approach to pilot testing with bilingual participants involves administering the target language version and the source language version to one (i.e., the same) group of bilingual participants (Kristjannson et al., 2003; Sireci, 1997). Although the same individuals are taking both tests, versions can be presented in counterbalanced order to avoid a practice effect for a particular version (Sireci, 1997). One can then compare the items from both language versions by examining the means and standard deviations for specific items as well as the factor structures of each language version (Kristjannson et al., 2003). This approach maximizes language group comparability because the researcher knows that the skills of the groups taking the measure in each language are the same (Sireci, 1997). However, this strategy is based on the assumption that the participants are equally proficient in each language, which is highly unlikely (Hambleton, 2004). Furthermore, findings from this pilot work may not be generalizable to the target population of monolingual individuals for whom the translated measure is being developed because the bilingual participants who are being pilot tested may have additional skills that the monolingual individuals do not have. For example, bilingual participants may be able to use their knowledge of both languages to help them determine the meaning of words or phrases, whereas monolingual participants will not have this advantage (Hambleton & Li, 2005).

Another strategy is to administer the two language versions of the measure to bilingual individuals who are randomly assigned to one of two different groups (Sireci, 1997). Each group takes either the source or target language version of the test, and then the item statistics and factor structure of each measure are compared. This strategy avoids practice effects because each group completes the measure only one time; however, equivalence in language ability for the groups must be assumed on the basis of the random assignment. A variation of this approach is to develop two measures, each composed of a random mixture of items from the source and target language versions of the measure. This strategy helps to account for the fact that it is highly unlikely that participants will be equally proficient in both languages. However, a significant limitation of these approaches is that a highly skilled bilingual sample is also likely to be highly educated, and their bilingual skills likely are accompanied by other skills that make them different from the target population of mono-lingual participants for which the measure is being translated. Thus, when a translated measure is pilot tested with bilingual participants, there is still some uncertainty regarding whether it will be appropriate for the intended population of participants.

Given the potential differences between bilingual and monolingual individuals, some researchers recommend using monolingual participants to pilot test translated measures because this group is more representative of the population for which the measures are being translated. One rec-ommendation involves a more qualitative approach, in which mono-lingual participants who mirror the target population are asked to review the translated measure and identify any grammatical lapses and awkward or confusing phrasing and to evaluate the clarity of instructions (Geisinger, 1994; Wang et al., 2006). Researchers gain this information with the use of individual interviews or focus group discussions in which participants discuss these issues with the researchers.

Another recommendation is to recruit monolingual participants from each language group and have members of each group complete the cor-responding language version of the measure. Researchers can compare item statistics across the two language versions and then carefully review and evaluate for change any items that behave differently across versions (Hambleton, 2004). An advantage of this approach is that the mono-lingual samples for the pilot testing are drawn from the source and target populations; thus, there is no concern regarding generalizability to the population of interest. A disadvantage, however, is that the researcher is unable to determine whether differences that emerge between items in the two measures are due to cultural differences (e.g., different levels of accul-turation or enculturation for members of each group) or to errors during the translation process. Furthermore, a large sample size for each group is necessary in order to conduct the statistical comparisons, so this may require a pilot sample that is larger than usual.

ANALYTIC STRATEGIES FOR ASSESSING DIFFERENT LANGUAGE VERSIONS OF A MEASURE

At the most basic level, researchers compare the two language versions of a measure by examining the degree of similarity in means and standard deviations of items across versions (Brislin, 1970; Hambleton, 2004). Others have recommended that in addition to this, one should compare the internal consistency of each language version by examining Cronbach's alphas across versions to determine whether they are comparably reliable (Bradley, 1994). However, evidence from these two procedures should not be considered sufficient for reaching a decision regarding the accuracy of a translated measure because there may be real differences on the construct of interest between individuals speaking different languages and because Cronbach's alpha does not consider the comparability of each interitem correlation among different language versions. A more rigorous strategy is to conduct factor analyses, which can provide preliminary information regarding the validity of the translated version; this is particularly useful if the measure comprises multiple subscales. If items from the translated measure do not load on the expected subscales, this could be an indication that the translation changed the meaning of those items and they are potentially assessing a different construct.

When sample size is too limited to conduct factor analysis, another strategy is to conduct interitem correlations for all items within each language version and compare correlations across language versions (Bradley, 1994). The magnitude of the effect size should be similar across versions and, for measures that comprise multiple subscales, items within the same subscale should correlate highly with one another and not as highly with items from other subscales. Thus, there are numerous strategies researchers can use to assess the equivalence of different language versions of a measure.

It is important to note that the analytical and methodological strategies just described may not be sufficient to fully address the equivalence of a translated and original language measure. Examining the similarity of the means and standard deviations assumes that the construct does not vary across individuals with differing degrees of connection to the ethnic and mainstream cultures. For example, a measure of familism might well have a different mean and standard deviation in a Latino or Asian American non–English-speaking sample when compared with a monolingual English-speaking counterpart because the latter may be more acculturated. In addition, examining the similarity of internal consistency coefficients is of limited utility because different combinations of interitem correlations can easily lead to similar Cronbach's alphas.

Fortunately, there has been substantial development of analytical methods (e.g., confirmatory factor analysis and item response theory analysis) more suited to the task of examining the equivalence of translated and original language measures (see Camilli & Shepard, 1994; Hines, 1993; Knight et al., 2002; Knight & Hill, 1998; Labouvie & Ruetsch, 1995; Malpass & Poortinga, 1986; McDonald, 1995; Reiss, Widaman, & Pugh, 1993; Widaman, 1995; Widaman & Reise, 1997). Hence, once a relatively sophisticated translation procedure is used to produce both an English language and a second language measure of the target construct, analyses of item (i.e., factorial invariance tests) and scale functioning (i.e., construct validity equivalence tests) and focus groups of monolingual individuals representative of the target population can be used to search for nonequivalencies that elude the bilingual translation team. That is, perhaps the best analytical approach for evaluating the quality and effectiveness of the translation procedures used by the research team is to evaluate the English language and the translated versions of the measure as a special case of the examination of measurement equivalence as described in chapter 3 of this volume.

ISSUES OF TRANSLATION WHEN CONDUCTING QUALITATIVE RESEARCH

Issues of translation also arise when researchers are using qualitative methods. As with quantitative research, those conducting qualitative research must translate their research instrument with caution. A difference, however, is that the instrument used in qualitative research is not a standardized measure but rather an interview protocol. In addition, researchers using qualitative methods must decide how they will handle the translation of data gathered during the study. This is primarily an issue when a study is being conducted in more than one language or if members of the research team do not speak the language in which data were gathered from participants. For example, data from a qualitative study including both English-speaking and Chinese-speaking participants will need to be translated either into English or into Chinese, depending on the language ability of the research team who will be analyzing the data. Similarly, if a study is being conducted with only Spanish-speaking participants, but the research team who will be analyzing the data includes individuals who speak only English, the data will need to be translated into English. Thus, with qualitative methods, translation issues carry on through the analysis phase if researchers will be analyzing the data in a language other than the one in which interviews were conducted.

Translating the Interview Protocol

Translation of the interview protocol in qualitative studies follows generally the same process as translation of measures. Researchers must consider conceptual equivalence; that is, is the construct meaningful in both language groups and meaningful to participants who speak the target language? Issues of semantic equivalence must also be considered, with particular attention to the meaning of each interview question and whether the manner in which the question is being asked in the target language has the same meaning when it is asked in the source language. However, qualitative researchers have the added advantage of being involved in a less formal and more intimate relationship with study participants. This means that they can look for cues that questions are confusing or nonsensical, and they can restate their question in different terms if necessary. In addition, participants are more likely to ask questions if material is confusing, and the participant and interviewer can discuss the intent of interview questions to resolve confusion before answers are provided.

Translating Participants' Data

Researchers recommend that the translation process for qualitative data include at least two steps: first, the researcher must translate the data that were transcribed verbatim into the language intended for analysis, and second, the translation must be double-checked for errors by a second, independent person who is a cultural insider to the participants of the study (Umaña-Taylor & Bámaca, 2004). The second step helps to ensure the cultural validity of the translation because a cultural outsider may not be familiar with the idioms and expressions of the particular national origin group being studied. Given the potential differences in dialect and expressions discussed previously, the second step is critical. For instance, in one study conducted with Puerto Rican participants (i.e., Umaña-Taylor & Bámaca, 2004), the word *palma* was initially translated by a non–Puerto Rican translator as *palm* (a technically correct Spanish translation); during the validity checking phase, however, a Puerto Rican translator changed the translation to indicate that the participant was referring to the symbol of a particular political party in Puerto Rico. Prior to this change, the statement in the transcript had little meaning; however, someone with knowledge of Puerto Rican culture was easily able to clarify the intended meaning. This would have gone undetected had the cultural validity step not been in place.

Using Data Analyses to Determine Equivalence

Beyond providing guidelines regarding the steps that researchers should follow when translating qualitative work, researchers also recommend various strategies to check whether translations are equivalent. One strategy is to use multiple coding teams during the analysis phase of the process (Twinn, 1997). One team would analyze the document that was translated into English, and a second team would analyze the document written in the original language in which the data were gathered. After analyses are complete, the results would be compared by assessing whether the same major and minor themes emerged in both analysis teams. However, this requires that a bilingual team compare the two sets of results because each will be in a different language. Twinn (1997) also recommended having two separate persons translate the original transcript into English and then having two analysis teams analyze the results using one of the translated English versions. Thus, all analyses are carried out in English, but there are two English versions being analyzed, and the results across these two versions are compared with one another. If the same major and minor themes emerge for the two teams, equivalence is assumed. Others who conduct qualitative research suggest that it may be impossible to achieve conceptual equivalence across languages because communication in any particular language carries with it a set of assumptions, feelings, and values that an outsider may be unlikely to detect (Temple & Young, 2004). One possible strategy to overcome this challenge, however, is to conduct qualitative research with teams of translators that include cultural insiders. Another major challenge associated with this approach, however, is the cost involved in staffing two separate analysis teams.

Selecting and Disclosing the Characteristics of the Research Team

Regardless of who comprises the research team, it is critical that researchers disclose the characteristics of the translators on the research team, as well as the process by which translation and cultural validity verification occurred, in order for consumers of the research to have the necessary information to evaluate its validity. Unfortunately, not all published studies provide this information and, in extreme cases, some published work does not indicate that there was any translation involved in the research process. In these cases, many erroneous assumptions are being made. Of most significant concern is the assumption that the characteristics of the translators who are conveying the meanings of the participants are unimportant to the research process when in fact they may influence how translators view the world and, therefore, how the translation of meaning is occurring (Temple & Young, 2004). Social characteristics such as national origin and SES, for example, position translators in a social world that may be considerably different from the experiences of study participants. Because the lens from which they view the world may be heavily influenced by these characteristics, it is critical to acknowledge this as a potential limitation of the translation process.

A final important consideration when translating qualitative research, one that is largely determined by characteristics of the research team, involves deciding at which point in the research process the translation will occur. Researchers who speak the language in which the data were gathered and have a research team who also speaks this language are able to analyze the data in the language in which data were gathered. In fact, some researchers believe this may be the most valid way to conduct the analyses, given that it ensures that participants' beliefs and ideas are being analyzed rather than translators' interpretations and translations of participants' beliefs and ideas (Temple & Young, 2004). Thus, conducting the translation later in the process (i.e., during manuscript preparation) may provide the most accurate account of participants' experiences because the potential for translators' interpretations to be introduced into the data being analyzed is eliminated.

IMPLICATIONS OF TRANSLATION FOR THE FOUR COMMON RESEARCH DESIGNS

The process of translation has unique implications for the common types of research designs discussed in chapter 1 of this volume. As previously discussed, the typical research goal of studies with a cross-group comparative design is to compare mean levels or interrelations among constructs across ethnic or economic groups. When using measures that have been translated, achieving conceptual equivalence between the translated and English-version measures is critical, especially when one of the groups being compared is more likely to complete the measure in a language other than English. For instance, if researchers are interested in comparing levels of self-esteem among Latino and African American adolescents, but a majority of the Latino participants completed the measure in Spanish, researchers will have trouble drawing conclusions from findings if the equivalence of measures has not been established. Specifically, if differences are detected, it is possible that differences are a result of inaccuracies in translation rather than actual differences in self-esteem; perhaps the Spanish version is actually measuring a construct other than self-esteem, and thus significant differences emerge as a result of different constructs being measured. Similarly, if differences do not emerge, it will be unclear whether there are no differences between groups or if the translation process introduced so much measurement error into the process that group differences simply could not be detected.

Similar concerns arise for within-group designs, when researchers are interested in making comparisons within ethnic groups. As introduced in chapter 1 of this volume, within-group designs are typically focused on examining processes within a specific group. However, oftentimes researchers will also look within the ethnic group to examine how members of the group differ from one another. For instance, if researchers studying Chinese American families are interested in comparing parents and children, but a majority of children completed the survey in English, and a majority of parents completed the survey in Chinese, then equivalence among language versions must be established before comparisons are made. This is not uncommon in studies of first- and second-generation immigrant families in which a majority of children complete the measures in English and a majority of parents complete the measures in their native language. If a goal of the study is to compare parents and children, and the two language versions of a particular measure are not equivalent, researchers will not know whether differences that emerge are the result of actual differences between parents and children on the construct of interest or the result of different constructs being measured in each of the language versions.

Translation, however, can introduce important measurement error or measurement bias into within-group designs even when researchers are not making within-group comparisons. For instance, in studies designed to examine the interrelations among a set of constructs among members of one ethnic group, and that include individuals who completed the measures in English or a second language, measurement error and measurement bias can obscure the findings if the two language versions are not equivalent. For example, if measures completed in Chinese are not assessing the same construct as those completed in English, but the data for participants who completed the measure in Chinese are aggregated with data for participants who completed the measures in English, then the observed relations between the total set of scores on the two measures may not represent the underlying nature of the relationship between the constructs assessed in either language.

Issues of equivalence for different language versions of measures are not typically a concern with national sample designs, which theoretically are designed to be representative of the U.S. population. Unfortunately, this is because large studies that use a nationally representative sample typically do not have non-English materials available for participants, and thus no translated measures are included in these studies. Therefore, the most significant concern with these national sample designs is that the sample is not in fact representative of the U.S. population because individuals who do not speak English are excluded from these studies.

Finally, inadvertently diverse designs also rarely have measures available in a language other than English, given that the diverse sample was achieved by happenstance and, thus, issues of language diversity were likely not considered in designing the study and preparing the research instruments. Thus, as is the case with national sample designs, issues of translation are not necessarily a concern for inadvertently diverse designs, but the generalizability of findings is a concern, given the exclusion of non–English speakers.

RECOMMENDATIONS FOR BEST PRACTICES AND FUTURE DIRECTIONS

The strategies researchers use when translating their research instruments and/or data will depend largely on the purpose of their research (e.g., cross-ethnic comparative study, research with an ethnic homogeneous population in which individuals have varied language abilities and preferences) and the characteristics of the research team (e.g., bilingual vs. monolingual, similar national and geographical origins). For example, if the goal of the research is cross-ethnic comparison, construct equivalence must first be established to ensure that the measure being translated to a different language for a different cultural group is assessing a construct that is meaningful to that population (Hambleton, 2004). An instrument can be adapted into a target language and culture, but a comparison of scores of the two language versions could be problematic if the conceptualizations of the construct differ in the two cultures being examined (Hambleton & Li, 2005). Thus, before translating a measure, it is critical to determine whether the construct being assessed is relevant for the target group. The issue of conceptual equivalence may be less of a problem when researchers are studying a construct within one cultural group (e.g., Mexican-origin families in the United States), but issues of semantic equivalence may be more important given that the items must reflect a similar meaning across different language versions of the measure. Thus, before attempting any translation, researchers must consider the types of equivalence that are most relevant to their research, as well as the translation strategies that will be most appropriate, given their goals.

Regardless of the strategy or strategies used, scholars agree that the primary goal of translation should be meaningful equivalence rather than a literal translation (Brislin, 1970; Hambleton & Li, 2005; Kristjannson et al., 2003). Items that are literally translated oftentimes do not represent the intended meaning, and/or are difficult to understand, in the target language (Hambleton & Li). Thus, the importance of meaningful rather than literal translation should be emphasized to all involved in the process of translation on a research team.

There also is consensus among scholars regarding the importance of taking into account the specific characteristics of the target population when selecting a translation team and selecting participants for pilot testing of instruments. Level of education, age group, occupation, previous knowledge of the topic, degree of bilingualism, and dialect experiences are a few examples of the characteristics that can introduce significant variability into the translation process (Prieto, 1992). For quantitative research, selecting translators and participants who mirror the characteristics of the target population, although costly, will significantly increase the generalizability of the measure to the intended population. For qualitative research, this strategy will help ensure that the questions being asked of research participants are meaningful in the target language and that the translated data represent an accurate depiction of participants' beliefs and experiences.

In closing, we offer two recommendations regarding how the field could move forward with regard to the translation of instruments and data. First, it will be critical for funding agencies to be informed about the time- and labor-intensive nature of translating measures given the need to explore and fix errors in translation as well as evaluate the equivalence of translated and original language measures. In an ideal scenario, researchers would use the most stringent strategies for translating measures and research protocols, involve a large and diverse translation team composed of experts in various aspects of the process, and conduct extensive pilot testing and measurement equivalence analyses to evaluate the equivalence of the different language versions before conducting hypothesis testing studies. This currently is not possible for a majority of research projects because of limited time and resources. These strategies and evaluations require significant preparation time for tasks such as selecting and hiring translators with appropriate skills and training translators and back-translators. Furthermore, pilot testing and measurement equivalence analyses also require considerable time and resources, and recruiting appropriate participants for pilot testing can be difficult, especially if researchers are trying to match pilot test participants to target participants on the numerous demographic characteristics discussed earlier. Finally, pilot testing may reveal additional changes necessary to the instrument or interview guide, which will entail a second round of pilot testing. An initial step toward securing the time and resources necessary to conduct translations appropriately involves educating funding agencies on the time- and labor-intensive nature of this process. For large quantitative projects, at least 1 year of preparation time is needed to get the measures designed, tested, revised, and finalized. For qualitative projects, sufficient time is necessary at the tail end of the project to verify the equivalence of the translated data. In addition, projects that involve translation require additional financial resources to find and hire the skilled translators whose characteristics match those of the target population. Thus, adequate resources for staff and pilot testing (e.g., recruitment, participant incentives) must be built into these budgets, and funding agencies must be made aware of these needs.

A final recommendation we propose is that researchers share their translated measures and provide a detailed account of how equivalence was assessed (e.g., intended population, characteristics of translation team, translation process followed, findings of pilot testing and measurement equivalence analyses). A national clearinghouse, whereby researchers could post their translated measures and the relevant equivalence testing information, would facilitate the process. If a rigorous translation process is followed, and the measure has been translated for a population that is similar to the population of interest (e.g., a measure translated for Mexican-origin populations in Arizona would likely be useful for Mexican-origin populations in California), then by sharing this information researchers could save considerable time and resources. In addition, a measure created for one Spanish-speaking group would provide a good starting point for researchers needing such a measure for another Spanish-speaking group, likely reducing the costs of creating a measure for the new group. Furthermore, journal editors should be encouraged to publish articles that focus on the process of translation, its methodological implications for research, and studies that have evaluated the equivalence of translated and English-language measures (for an example, see Peña, 2007). This sharing of information could contribute significantly to advancing the field because researchers could spend the saved time and resources on advancing other aspects of their research with linguistically diverse populations.

6

Putting Research Into Action: Preventive Intervention Research

Preventive intervention programs are essential for reducing the incidence, duration, or intensity of undesirable outcomes such as delinquency, school failure or dropout, physical health problems, and mental health problems. Because ethnic minority and economically disadvantaged populations are at greater risk for these outcomes, the U.S. Surgeon General and others have called for an increased focus on prevention and services delivery research with these populations (e.g., M. H. Case & Robinson, 2003; Hollon et al., 2002; T. G. Thompson, 2001). In addition, ethnic minority and economically disadvantaged groups are more ambivalent than others about seeking services, or they cannot take advantage of available services because of costs, a lack of insurance, or their status as undocumented persons.

At present, the field of preventive intervention science is significantly limited with regard to prevention efforts with diverse populations. Most preventive interventions are designed without attention to cultural differences or diversity in socioeconomic class. Thus, there is a need to adapt, develop, and test approaches with diverse populations that hold promise as preventive interventions. Cultural competency is an important aspect of this process. Researchers must consider adaptations that are culturally relevant to the groups in question and, furthermore, consider culturally appropriate methods of delivering the program to the groups of interest. Accordingly, in this chapter we review the state of the field with regard to preventive intervention research with ethnic minority and economically disadvantaged populations. Specifically, we discuss the need to increase prevention efforts with diverse populations; present strategies for adapting, developing, and delivering programs to diverse groups; and provide an overview of challenges inherent to such adaptations. We conclude the chapter with a discussion of a culturally adapted depression prevention program designed for use with African American and Latino children. It is important to note that most of the literature on prevention research has focused on adaptations with respect to ethnic minority group members rather than economically disadvantaged groups; however, in the discussion that follows we have attempted to extend these ideas to economically disadvantaged groups, where applicable.

THE NEED FOR PREVENTION EFFORTS WITH ETHNICALLY DIVERSE AND ECONOMICALLY DISADVANTAGED POPULATIONS

Scholars agree that the field of prevention science is extremely limited with respect to the inclusion of members of ethnic minority and economically disadvantaged populations in preventive intervention programs (e.g., Hollon et al., 2002; Kumpfer, Alvarado, Smith, & Bellamy, 2002; Lopez, Edwards, Pedrotti, Ito, & Rasmussen, 2002; Miranda, Nakamura, & Bernal, 2003; Turner, 2000). Some argue that preventive interventions are particularly important for ethnic minority and other special populations who are more ambivalent about seeking psychological services (M. H. Case & Robinson, 2003; T. G. Thompson, 2001). Furthermore, scholars indicate that poverty and its correlates (e.g., exposure to violence) are often identified as risk factors on which researchers must focus because they greatly increase the risk for negative outcomes (e.g., Hollon et al., 2002), thus supporting the need for preventive interventions tailored toward economically disadvantaged populations. The shortage of existing programs tested with and/or tailored to ethnic minority and economically disadvantaged populations poses a number of significant problems. Of particular concern is that relatively little is known about the effectiveness of evidence-based interventions with members of many at-risk populations (U.S. Department of Health and Human Services, 2001).

To use the area of mental health as an example, the National Institute of Mental Health (NIMH) recently assembled a work group charged with reviewing the state of psychosocial interventions for mood disorders and considering how NIMH could improve the knowledge base (Hollon et al., 2002). The work group was particularly concerned with the finding that members of underrepresented groups were at greatest risk of not receiving efficacious treatment, likely because of their limited inclusion in randomized clinical trials and the resulting lack of knowledge concerning effective treatment (Hollon et al., 2002). For instance, most studies merely enrolled representative numbers of ethnic minorities in preventive intervention research, which did not result in a sample of sufficient size to test whether the program was efficacious with specific groups (Miranda et al., 2003). As a result, one of the major recommendations made to NIMH was the need for development of interventions for, and validation of existing interventions with, populations such as ethnic minorities and economically disadvantaged groups (Hollon et al., 2002). This is consistent with others' suggestions regarding the need to adapt, develop, and test with ethnic minority populations approaches that hold promise as preventive interventions (Roselló & Bernal, 1999). Similar recommendations have been made by scholars who focus on preventive interventions in the area of substance abuse (e.g., Catalano et al., 1993; Resnicow, Soler, Braithwaite, Ahluwalia, & Butler, 2000) and youth violence (e.g., Reese, Vera, & Hasbrouck, 2003) as well as by professionals who conduct family-based interventions (e.g., Kumpfer et al., 2002; Turner, 2000). Thus, it is clear that scholars are in agreement regarding the need for culturally adapted preventive intervention programs. Prior to discussing the elements of programs that must be considered for adaptation and the types of adaptations involved in making a program culturally relevant, we review basic terminology and present the prevention research cycle.

A REVIEW OF BASIC TERMS AND THE PREVENTION RESEARCH CYCLE

Intervention research can be viewed along a spectrum that includes prevention, treatment, and maintenance (Muñoz, Mrazek, & Haggerty, 1996). *Preventive interventions* are designed to occur before the onset of health or behavior problems, *treatment interventions* focus on alleviating or eliminating episodes or symptoms of a problem or disorder, and *maintenance interventions* typically occur after the acute episode of a disorder has subsided. Maintenance interventions may be designed to reduce relapse and focus on rehabilitation services. Our focus in this chapter is on preventive interventions, which can be further divided into three subcategories: (a) *universal,* (b) *selective,* and (c) *indicated* (Muñoz et al., 1996). Universal preventive interventions are targeted to the general public or populations that have not been identified on the basis of increased risk. Selective preventive interventions are targeted to a group whose risk for developing a particular disorder is higher than average, and indicated preventive interventions are targeted to high-risk individuals who have detectable signs of a disorder but do not yet meet diagnostic criteria.

Regardless of the category of risk for which the preventive intervention is being developed and conducted, most researchers follow a general prevention research cycle. The stages of the prevention research cycle are commonly described as involving four stages: (a) *generative,* (b) *program development,* (c) *implementation,* and (d) *diffusion.* The generative stage includes identifying the problem, reviewing the potential risk and protective processes associated with the problem or disorder, and developing a theory of the causal processes that place a group at heightened risk for negative outcomes (Mrazek & Haggerty, 1994; Roosa, Wolchik, & Sandler, 1997). Research conducted and/or reviewed during this phase that informs researchers of the mechanisms to target in an intervention is referred to as *generative research.* On the basis of findings from generative research, and using a theoretical model to guide intervention development (i.e., referred to as a *small theory of intervention;* Roosa et al., 1997), researchers then enter the program development stage, which focuses on designing the intervention. During this stage researchers design behavior change strategies based on the key elements of the small theory of the intervention, recruit and train staff, identify and recruit potential participants, and conduct pilot studies. Experimental field trials are then implemented to test whether the program is effective in changing putative causal processes and targeted outcomes. During the stage of implementation, researchers conduct multiple generations of field trials to ensure continued efficacy and to distinguish core elements from adaptable characteristics. The final step is a diffusion stage, in which a standardized program is implemented on a large scale and in various naturalistic community settings; this is also referred to as *dissemination of a program* (Roosa et al., 1997). The discussion of cultural adaptation that follows focuses largely on how ethnic and economic diversity are critical to consider in the first three stages of the prevention research cycle; failure to consider these factors will pose considerable problems for the final stage, which involves large-scale dissemination of programs.

CULTURAL ADAPTATION

Multiple program elements must be evaluated when one is determining their appropriateness for ethnic minority or economically disadvantaged populations. These program elements have implications for each stage of the prevention research cycle. For instance, researchers must determine whether the content, method of delivery, recruitment strategies, and the approach for retaining program participants will be relevant to the group of interest. To make the program relevant to and effective with a particular ethnic or economic group, researchers must often make adaptations to one or more program elements. In fact, some argue that to achieve cultural competence, intervention researchers must integrate culture into each level of the research cycle (Yasui & Dishion, 2007). Resnicow and colleagues (Resnicow, Baranowski, Ahluwalia, & Braithwaite, 1999; Resnicow et al., 2000) have explained that adaptations can involve *surface structure adaptations* or *deep structure adaptations*. Surface structure adaptations focus on matching intervention materials and messages to social and behavioral characteristics of a target population. For example, a surface structure adaptation might involve having video educational materials reflect the ethnicity of group participants such that actors in the video are of the same ethnicity as members of the intervention group. This also includes identifying the settings and channels (e.g., media) that are most appropriate for delivery of messages and programs for the particular population. The surface structure dimension of cultural adaptation is achieved by means of expert and community review as well as the involvement of the target population in the program. Modifying delivery is an example of a surface structure adaptation; this may involve presenting the same program content but delivering it with changes in characteristics of the person or persons delivering the program, the channel of delivery, and/or the location of delivery (Castro, Barrera, & Martinez, 2004).

Other researchers argue that cultural adaptations must move beyond surface structure changes and incorporate deep structure changes, whereby core values, beliefs, norms, and other significant aspects of worldviews and lifestyles are incorporated (e.g., Castro et al., 2004). Deep structure adaptations are more focused on how cultural, social, psychological, environmental, and historical factors might influence behaviors differently across different cultural groups (Resnicow et al., 2000). For example, an intervention that originally involved individual learning activities may be revamped to include group-focused learning activities because the targeted participants are members of an ethnic group known for a more collectivistic or interdependent orientation. In fact, research in education suggests that cooperative learning is a generally effective instructional tactic (see Slavin, 1980), but it is thought to be particularly useful with Hispanic American and Native American students because of these cultural groups' emphasis on cooperation and sharing, which may make these students better prepared than others to work as part of a group (Snowman & Biehler, 1997). The need for deep structure adaptations is typically discovered in the generative phase of the research cycle, when researchers are most likely to recognize that the processes for intervention may be different for ethnic or economically diverse groups. Deep structure adaptations typically involve modifying the content of the program. Modification of content is necessary when a group needs or wants certain content not offered by the original model program; this content can be incorporated throughout the curriculum or designed as a complete supplemental module (Castro et al., 2004). Resnicow and colleagues (Resnicow et al., 1999, 2000) have indicated that because surface structure adaptations generally increase receptivity and comprehension of the program, they tend to establish feasibility, whereas deep structure adaptations determine program impact because they increase salience for the relations of interest due to their cultural relevance.

In general, deep structure adaptations pertain mainly to the content of the intervention (i.e., the generative and program development stages of the research cycle), whereas surface structure adaptations typically address elements associated with delivery of the program (i.e., the implementation and dissemination stages of the research cycle). In most cases, deep structure and surface structure adaptations are equally necessary when adapting a program. Because the cultural context of the group of interest must be considered throughout the entire research process to maximize the relevance and efficacy of the program (G. Bernal, Bonilla, & Bellido, 1995), and given the often vast differences in cultural context between the ethnic or economic group of interest and the group with which the program was initially developed (i.e., typically a White middle-class sample), both surface structure and deep structure adaptations will be necessary to make a program culturally relevant and efficacious with a particular ethnic or economic group.

Regardless of whether the adaptations are deep structure or surface structure, scholars recognize the need for making cultural adaptations to existing programs in order to increase their relevance to and effectiveness with ethnic minority or economically disadvantaged groups. Thus, the question is not whether programs will be adapted but whether they will be adapted in a manner that is scientifically rigorous and maintains fidelity (Castro et al., 2004). As the field has advanced, scholars have contributed to the discourse on this topic by providing numerous recommendations for cultural adaptation of existing preventive intervention programs. In the next section, we review these recommendations and discuss which aspects of a program are typically affected, whether the recommendation addresses surface structure or deep structure adaptations, and which phases of the research cycle are usually involved.

RECOMMENDATIONS AND STRATEGIES FOR ADAPTING, DEVELOPING, AND DELIVERING PROGRAMS

Given the considerable concern regarding inclusion of individuals from ethnic minority and economically disadvantaged populations in intervention research, scholars have posed a number of recommendations, strategies, and issues that one should consider when adapting or developing a preventive intervention program. The most common issues center on considering the cultural context and using it to inform all aspects of intervention development and implementation, collaborating with the community and allowing those collaborations to influence intervention development and implementation, offering materials in participants' language of preference, determining where to administer programs, revising target variables or intervention design elements to be consistent with the needs of the target population, and considering the use of ethnically homogeneous designs.

The most general recommendation offered by scholars involves considering the cultural context within which individuals' lives are embedded when determining how to adapt or develop a particular program for a specific population. Although this may seem as if it would be a given for anyone considering administering a program to members of ethnic minority groups, such has not been the case; as a result, scholars include it as one of the primary recommendations for prevention work with minority populations (e.g., G. Bernal et al., 1995; M. H. Case & Robinson, 2003; Dumka, Lopez, & Carter, 2002; Lopez et al., 2002). It is recommended that researchers revise a program to be administered to a particular group only after careful examination of the cultural context. Consideration of the cultural context can lead to both surface structure and deep structure adaptations. As described earlier, during the generative phase of the research cycle, after reviewing existing research and considering the cultural context of their target participants, researchers may realize that the original intervention program may not be effective with a particular ethnic or economic group. For example, an intervention administered to Latino youth may need to be revised to become a family-based program, given the importance of the family in Latino cultures (G. Bernal et al., 1995). Thus, in the generative stage of the research cycle researchers would determine whether the causal processes and mechanisms that initially informed the development of the program would be applicable to Latino youth. If not, the intervention would be adapted to be applicable to Latino youth during the program development phase of the research cycle.

Consideration of the cultural context can also lead to revisions of the methods by which the program is delivered and the strategies that

174

researchers use to retain participants in the program (i.e., surface struc-ture), which would pertain to the implementation and dissemination stages of the research cycle. In their prevention work with Latino adoles-cents, Zambrana and Aguirre-Molina (1987) maintained participants' interest in the program by integrating aspects of their cultural back-grounds and their surrounding community into the program. For exam-ple, because many of the Latino youth in their program were racially Black, they emphasized the African roots of Latino culture in the cultural awareness component of their intervention program. Thus, the concep-tual structure of the intervention did not change, but the symbols they used to deliver the information were revised to be consistent with the cul-tural context. Because consideration of the cultural context is such a broad recommendation, the suggestions that follow can be considered specific examples of how to consider the cultural context in adapting or develop-ing interventions that are culturally relevant.

Collaborating With the Community

Similar to recommendations for facilitating recruitment and retention of participants in research (see chap. 2, this volume), scholars recom-mend working in collaboration with members of the community to earn trust and demonstrate reciprocity between the researcher and commu-nity members when conducting preventive interventions (M. H. Case & Robinson, 2003). Community collaboration can affect each stage of the prevention research cycle. In the generative and program development stages of the research cycle, community collaboration is critical because it allows researchers to gain a better understanding of the participants for whom the intervention is planned (Dumka et al., 2002). Scholars recom-mend making contributions to the community before undergoing the research process (Reese & Vera, 2007). For example, volunteering at com-munity events can provide researchers with an inside view of the commu-nity and demonstrate that they have a certain level of commitment to the community. These efforts help establish trust with the community. Fur-thermore, some scholars recommend using qualitative methods, such as focus groups, to explore important predictor variables that are culture specific and should be included in the program development stage (Dumka, Roosa, Michaels, & Suh, 1995; Lengua et al., 1992; Resnicow et al., 1999).

With respect to the implementation stage, scholars argue that establishing trust between the researcher and participants is a critical necessary step toward successful program implementation with ethnic minority and economically disadvantaged populations (Dumka et al., 1995; Lopez et al., 2002). Community advisory boards can assist in identifying locations from which to offer programs that will not exclude particular groups of potential participants (Vera, 2007). Others suggest that members of the community be recruited to facilitate implementation of the intervention (Reese & Vera, 2007). For example, in a parenting intervention program for low-income ethnically diverse families, Dumka et al. (1995) hired women who lived in the target community and represented the ethnic groups in the study to assist with tasks such as recruitment and home visits. Finally, some researchers recommend that research findings be shared with community members so that alternative explanations for findings can be considered (Lopez et al., 2002). In other words, participants are asked for their interpretations of the research findings. These interpretations may improve researchers' understanding of the phenomenon being studied within the context of this population and add to the development of cross-cultural theory. By demonstrating a genuine interest in participants' perspectives, insiders' interpretations also may benefit the research process by increasing participants' trust of the research team and, in turn, facilitating participation and retention in longitudinal studies. Thus, the value of incorporating members of the target community throughout the entire prevention research cycle for programs with minority populations is a consistent theme in the literature. Community collaboration can lead to surface structure adaptations to programs whereby community members inform researchers about things such as culturally appropriate symbols and recruitment methods. However, community collaboration can also lead to deep structure adaptations if community members are relied on to provide information regarding their perceptions of characteristics that place members of the target population at risk for the variable under study or some other more substantive issue that would change the variable or variables targeted in the intervention (Resnicow et al., 1999).

Language

In general, issues related to language of delivery typically affect the program development stage of the research cycle and carry through to the implementation and dissemination stages. Many scholars argue that making the program available in participants' language of preference is a requisite of any culturally adapted intervention (G. Bernal et al., 1995; Miranda et al., 2003; Sabogal, Otero-Sabogal, Pasick, Jenkins, & Pérez-Stable, 1996). This need can be determined only after careful study of the target population. Researchers must become intimately familiar with the target group to understand the language needs of the community; a simple survey of the population asking about language preference will likely not be sufficient. For example, in a seemingly acculturated Latino community, a quick survey of language preference may indicate that participants prefer a program in English; however, on delivery of the program the researchers may find that participants frequently switch back and forth between Spanish and English. If research group leaders are not proficient in Spanish, this could create a barrier between them and the participants, and it could minimize the effectiveness of the program because participants are not able to express themselves in their preferred manner. If researchers had conducted a more extensive study of the community, this characteristic of the population may have been uncovered and the potential threat to the delivery of the program averted.

If a researcher determines that multiple language versions of a program are necessary, or that the program should be disseminated in a language other than the language in which it was initially developed (i.e., typically English), then he or she will need to translate the program to the desired language. Consistent with our discussion in chapter 5 of this volume, scholars caution against literal translations and emphasize that particular attention be paid to recruitment materials that, if translated incorrectly, can have negative effects on recruitment and participation (Sabogal et al., 1996). For instance, a health education program delivered to Vietnamese women translated a breast cancer screening brochure to read, "There is only one kind of woman at risk for breast cancer," and depicted four women who were not Vietnamese. The intended meaning in the original English version was to demonstrate that all women are at risk for breast cancer; however, the Vietnamese translation had spelling and grammatical errors and did not portray Vietnamese women. Thus, the intended meaning for the Vietnamese community was lost completely (Sabogal et al., 1996). Furthermore, if translations are necessary, and especially if the program will be delivered in multiple languages, then measurement equivalence must be established for the scales that are used to evaluate the efficacy and effectiveness of the program (for a discussion of measurement equivalence, see chap. 4, this volume). Examination of equivalence would take place during the implementation stage of the research cycle and, if the results supported equivalence, would provide confidence that large-scale dissemination to linguistically diverse groups would be possible.

Tailoring all aspects of the intervention program to be administered in multiple languages is a surface structure adaptation; however, this type of adaptation can have profound effects on the accessibility of the program to the populations that are most in need of the service. This will be a labor-intensive task because researchers will need to ensure that the language used is culturally consistent with the target population. This process entails involving members of the community to provide cultural validity checks to ensure that the nuances of the economic class and ethnic culture of the target population are captured in the translation. Although adaptations that involve changes to the language of delivery are labor intensive, this is a critical aspect of adaptation that will determine whether the intervention is received as intended (G. Bernal et al., 1995).

Where to Administer Programs

The issue of where to administer preventive intervention programs is complex and affects the implementation and dissemination stages of the research cycle. Some researchers recommend administering programs in schools, churches, or community centers where individuals feel comfortable and are in regular attendance (Cardemil, Reivich, & Seligman, 2002; Muñoz, Penilla, & Urizar, 2002; Zambrana & Aguirre-Molina, 1987). Researchers argue that administering programs in schools, for example, gives programs a high likelihood of dissemination and may increase service utilization in at-risk populations because the vast majority of children attend school (Muñoz et al., 2002) and because programs that are school based are less likely to conflict with other obligations (e.g., housework) that are typically done on weekends or evenings (Zambrana & Aguirre-Molina, 1987). Others, however, argue that administering programs in such locations may actually miss the individuals who are at greatest risk because they may be less likely to be regularly attending school or engaged in community organizations (e.g., Reese et al., 2003; Vera, 2007). Furthermore, programs may appear efficacious with a school-based population, whereas there may be something about the population of youth who are not engaged in school that would minimize the generalizability of the results of the program to them (for a discussion of the representativeness of a sample, see chap. 2, this volume). Put differently, relying on school- or community-based locations for delivering programs may compromise the external validity of the program. Given that the experimental field trials conducted in the implementation stage of the research cycle ultimately inform the standardized program that will be disseminated, it is critical that researchers carefully consider the locations where the program is administered and that they thoroughly examine the potential effects of location on the effectiveness of their program.

Revising Target Variables or Intervention Design

Community collaboration efforts and findings from community-based research often lead to the need to revise core elements of an intervention to make it culturally relevant and attractive to a target population. These deep structure adaptations can involve introducing new core elements to the intervention, for example, or changing the type of intervention (e.g., from an individual to a family-based program). Provided that these adaptations are guided by culturally informed theory and evidence during the generative stage of the research cycle, they will likely make significant contributions to prevention science (Castro et al., 2004). For instance, some scholars recommend adopting family-based intervention strategies when considering prevention programs for ethnic minority populations (Turner, 2000). This is based on the notion that families play a central role in shaping the lives of ethnic minority individuals. Thus, family involvement in prevention programs is considered by many researchers to be an aspect of the cultural context that is relevant to all ethnic minority families (see Kumpfer et al., 2002). Zambrana and Aguirre-Molina (1987) found that feedback from participants in an alcohol abuse prevention program supported the notion that family involvement is essential for programs engaging individuals from ethnic minority groups: Participants reported that involving members of their family in the program was critical for their own involvement.

Another recommendation that is addressed during the generative stage of the research cycle involves developing an increased understanding of areas of strength and resiliency among ethnic minorities and using participants' natural resiliency in the design and implementation of prevention strategies (M. H. Case & Robinson, 2003). Building on the cultural strengths that participants possess could increase their connection to the program, as well as the program's effectiveness. For example, a set of potential variables to target among ethnic and racial minority youth may be ethnic and racial identities, such as the degree to which individuals have explored, resolved, and affirm their ethnic group membership (Umaña-Taylor, Yazedjian, & Bámaca-Gómez, 2004). Ethnic and racial identity have been demonstrated to serve as protective factors for multiple groups of ethnic minority youth (Mossakowski, 2003; Noh, Beiser, Kaspar, Hou, & Rummens, 1999; Romero & Roberts, 2003; Sellers, Caldwell, Schmeelk-Cone, & Zimmerman, 2003; Sellers & Shelton, 2003); thus these may be ideal variables to consider for intervention because they build on youth's cultural strengths, and preliminary work has demonstrated their protective nature. Thus, implementing interventions in a manner that fosters exploration of one's ethnic background may enhance other program elements designed to increase self-actualization.

Another potential adaptation strategy in the program development stage involves reconsidering the method of delivery for an intervention based on the needs of the target population. For one program, researchers concluded that a combination of learning approaches was most effective, compared with an approach that focused on verbal activities alone (Zambrana & Aguirre-Molina, 1987). Thus, during the program development stage of the research cycle the method of instruction was changed to include more active and interactive (e.g., field trips, workshops) methods in addition to verbal activities.

Ethnically Homogeneous Designs

Finally, some scholars argue for ethnically homogeneous designs, noting that the diversity among ethnic groups has the potential to confound results if not carefully considered (G. Bernal & Scharrón-Del-Rio, 2001; Lopez et al., 2002). Similarly, considering the diversity within specific ethnic groups is critical because this also has the potential to introduce variability that could confound the results. For instance, scholars suggest that differences in acculturation, bicultural competence, and ethnic identity must be considered in all programs involving ethnic minority group members because these variables could introduce significant variability into the relations of interest (M. H. Case & Robinson, 2003; Lopez et al., 2002; Resnicow et al., 2000; Santisteban, Muir-Malcolm, Mitrani, & Szapocznik, 2001). Of significant concern is that it is not possible to separate out the influences of the demographic characteristics that introduce considerable variability into individuals' lives (e.g., social class, acculturation) because their influences are so intertwined that it is methodologically and statistically impossible to determine their separate influence (Roosa, Morgan-Lopez, Cree, & Specter, 2002). However, cross-group comparative studies and in-depth studies of single specific ethnic groups may advance our understanding of the generalizability across subgroups, and they can facilitate the development of generalizable interventions rather than focusing on making adaptations solely to fit one subpopulation. Adaptations tailored toward one specific group are limited because they are more difficult to implement to ethnically and economically diverse audiences.

Consideration of the diversity among and within ethnic groups is important for all stages of the prevention research cycle. Because ethnically homogeneous intervention designs are not ideal because of concerns about creating programs that are so specific to certain groups that they are not easily administered to other populations (Roosa et al., 2002), some researchers have recommended strategies that would acknowledge the diversity that exists within groups and move the field forward with respect to understanding whether programs could be delivered to diverse populations. One strategy we recommend during the generative and program development stages of the research cycle is to use existing research conducted with diverse groups to guide the development of preventive interventions for diverse populations. This minimizes the need for developing and testing ethnically homogeneous designs that may or may not be efficacious and generalize to other populations. For example, drug abuse prevalence and incidence data for specific ethnic and economic groups can provide information on the developmental appropriateness and timing of prevention interventions for specific groups (Catalano et al., 1993). Furthermore, findings from existing generative studies conducted with ethnically homogeneous samples can be examined to identify common risk factors across different cultural groups, which can then help establish intervention priorities (Catalano et al., 1993). Sabogal et al. (1996) indicated that in some circumstances culture-specific materials are necessary (e.g., tailored specifically toward Cuban American participants, with references to specific concerns unique to the Cuban community and dialect-specific translation), but in other cases culturally universal materials may be appropriate (e.g., tailored toward a general Latino American population and emphasizing a common value across Latino groups, such as respect for elder family members). These decisions can be informed by referring to previous studies in which the target variables have been examined with diverse populations.

In terms of implementation and dissemination, one strategy is to assume that the critical ingredients of care (to use mental health care as an example) are likely to work similarly for most human beings, especially when there is no culturally based reason to assume otherwise (e.g., assertiveness training can be more or less useful for individuals from certain cultural groups that do not encourage assertive behavior; Miranda et al., 2003). Researchers working under this assumption would test effectiveness studies with diverse populations and document when programs are not working well for specific populations. On the basis of those findings, focused studies could then be conducted with diverse groups to determine program elements that must be adapted. It is important to recognize that this requires oversampling of ethnic minority and economically disadvantaged populations, and large enough sample sizes for all groups, to allow comparison across groups. On the basis of field studies conducted during the implementation stage of the prevention research cycle, researchers would devise the standardized program to be disseminated widely to diverse groups.

CHALLENGES TO OVERCOME AND DIRECTIONS FOR FUTURE RESEARCH

Preventive interventions that do not consider culture risk losing community participation in their programs; however, culturally focused preventive interventions that are unscientific will not guarantee program effectiveness (Castro et al., 2004). Thus, a balance between adapting interventions to be culturally relevant and maintaining fidelity of implementation is necessary. Castro et al. (2004) recommended developing hybrid prevention programs that build in adaptation to enhance program fit while maximizing fidelity of implementation and program effectiveness. Although cultural adaptations of existing programs have led to more success in recruitment and retention, when these cultural adaptations are accompanied by, for example, reducing dosage or eliminating critical core content, the positive outcomes of the intervention have been diminished (Kumpfer et al., 2002). Cultural adaptations that reduce dosage (e.g., provide fewer original-content focused sessions) typically do so as a result of having to balance the need to add program sessions that focus on unique cultural needs (e.g., sessions focused on strengthening family values) and to keep the length of the curriculum manageable; thus, sessions that were original to the program inadvertently get cut, and thus original dosage is reduced. In their review of several cultural adaptations, Kumpfer et al. (2002) concluded that the cultural adaptations reviewed were generally associated with better recruitment and retention rates but that the original, nonadapted versions demonstrated slightly better outcomes. Thus, they recommended that researchers implement cultural adaptations that maintain fidelity rather than using programs that ultimately reduce dosage or cut core elements.

The most significant limitation with the existing body of work is the lack of studies that have compared the efficacy of culturally adapted programs with programs that do not have such an adaptation. In fact, scholars indicate that there are no randomized control trials comparing the efficacy of a culturally adapted version of a family-based preventive intervention with a generic version (Kumpfer et al., 2002); the same criticism has been raised with respect to culturally sensitive therapeutic interventions (Cardemil, 2008). Most researchers adapt a program and test the efficacy of the adapted program rather than simultaneously delivering a nonadapted version of the program to members of the same population. Thus, there is a dire need for controlled trials to determine whether culturally sensitive programs are indeed more effective than generic programs (Cardemil, 2008; Dumka et al., 2002; Resnicow et al., 2000).

CASE STUDY: A CULTURALLY ADAPTED DEPRESSION PREVENTION PROGRAM DESIGNED FOR USE WITH LOW-INCOME AFRICAN AMERICAN AND LATINO CHILDREN

It is useful to provide an example of a preventive intervention adapted for use with low-income African American and Latino children because it nicely illustrates how each stage of the prevention research process was affected during the cultural adaptation process. Cardemil, Reivich, and Seligman (2002) modified the Penn Resiliency Program (PRP; a school-based depression prevention program) to make it culturally appropriate for African American and Latino low-income middle school students. The PRP was designed to teach cognitive–behavioral and social problem-solving techniques (e.g., learning how to realistically appraise situations and apply appropriate problem-solving strategies, such as seeking help from a teacher or other adult) to prevent depression symptoms. Its effectiveness with middle school children has been demonstrated in existing work (e.g., Gillham, Reivich, Jaycox, & Seligman, 1995; Jaycox, Reivich, Gillham, & Seligman, 1994). However, the program has been tested with samples composed predominantly of European American children. Given the increased risk for depressive symptoms among low-income populations, in which African

Americans and Latinos are overrepresented, and the underutilization of mental health services by both low-income and ethnic minority individuals, a preventive intervention program tailored toward low-income African American and Latino participants was needed. Therefore, Cardemil et al. made surface structure adaptations to the original program and implemented the adapted program in two Philadelphia urban schools.

Adaptations included changing the ethnicity–race of characters used in examples so that they were consistent with participants' racial and ethnic backgrounds and tailoring discussions toward issues that were particularly salient to participants given their low-income urban environment (e.g., many were growing up in single-parent homes). Furthermore, because many children in this setting resorted to physical confrontation when they encountered a peer conflict, a cartoon character who typically resorted to physical confrontation was introduced as part of the program and was referred to throughout the sessions. Group leaders received extensive training, and considerable care was taken to prevent intervention providers from imposing suburban, middle-class values or perspectives on participants (e.g., assuming that all children live in two-parent homes, that children can talk freely with parents about family conflict without concerns about rigid hierarchical relationships between parents and children). In addition, method of delivery was modified to be consistent with the needs of the target populations. For instance, after careful consultation with principals and teachers about the nature of the sample, Cardemil et al. (2002) determined that the program should be delivered during school hours; otherwise, the students simply would not attend. Furthermore, research staff made weekly phone calls to participants to remind them to complete assignments; this was deemed necessary because a majority of children were not completing their homework assignments without reminder calls. Thus, the cultural adaptation by Cardemil et al. involved a number of the recommendations reviewed earlier, such as carefully considering the cultural context by evaluating the needs of the community and the type of program necessary. Furthermore, in the program development stage of the cycle, they involved the community in the research process by spending significant time consulting with principals, teachers, and parents of the children, to determine the best ways to administer their program.

With respect to the implementation stage of the research cycle, Cardemil and colleagues (Cardemil et al., 2002; Cardemil, Reivich, Beevers, Seligman, & James, 2007) tested the efficacy of the culturally adapted PRP at 3 months, 6 months, 1 year, and 2 years. The findings generally demonstrated that compared with the control group, there was a beneficial effect for the Latino children at 3 months, 6 months, and 1 year, but African American children did not differ significantly from their control group at any point over the 2-year period (Cardemil et al., 2002, 2007). The different findings for the two groups raised a number of questions, some of which pertain to the adequacy of the cultural adaptation of the program for each of the groups.

First, it is important to note that although the program demonstrated beneficial effects for Latino children, it is not possible to conclude that the cultural adaptation in and of itself made the program work for Latino children. A controlled trial in which the culturally adapted version is compared with the original version to determine whether, in fact, there is value added by culturally adapting the program clearly is needed. It is possible that the cultural adaptations Cardemil et al. (2002) made facilitated retention and recruitment but did not meaningfully affect the program's efficacy. Put differently, the beneficial effects of the intervention for Latino children may have been just as strong with the original PRP as they were with the culturally adapted version. As we mentioned earlier, this is one of the most significant limitations in the existing empirical work; no controlled studies have compared the effectiveness of culturally adapted interventions to generic versions of the same programs.

Furthermore, it is possible that the theory of intervention is valid for low-income Latino children but not valid for low-income African American children; therefore, deep structure adaptations may be necessary to make the program efficacious with low-income African American children. Perhaps low-income African American children do not respond to cognitive behavioral approaches, and other therapeutic intervention approaches are necessary to reduce depressive symptoms in this population (Cardemil et al., 2002). Although surface structure adaptations may make the program superficially relevant to African American youth with respect to the examples used and the "face" of the program, the theory of intervention may not be relevant to African American youth and thus has no beneficial impact. Some researchers (e.g., Miranda et al., 2003) would recommend that this is the point at which an ethnically homogeneous study is necessary, given that the program elements did not work with a specific population. Thus, researchers should move toward conducting within-group studies to determine what types of interventions have the potential to be efficacious with low-income African American children.

Further evidence for the need to conduct ethnically homogeneous studies and to more carefully explore processes within an ethnic group is provided by the finding that African American children in Cardemil et al.'s (2002) program, like their Latino counterparts, did improve over the course of the intervention. However, the critical difference was that the African American children in the experimental condition, compared with their African American counterparts in the control group, showed no improvement (E. V. Cardemil, personal communication, October 31, 2008). Thus, the adapted PRP could not produce a differential improvement with African American children because their control counterparts were showing a similar trajectory of symptom improvement. It is possible that the improvement among African American children in the control group is due to cultural factors that influence the development and expression of depressive symptoms (E. V. Cardemil, personal communication, October 31, 2008). This is consistent with scholars' recommendations to ground cultural adaptations in the literature that is specific to the ethnic or racial group of interest (Lau, 2006).

Another possibility, although clearly speculative, is that the cultural adaptations made to the program were more relevant for low-income Latino children, making the program culturally insensitive to African American children. In this case, there would be no value added for the African American children and, hence, the improvements over time for the experimental group mirrored those of the control group. Perhaps the original PRP would have had beneficial effects with the African American group. Although costly, future studies that test a culturally adapted program should include three groups: (a) a group that receives the culturally adapted program, (b) a group that receives a generic version of the program, and (c) a control group. Use of this design is the only way we will move the field forward with respect to understanding the efficacy of existing intervention programs with ethnic and economically diverse populations, as well as the value added by culturally adapting existing programs. Finally, before Cardemil et al.'s (2002) cultural adaptation of the PRP can enter the dissemination stage of the research cycle, a better understanding of the effectiveness of the culturally adapted program is needed because current findings suggest that the program should be disseminated only to low-income Latino children.

APPLICATION OF THE FOUR TYPES OF RESEARCH TO THE CULTURAL ADAPTATION OF PREVENTIVE INTERVENTIONS

As presented earlier, some scholars recommend cross-group comparative designs as an ideal initial step for examining preventive intervention programs with diverse populations. Thus, prior to making cultural adaptations, researchers should work under the assumption that the theory of intervention is applicable to all groups (Miranda et al., 2003). It is only when a program is found to function differently for certain groups that researchers should move toward within-group designs to determine which aspects of the program may or may not be efficacious for a particular group. The benefits of using a cross-group comparative design include being able to compare ethnic and economic groups and, assuming random assignment to each condition, being able to draw conclusions regarding the efficacy of programs across multiple groups. If the program is found to be similarly efficacious, cross-group comparative designs are cost effective and more manageable to disseminate and transport, given their applicability to multiple, diverse groups. However, as described earlier, some would argue that it is not possible to conduct a culturally sensitive cross-group comparative design, given that existing work demonstrates the benefits of tailoring programs to match the characteristics of specific ethnic groups. Others, however, point out that the existing empirical work demonstrates benefits only with respect to retention and recruitment and that it is not clear whether programs that are culturally adapted are in fact more efficacious than those that are not culturally adapted (Kumpfer et al., 2002). Our perspective is that studies that include three conditions (i.e., test the efficacy of a culturally adapted program, a control group, and a group that received a generic [not culturally adapted] version of the program) are necessary in order to make a recommendation regarding the benefits of cross-group comparative designs. There is some evidence that cultural adaptations increase retention and facilitate recruitment, but to our knowledge no studies have tested the efficacy of a culturally adapted program against a control group and against a group that received a generic (not culturally adapted) version of the program; thus, the value added by cultural adaptations (with respect to efficacy) is unknown.

National sample designs are typically used to conduct generative research, out of which the small theories of intervention may develop. Thus, they are not relevant to our present discussion. Within-group designs, however, are viewed by some people as an ideal way to test preventive intervention programs because they allow for specific tailoring to meet the needs of the specific ethnic and economic group of interest. Although within-group designs allow prevention scientists to tailor a program in a manner that makes it highly relevant for a specific group, this strength is also a limitation because it considerably limits the generalizability of the program. Furthermore, the potential lack of generalizability raises practical concerns regarding dissemination of such a specific program. Thus, some recommend that within-group designs should be conducted only after findings from cross-group comparative designs have informed researchers of a lack of efficacy of a prevention program for a specific group; then the within-group design could be implemented to better understand the processes and specific variables to target for the group of interest.

Finally, inadvertently diverse designs are likely not informative regarding the efficacy of preventive interventions across diverse ethnic and economic groups because of sample size restrictions. Sample sizes for each ethnic and economic group are likely not large enough to permit one to meaningfully compare the efficacy of the program across groups, given that preventive intervention programs typically do not have large sample sizes because of the labor- and time-intensive nature of the programs. Thus, an inadvertently diverse sample is likely to amount to a few participants from each ethnic or economic group who are contributing to the diversity, which is not sufficient to test group differences and draw meaningful conclusions.

SUMMARY

Culturally adapting preventive interventions is difficult, but it is vital to providing aid to local communities as well as to gaining a broader understanding of subtle interactions between race, ethnicity, and socioeconomic status and individuals' responses to intervention efforts. As we reviewed at the beginning of this chapter, scholars are in agreement across disciplines and substantive areas of research that there is a dire need to develop and/or adapt preventive interventions that can be delivered to ethnic minority and economically disadvantaged populations. Given the lack of research, it is unclear whether the benefits of culturally adapted interventions reach beyond favorable retention and recruitment outcomes. Although retention and recruitment are important aspects of program implementation, a necessary direction for further research will be the testing the efficacy of culturally adapted programs compared with the efficacy of generic versions of the same program, as well as a control group that receives no intervention. Until this design is implemented, we will remain uninformed regarding the value added, with respect to efficacy, by culturally adapting an existing efficacious program.

Epilogue

The rapidly changing demographics of the United States have led to a great deal of interest in research focusing on ethnic minority and economically disadvantaged populations. Researchers increasingly are considering the utility of studying members of these populations either for evaluating the breadth of current psychological or social science theories of for addressing the development of new theoretical propositions that apply to a more diverse subset of the overall population. Some of this research is also more pragmatically directed either at addressing societal problems or assets originating from these populations. These interests, combined with a growing emphasis on fairness and adequate representation of the overall population in research, have created a research context in which scholars are increasingly including ethnic minorities and economically disadvantaged participants in their studies.

The chapters in this book were designed to provide not only an overview of the challenges facing researchers as they attempt to conduct research with ethnic minority and economically disadvantaged populations but also best practice recommendations that can facilitate their efforts. Although conducting research with members of ethnic minority and economically disadvantaged populations can seem to be a daunting task given the challenges associated with sampling, recruitment, retention, and measurement, as we have alluded to throughout this book, our personal experiences conducting research with these populations have been extremely rewarding. It is also likely that the increased interest in these populations will open the door to a wide variety of new paths that will allow many others to develop an interesting and rewarding research career. Furthermore, our sciences cannot be considered complete or accurate until they have demonstrated their applicability to the whole population instead of only to, or primarily to, the middle-class European American majority.

Together, the chapters in this book identify the level of sophistication that currently characterizes research on ethnic minority and economically disadvantaged populations. For example, in chapter 2 we highlighted critical areas in which we have lapsed, but we also provided examples of how research designs can be strengthened with respect to sampling, recruitment, and retention of members of ethnic minority and economically disadvantaged populations. A common theme throughout this chapter was the importance of gaining a more nuanced understanding of ethnic minority and economically disadvantaged research participants who may be included in research studies (e.g., their beliefs and values) in order to more accurately sample, recruit, and retain the population and, equally important, involve members of the community as advisors or collaborators in one's research endeavors. Similarly, we highlighted in this chapter the fundamental value of treating all potential research participants with respect; in the cases of ethnic minority and economically disadvantaged populations, this means being aware of and showing respect for any differences between them and the majority population. In chapter 2 we also provided numerous best practice strategies for researchers. At a basic level, we believe that all researchers can contribute to improvements in recruitment and retention in the social sciences by systematically describing their recruitment and retention processes as well as reporting, when appropriate, the results of these procedures for specific ethnic minority or economic subgroups. We are optimistic that by increasing the communication among researchers, with respect to sampling, recruitment, and retention successes (and failures), we will move science forward.

Similarly, in chapter 3 we reviewed concerns for research with human participants, particularly when researchers are studying populations that have historically lacked protection and fair treatment. In this chapter, we emphasized the value of communicating with persons who feel disempowered or who come from cultural backgrounds that did not prepare them for exercising their right to refuse to participate in research; such an approach will contribute to better practices in social science research. Furthermore, and similar to recommendations provided in chapter 2, we emphasized the value gained by conducting research in partnership with community groups or by consulting with community advisory boards or other representatives of the targeted minority and economically disadvantaged populations. This approach can provide insights into the targeted group that may help identify ethical concerns and insiders' perspectives on other potential ethical concerns.

In chapters 4 and 5, we provided overviews of methodological challenges involved with measurement in studies that include ethnic minority and economically disadvantaged populations. Our intentions in chapter 4 were to provide readers with a useful overview of different strategies that have been used to evaluate the equivalence of measures used with diverse groups as well as a critique of the most commonly used strategies; we also shared our perspectives on what we view as the most rigorous approaches to establishing measurement equivalence. Chapter 5 followed nicely from chapter 4 because, in essence, translation of measures is a special case of measurement equivalence. In chapter 5 we reviewed different strategies that researchers can use to translate their measures. We recognize that the most highly recommended approaches also are the most time and cost intensive; nevertheless, we maintain that translation of measures, and establishing the equivalence of translated measures administered to ethnically and economically diverse groups, is absolutely necessary in order to have confidence in the scientific inferences that will be drawn from these research studies. Establishing measurement equivalence through effective translation processes and/or statistical processes is fundamental to establishing the validity of research results that includes individuals from outside the majority population. Although establishing measurement equivalence requires a substantial research effort, analytical techniques and theoretical guidance for addressing these issues are continually being developed and are becoming increasingly accessible to researchers. It is our hope that these chapters will provide readers with useful tools that will clarify the types of analyses necessary to examine equivalence and, furthermore, provide readers with a clearer understanding of the value and importance of measurement equivalence.

Our book ends with a chapter on translational research. We felt this was a necessary chapter in a book focused on studying ethnic minority and economically disadvantaged populations because scholars agree, across disciplines and substantive areas of interest, that there is a dire need to develop and/or adapt preventive interventions that can be delivered to ethnic minority and economically disadvantaged populations. Our review of the existing work suggests that because of limited research, it is unclear whether the benefits of culturally adapted interventions reach beyond favorable retention and recruitment outcomes. We recognize the value of increasing retention and recruitment of members of ethnic minority and economically disadvantaged groups for program implementation; nevertheless, a necessary direction for further research will be testing the efficacy of culturally adapted programs against the efficacy of generic versions of the same program. Such designs will increase our understanding of the value added, with respect to efficacy, when cultural adaptations of existing preventive interventions are implemented.

More generally, we believe that funding agencies must recognize the labor-intensive nature of conducting high-quality research with ethnic minority and economically disadvantaged populations (e.g., increased difficulties associated with sampling, recruitment, retention, translation, and measurement). This recognition must come in the form of more flexible funding allowances (with respect to time and financial resources) that allow for longer development periods (e.g., time built into the grant for measure development) and larger budgets that can absorb costs associated with hiring qualified translation staff and community advisory boards as consultants, for example. Although we feel strongly about the need for institutional change, we also hold ourselves, as researchers, responsible for doing a better job of communicating amongst ourselves and sharing information across research sites with respect to strategies used and their resulting outcomes in terms of sampling, recruitment, retention, translation, and measurement. This sharing of information across sites will not only contribute significantly to advancing the field but also will be cost effective.

It is our hope that this book helps move research with ethnic minority and disadvantaged populations forward in both sophistication and volume. Because these populations are included in our research in larger numbers, we will not be surprised if currently popular theories in the social sciences will need modifications, if approaches to interventions with these populations change and improve, and if public policy recommendations do a better job of representing the needs of these populations. We have a long way to go to reach a state of equity in access to research participation and the benefits that come from research, but numerous researchers have laid the foundation for swift growth and improvement in these areas in coming years. We hope that this book makes at least a modest contribution to these improvements.

References

Adamopoulos, J., & Lonner, W. J. (2001). Culture and psychology at a cross-road: Historical perspective and theoretical analysis. In D. Matsumoto (Ed.), *The handbook of culture and psychology* (pp. 11–34). New York: Oxford University Press.

Aiken, L. S., & West, S. G. (1991). *Multiple regression: Testing and interpreting interactions.* Newbury Park, CA: Sage.

Amato, P. R., & Zuo, J. (1992). Rural poverty, urban poverty, and psychological well-being. *Sociological Quarterly, 33,* 229–240.

Ambrose, N. G., & Yairi, E. (2002). The Tudor Study: Data and ethics. *American Journal of Speech-Language Pathology, 11,* 190–203.

Arean, P. A., & Gallagher-Thompson, D. (1996). Issues and recommendations for recruitment of older ethnic minority adults into clinical research. *Journal of Consulting and Clinical Psychology, 64,* 875–880.

Baldwin, A. L., Baldwin, C., & Cole, R. E. (1990). Stress-resistant families and stress-resistant children. In J. Rolf, A. S. Masten, D. Cicchetti, K. H. Neuchterlein, & S. Weintraub (Eds.), *Risk and protective factors in the development of psychopathology* (pp. 257–280). New York: Cambridge University Press.

Baldwin, A. L., Baldwin, C. P., Kasser, T., Zax, M., Sameroff, A., & Seifer, R. (1993). Contextual risk and resiliency during late adolescence. *Development and Psychopathology, 5,* 741–761.

Beals, J., Manson, S. M., Whitesell, N. R., Mitchell, C. M., Novins, D. K., Simpson, S., et al. (2005). Prevalence of major depressive episode in two American Indian reservation populations: Unexpected findings with a structured interview. *American Journal of Psychiatry, 162,* 1713–1722.

Benet-Martinez, V., Leu, J., Lee, F., & Morris, M. W. (2002). Negotiating biculturalism: Cultural frame switching in biculturals with oppositional versus compatible cultural identities. *Journal of Cross-Cultural Psychology, 33,* 492–516.

Berg, B. L. (1995). *Qualitative research methods for the social sciences* (2nd ed.). Boston: Allyn & Bacon.

Bernal, G., Bonilla, J., & Bellido, C. (1995). Ecological validity and cultural sensitivity for outcome research: Issues for the cultural adaptation and development of psychosocial treatments with Hispanics. *Journal of Abnormal Child Psychology, 23,* 67–82.

Bernal, G., & Scharrón-Del-Rio, M. R. (2001). Are empirically supported treatments valid for ethnic minorities? Toward an alternative approach for treatment research. *Cultural Diversity and Ethnic Minority Psychology, 7,* 328–342.

Bernal, M. E., & Knight, G. P. (Eds.). (1993). *Ethnic identity: Formation and transmission among Hispanics and other minorities.* Albany: State University of New York Press.

Bernstein, N. (2007, April 10). U.S. raid on immigrant household deepens anger and mistrust on L. I. *New York Times,* B1.

Berry, J. W. (2006). Acculturation: A conceptual overview. In M. H. Bornstein & L. R. Cote (Eds.), *Acculturation and parent–child relationships* (pp. 13–32). Mahwah, NJ: Erlbaum.

Bollen, K. A. (1989). *Structural equations with latent variables.* New York: Wiley.

Bradley, C. (1994). Translation of questionnaires for use in different languages and cultures. In C. Bradley (Ed.), *Handbook of psychology and diabetes: A guide to psychological measurement in diabetes research and practice* (pp. 43–55). Chur, Switzerland: Harwood Academic.

Breese, P. E., Burman, W. J., Goldberg, S., & Weis, S. E. (2007). Education level, primary language, and comprehension of the informed consent process. *Journal of Empirical Research on Human Research Ethics, 2,* 69–79.

Brislin, R.W. (1970). Back-translation for cross-cultural research. *Journal of Cross-Cultural Psychology, 1,* 185–216.

Broman, C. L., Reckase, M. D., & Freedman-Doan, C. R. (2006). The role of parenting in drug use among Black, Latino, and White adolescents. *Journal of Ethnicity in Substance Abuse, 5,* 39–50.

Brooks-Gunn, J., Klebanov, P., Liaw, F., & Duncan, G. (1995). Toward an understanding of the effects of poverty upon children. In H. E. Fitzgerald, B. M. Lester, & B. Zuckerman (Eds.), *Children of poverty: Research, health, and policy issues* (pp. 3–41). New York: Garland.

Browne, M. W., & Cudeck, R. (1993). Alternative ways of assessing model fit. In K. Bollen & S. Long (Eds.), *Testing structural equation models* (pp. 136–159). Newbury Park, CA: Sage.

Bryant, A. L., Schulenberg, J. E., O'Malley, P. M., Bachman, J. G., & Johnston, L. D. (2003). How academic achievement, attitudes, and behaviors relate to the course of substance use during adolescence: A 6-year, multiwave national longitudinal study. *Journal of Research on Adolescence, 13,* 361–397.

Bryman, A., & Burgess, R. (Eds.). (1994). *Analyzing qualitative data.* New York: Routledge.

Byrne, B. M., Shavelson, R. J., & Muthén, B. (1989). Testing for the equivalence of factor covariance and mean structures: The issue of partial measurement invariance. *Psychological Bulletin, 105,* 456–466.

Camilli, G., & Shepard, L. A. (1994). *Methods for identifying biased test items.* Thousand Oaks, CA: Sage.

Capaldi, D., & Patterson, G. R. (1987). An approach to the problem to recruitment and retention rates for longitudinal research. *Behavioral Assessment, 9,* 169–177.

Cardemil, E. V. (2008). Commentary: Culturally sensitive treatments: Need for an organizing framework. *Culture & Psychology, 14,* 357–367.

Cardemil, E. V., Reivich, K. J., Beevers, C. G., Seligman, M. E. P., & James, J. (2007). The prevention of depressive symptoms in low-income, minority children: Two-year follow-up. *Behaviour Research and Therapy, 45,* 313–327.

Cardemil, E. V., Reivich, K. J., & Seligman, M. E. P. (2002). The prevention of depressive symptoms in low-income minority middle school students. *Prevention & Treatment, 5,* Article 8.

Carnegie Task Force. (1994). *Starting points: Meeting the needs of our young children.* New York: Carnegie Corporation.

Case, L., & Smith, T. B. (2000). Ethnic representation in a sample of the literature of applied psychology. *Journal of Consulting and Clinical Psychology, 64,* 1107–1110.

Case, M. H., & Robinson, W. L. (2003). Interventions with ethnic minority populations: The legacy and promise of community psychology. In G. Bernal, J. E. Trimble, A. K. Burlew, & F. T. L. Leong (Eds.), *Handbook of racial and ethnic minority psychology* (pp. 573–590). Thousand Oaks, CA: Sage.

Castro, F. G., Barrera, M., & Martinez, C. R. (2004). The cultural adaptation of prevention interventions: Resolving tensions between fidelity and fit. *Prevention Science, 5,* 41–45.

Catalano, R. F., Hawkins, J. D., Krenz, C., Gillmore, M., Morrison, D., Wells, E., & Abbott, R. (1993). Using research to guide culturally appropriate drug abuse prevention. *Journal of Consulting and Clinical Psychology, 61,* 804–811.

Cauce, A. M., Coronado, N., & Watson, J. (1998). Conceptual, methodological, and statistical issues in culturally competent research. In M. Hernandez & M. Isaacs (Eds.), *Promoting cultural competence in children's mental health services* (pp. 305–329). Baltimore: Paul H. Brookes.

Cauce, A. M., Ryan, K. D., & Grove, K. (1998). Children and adolescents of color, where are you? Participation, selection, recruitment, and retention in developmental research. In V. C. McLoyd & L. Steinberg (Eds.), *Studying minority adolescents: Conceptual, methodological, and theoretical issues* (pp. 147–166). Mahwah, NJ: Erlbaum.

Cheung, G. W., & Rensvold, R. B. (2002). Evaluating goodness-of-fit indexes for testing measurement invariance. *Structural Equation Modeling, 9,* 233–255.

Clifton, J. (1989). *Being and becoming Indian: Biographical studies of North American frontiers.* Chicago: Dorsey Press.

Coen, A. S., Patrick, D. C., & Shern, D. L. (1996). Minimizing attrition in longitudinal studies of special populations: An integrated management approach. *Evaluation and Program Planning, 19,* 309–319.

Conger, R. D., & Conger, K. J. (2002). Resilience in Midwestern families: Selected findings from the first decade of a prospective, longitudinal study. *Journal of Marriage and Family, 64,* 361–373.

Corbie-Smith, G., Thomas, S. B., Williams, M. V., & Moody-Ayers, S. (1999). Attitudes and beliefs of African Americans toward participation in medical research. *Journal of General Internal Medicine, 14,* 537–546.

Cronbach, L. J. (1970). *Essentials of psychological testing* (3rd ed.). New York: Harper & Row.

Cunradi, C. B., Caetano, R., Clark, C., & Shafer, J. (2000). Neighborhood poverty as a predictor of intimate partner violence among White, Black, and Hispanic couples in the United States: A multilevel analysis. *Annals of Epidemiology, 10,* 297–308.

Dumka, L., Garza, C., Roosa, M. W., & Stoerzinger, H. (1997). Recruiting and retaining high risk populations into preventive interventions. *Journal of Primary Prevention, 18,* 25–39.

Dumka, L. E., Lopez, V. A., & Carter, S. J. (2002). Parenting interventions adapted for Latino families: Progress and prospects. In J. M. Contreras, K. A. Kerns, & A. M. Neal-Barnett (Eds.), *Latino children and families in the United States: Current research and future directions* (pp. 203–231). Westport, CT: Praeger.

Dumka, L. E., Roosa, M. W., Michaels, M. L., & Suh, K. W. (1995). Using research and theory to develop prevention programs for high risk families. *Family Relations, 44,* 78–86.

Erkut, S., Alarcón, O., Coll, C. G., Tropp, L. R., & García, H. A. V. (1999). The dual-focus approach to creating bilingual measures. *Journal of Cross-Cultural Psychology, 30,* 206–218.

Farley, R. (1997). Racial trends and differences in the United States 30 years after the civil rights decade. *Social Science Research, 26,* 235–262.

Feldman, M. S. (1995). *Strategies for interpreting qualitative data.* Thousand Oaks, CA: Sage.

Fetterman, D. M. (1989). *Ethnography: Step by step.* Newbury Park, CA: Sage.

Fisher, C. B., Hoagwood, K., Boyce, C., Duster, T., Frank, D. A., Grisso, T., et al. (2002). Research ethics for mental health science involving ethnic minority children and youths. *American Psychologist, 57,* 1024–1040.

Flaskerud, J. H., & Nyamathi, A. M. (2000). Attaining gender and ethnic diversity in health intervention research: Cultural responsiveness versus resource provision. *Advances in Nursing Science, 22*(4), 1–15.

Gallagher-Thompson, D., Rabinowitz, Y., Tang, P. C., Tse, C., Kwo, E., Hsu, S., et al. (2006). Recruiting Chinese Americans for dementia caregiver research: Suggestions for success. *American Journal of Geriatric Psychiatry, 14,* 676–683.

Gallagher-Thompson, D., Singer, L. S., Depp, C., Mausbach, B. T., Cardenas, V., & Coon, D. W. (2004). Effective recruitment strategies for Latino and Caucasian dementia family caregivers in intervention research. *American Journal of Geriatric Psychiatry, 12,* 484–490.

Gavaghan, H. (1995, January 19). Clinical trials face a lack of minority group volunteers. *Nature, 373,* 178.

Geisinger, K. F. (1994). Cross-cultural normative assessment: Translation and adaptation issues influencing the normative interpretation of assessment instruments. *Psychological Assessment, 6,* 304–312.

Gillham, J. E., Reivich, K. J., Jaycox, L. H., & Seligman, M. E. P. (1995). Prevention of depressive symptoms in school children: Two-year follow-up. *Psychological Science, 6,* 343–351.

Gilliss, C. L., Lee, K. A., Gutierrez, Y., Taylor, D., Beyene, Y., Neuhaus, J., & Murrell, N. (2001). Recruitment and retention of healthy minority women into community-based longitudinal Research. *Journal of Women's Health & Gender-Based Medicine, 10,* 77–85.

Gone, J. (2006). Research reservations: Response and responsibility in an American Indian community. *American Journal of Community Psychology, 37,* 333–340.

Gonzales, N. A., Cauce, A. M., Friedman, R., & Mason, C. A. (1996). Family, peer and neighborhood influences on academic achievement among African-American adolescents. *American Journal of Community Psychology, 24,* 365–387.

Gonzales, N. A., Fabrett, F. C., & Knight, G. P. (in press). Acculturation, enculturation and the psycholosocial adaptation of Latino youth. In F. Villaruel, G. Carlo, M. Azmitia, J. Grau, N. Cabrera, & J. Chahin (Eds.), *Handbook of U.S. Latino psychology.* Thousand Oaks, CA: Sage.

Gonzales, N. A., Gunnoe, M. L., Samaniego, R., & Jackson, K. (1995, June). *Validation of a multicultural event schedule for adolescents.* Paper presented at the Fifth Biennial Conference of the Society for Community Research and Action, Chicago.

Gonzales, N. A., Knight, G. P., Morgan-Lopez, A., Saenz, D., & Sirolli, A. A. (2002). Acculturation and the mental health of Latino youths: An integration and critique of the literature. In J. M. Contreras, K. A. Kerns, & A. M. Neal-Barnett (Eds.), *Latino children and families in the United States: Current research and future directions* (pp. 45–74). Westport, CT: Praeger.

Gonzalez-Ramos, G., Zayas, L. H., & Cohen, E. V. (1998). Child-rearing values of low-income, urban Puerto Rican mothers of preschool children. *Professional Psychology: Research and Practice, 29*, 377–382.

Guerra, N. G., & Knox, L. (2008). How culture impacts the dissemination and implementation of innovation: A case study of the Families and School Together program (FAST) for preventing violence with immigrant Latino youth. *American Journal of Community Psychology, 41*, 304–313.

Halgunseth, L. C., Ispa, J. M., & Rudy, D. (2006). Parental control in Latino families: An integrated review of the literature. *Child Development, 77*, 1282–1297.

Hambleton, R.K. (2004). Issues, designs, and technical guidelines for adapting tests into multiple languages and cultures. In R. K. Hambleton, P. Merenda, & C. Spielberger (Eds.), *Adapting educational and psychological tests for cross-cultural assessment* (pp. 3–38). Mahwah, NJ: Erlbaum.

Hambleton, R. K., & Li, S. (2005). Translation and adaptation issues and methods for educational and psychological tests. In C. L. Frisby & C. R. Reynolds (Eds.), *Comprehensive handbook of multicultural school psychology* (pp. 881–903). New York: Wiley.

Hambleton, R. K., Swaminathan, H., & Rogers, H. J. (1991). *Fundamentals of item response theory*. Newbury Park, CA: Sage.

Hampson, S. E., Dubanoski, J. P., Hamada, W., Marsella, A. J., Matsukawa, J., Suarez, E., & Goldberg, L. R. (2001). Where are they now? Locating former elementary-school students after nearly 40 years for a longitudinal study of personality and health. *Journal of Research in Personality, 35*, 375–387.

Harrison, A. O., Wilson, M. N., Pine, C. N., Chan, S. Q., & Buriel, R. (1990). Family ecologies of ethnic minority children. *Child Development, 61*, 347–362.

Hines, A. M. (1993). Linking qualitative and quantitative methods in cross-cultural survey research: Techniques from cognitive science. *American Journal of Community Psychology, 21*, 729–746.

Hinton, L., Guo, Z., Hillygus, J., & Levkoff, S. (2000). Working with culture: A qualitative analysis of barriers to the recruitment of Chinese-American family caregivers for dementia research. *Journal of Cross-Cultural Gerontology, 15*, 119–137.

Hollon, S. D., Muñoz, R. F., Barlow, D. H., Beardslee, W. R., Bell, C. C., Bernal, G., et al. (2002). Psychosocial intervention development for the prevention and treatment of depression: Promoting innovation and increasing access. *Biological Psychiatry, 52,* 610–630.

Hong, Y., Morris, M. W., Chiu, C., & Benet-Martinez, V. (2000). Multicultural minds: A dynamic constructivist approach to culture and cognition. *American Psychologist, 55,* 709–720.

Hughes, D., Seidman, E., & Williams, N. (1993). Cultural phenomena and the research enterprise: Toward a culturally anchored methodology. *American Journal of Community Psychology, 21,* 687–704.

Hui, C. H., & Triandis, H. C. (1985). Measurement in cross-cultural psychology: A review and comparison of strategies. *Journal of Cross-Cultural Psychology, 16,* 131–152.

Hui, C. H., & Triandis, H. C. (1989). Effects of culture and response format on extreme response style. *Journal of Cross-Cultural Psychology, 20,* 296–309.

Hussain-Gambles, M., Atkin, K., & Leese, B. (2004). Why ethnic minority groups are under-represented in clinical trials: A review of the literature. *Health and Social Care in the Community, 12,* 382–388.

Jaycox, L. H., Reivich, K. J., Gillham, J., & Seligman, M. E. P. (1994). Prevention of depressive symptoms in school children. *Behaviour Research and Therapy, 32,* 801–816.

Joiner, T. E., Perez, M., Wagner, K. D., Berenson, A., & Marquina, G. S. (2001). On fatalism, pessimism, and depressive symptoms among Mexican-American and other adolescents attending an obstetrics–gynecology clinic. *Behaviour Research and Therapy, 39,* 887–896.

Jones, J. H. (1981). *Bad blood: The Tuskegee syphilis experiment.* New York: Free Press.

Katz, R. V., Kegeles, S. S., Kressin, N. R., Green, B. L., Wang, M. Q., James, S. A., et al. (2006). The Tuskegee Legacy Project: Willingness of minorities to participate in biomedical research. *Journal of Health Care for the Poor and Underserved, 17,* 698–715.

Keller, C. S., Gonzales, A., & Fleuriet, K. J. (2005). Retention of minority participants in clinical research studies. *Western Journal of Nursing Research, 27,* 292–306.

Kline, R. B. (1998). *Principles and practice of structural equation modeling.* New York: Guilford Press.

Knight, G. P., & Hill, N. E. (1998). Measurement equivalence in research involving minority adolescents. In V.C. McLoyd & L. Steinberg (Eds.), *Studying minority adolescents: Conceptual, methodological, and theoretical issues* (pp. 183–210). Mahwah, NJ: Erlbaum.

Knight, G. P., Roosa, M. W., Calderón, C. O., & Gonzales, N. A. (in press). Methodological issues in research on Latino populations. In F. Villaruel, G. Carlo, M. Azmitia, J. Grau, N. Cabrera, & J. Chahin (Eds.), *Handbook of U.S. Latino psychology*. Thousand Oaks, CA: Sage.

Knight, G. P., Tein, J.-Y., Prost, J., & Gonzales, N. A. (2002). Measurement equivalence and research on Latino children and families: The importance of culturally informed theory. In J. M. Contreras, K. A. Kerns, & A. M. Neal-Barnett (Eds.), *Latino children and families in the United States: Current research and future directions* (pp. 181–201). Westport, CT: Praeger.

Knight, G. P., Virdin, L. M., Ocampo, K. A., & Roosa, M. (1994). An examination of the cross-ethnic equivalence of measures of negative life events and mental health among Hispanic and Anglo American children. *American Journal of Community Psychology, 22,* 767–783.

Knight, G. P., Virdin, L. M., & Roosa, M. (1994). Socialization and family correlates of mental health outcomes among Hispanic and Anglo American children: Consideration of cross-ethnic scalar equivalence. *Child Development, 65,* 212–224.

Koch, E. (1996). *Promotoras and community health advisors: Program challenge in an age of change.* Washington, DC: Project on Sustainable Services, Georgetown University Law Center.

Kristjansson, E. A., Desrochers, A., & Zumbo, B. (2003). Translating and adapting measurement instruments for cross-linguistic and cross-cultural research: A guide for practitioners. *Canadian Journal of Nursing Research, 35,* 127–142.

Kumpfer, K. L., Alvarado, R., Smith, P., & Bellamy, N. (2002). Cultural sensitivity and adaptation in family-based prevention interventions. *Prevention Science, 3,* 241–246.

Labouvie, E., & Ruetsch, C. (1995). Testing the equivalence of measurement scales: Simple structure and metric invariance reconsidered. *Multivariate Behavioral Research, 30,* 63–70.

Lamborn, S. D., Dornbusch, S. M., & Steinberg, L. (1996). Ethnicity and community context as moderators of the relations between family decision making and adolescent adjustment. *Child Development, 67,* 283–301.

Lau, A. S. (2006). Making the case for selective and directed cultural adaptations of evidence-based treatments: Examples from parent training. *Clinical Psychology: Science and Practice, 13,* 295–310.

Lau, A. W., & Gallagher-Thompson, D. (2002). Ethnic minority older adults in clinical and research programs: Issues and recommendations. *The Behavior Therapist, 25,* 10–11, 16.

Lazarus, R. S., & Folkman, S. (1984). *Stress, appraisal, and coping.* New York: Springer Publishing Company.

Lengua, L. J., Roosa, M. W., Shupak-Neuberg, E., Michaels, M. L., Berg, C. N., & Weschler, L. F. (1992). Using focus groups to guide the development of a parenting program for difficult-to-reach, high-risk families. *Family Relations, 41*, 163–168.

Levkoff, S., & Sanchez, H. (2003). Lessons learned about minority recruitment and retention from the Centers on Minority Aging and Health. *The Gerontologist, 43*, 18–26.

Little, T. D., Preacher, K. J., Selig, J. P., & Card, N. A. (2007). New developments in latent variable panel analyses of longitudinal data. *International Journal of Behavioral Development, 31*, 357–365.

Lopez, S. J., Edwards, L. M., Pedrotti, J. T., Ito, A., & Rasmussen, H. N. (2002). Culture counts: Examinations of recent applications of the Penn Resiliency Program or, toward a rubric for examining cultural appropriateness of prevention programming. *Prevention & Treatment, 5*, Article 12.

Lord, F. M. (1980). *Applications of item response theory to practical testing problems.* Hillsdale, NJ: Erlbaum.

Macfarquhar, N. (2007, August 24). Detention was wrong, and U.S. apologizes. *New York Times*, p. A17.

Maloney, D. M. (2006). Court says it's possible that children were used like canaries in a mine—To warn of danger. *Human Research Report, 21*, 8.

Malpass, R. S., & Poortinga, Y. H. (1986). Strategies for design and analysis. In W. J. Lonner & J. W. Berry (Eds.), *Field methods in cross-cultural research* (pp. 47–84). Newbury Park, CA: Sage.

Manson, S. M., Garroutte, E., Goins, R. T., & Henderson, P. N. (2004). Access, relevance, and control in the research process: Lessons from Indian country. *Journal of Aging and Health, 16*, 58S–77S.

Marín, G., Gamba, R. J., & Marín, B. V. (1992). Extreme response style and acquiescence among Hispanics: The role of acculturation and education. *Journal of Cross-Cultural Psychology, 23*, 498–509.

Marín, G., & Marín, B. V. (1991). *Research with Hispanic populations.* Thousand Oaks, CA: Sage.

Massey, D. S., & Denton, N. A. (1987). Trends in the residential segregation of Blacks, Hispanics, and Asians: 1970–1980. *American Sociological Review, 52*, 802–825.

Maxwell, A. E., Bastani, R., Vida, P., & Warda, U. S. (2005). Strategies to recruit and retain older Filipino-American immigrants for a cancer screening study. *Journal of Community Health, 30*, 167–179.

McDonald, R. P. (1995). Testing for approximate dimensionality. In D. Laveault, B. D. Sumbo, M. E. Gessaroli, & M. W. Boss (Eds.), *Modern theories of measurement: Problems and issues* (pp. 63–86). Ottawa, Ontario, Canada: Edumetric Research Group, University of Ottawa.

McDonald, R. P. (1999). *Test theory: A unified treatment.* Mahwah, NJ: Erlbaum.

McLanahan, S. (1985). Family structure and the reproduction of poverty. *American Journal of Sociology, 90,* 873–890.

McLoyd, V. C. (1990). Minority children: Introduction to the special issue. *Child Development, 61,* 263–266.

McLoyd, V. C. (1998). Socioeconomic disadvantage and child development. *American Psychologist, 53,* 185–204.

McLoyd, V. C., Cauce, A. M., Takeuchi, D., & Wilson, L. (2000). Marital processes and parental socialization in families of color: A decade review of research. *Journal of Marriage and Family, 62,* 1070–1093.

Michaels, M, Barr, A., Roosa, M., & Knight, G. P. (2007). Self-esteem: Assessing measurement equivalence in a multi-ethnic sample of youth. *Journal of Early Adolescence, 27,* 269–295.

Millsap, R. E. (1997). Invariance in measurement and prediction: Their relationship in the single-factor case. *Psychological Methods, 2,* 248–260.

Millsap, R. E., & Kwok, O-M. (2004). Evaluating the impact of partial factorial invariance on selection in two populations. *Psychological Methods, 9,* 93–115.

Miranda, J., Azocar, F., Organista, K. C., Munoz, R. F., & Lieberman, A. (1996). Recruiting and retaining low-income Latinos in psychotherapy research. *Journal of Consulting and Clinical Psychology, 64,* 868–874.

Miranda, J., Nakamura, R., & Bernal, G. (2003). Including ethnic minorities in mental health intervention research: A practical approach to a long-standing problem. *Culture, Medicine, and Psychiatry, 27,* 467–486.

Mossakowski, K. N. (2003). Coping with perceived discrimination: Does ethnic identity protect mental health? *Journal of Health and Social Behavior, 44,* 318–331.

Muñoz, R. F., Mrazek, P. J., & Haggerty, R. J. (1996). Institute of Medicine report on prevention of mental disorders: Summary and commentary. *American Psychologist, 51,* 1116–1122.

Muñoz, R. F., Penilla, C., & Urizar, G. (2002). Expanding depression prevention research with children of diverse cultures. *Prevention and Treatment, 5,* 35–47.

Mzarek, P. J., & Haggerty, R. J. (1994). *Reducing risks for mental health disorders: Frontiers for preventive intervention research.* Washington, DC: National Academy Press.

Nagayama Hall, G. C., & Maramba, G. G. (2001). In search of cultural diversity: Recent literature in cross-cultural and ethnic minority psychology. *Cultural Diversity and Ethnic Minority Psychology, 7,* 12–26.

National Commission for the Protection of Human Subjects of Biomedical and Behavioral Research. (1979). *The Belmont Report: Ethical principles and guidelines for the protection of human subjects of research.* Washington, DC: U. S. Department of Health and Human Services.

Nelson, R. M. (2001). Nontherapeutic research, minimal risk, and the Kennedy Krieger Lead Abatement Study. *IRB: Ethics and Human Research, 23,* 7–11.

Noh, S., Beiser, M., Kaspar, V., Hou, F., & Rummens, J. (1999). Perceived racial discrimination, depression, and coping: A study of Southeast Asian refugees in Canada. *Journal of Health and Social Behavior, 40,* 193–207.

Norton, I. M., & Manson, S. M. (1996). Research in American Indian and Alaska Native communities: Navigating the cultural universe of values and process. *Journal of Consulting and Clinical Psychology, 64,* 856–860.

Nunnally, J. C. (1967). *Psychometric theory.* New York: McGraw-Hill.

Peña, E. D. (2007). Lost in translation: Methodological considerations in cross-cultural research. *Child Development, 78,* 1255–1264.

Picot, S. J. F., Tierney, J., Mirpourian, N., Ericsson, J. M., Wright, J. T., & Powel, L. L. (2002). Engaging Black older adults and caregivers in urban communities in health research. *Journal of Gerontological Nursing, 28,* 19–27.

Prelow, M. H., Tein, J.-Y., Roosa, M. W., & Wood, J. (2000). Do coping styles differ across sociocultural groups? The role of measurement equivalence in making this judgment. *American Journal of Community Psychology, 28,* 225–244.

Prieto, A. J. (1992). A method for translation of instruments to other languages. *Adult Education Quarterly, 43,* 1–14.

Protection of Human Subjects, 45 C.F.R. §46 (2005).

Quintana, S. M., Aboud, F. E., Chao, R. K., Contreras-Grau, J., Cross, W. E., Hudley, C., et al. (2006). Race, ethnicity, and culture in child development: Contemporary research and future directions. *Child Development, 77,* 1129–1141.

Ramirez-Esparza, N., Gosling, S. D., Benet-Martinez, V., Potter, J. P., & Pennebaker, J. W. (2006). Do bilinguals have two personalities? A special case of cultural frame switching. *Journal of Research in Personality, 40,* 99–120.

Reese, L. E., & Vera, E. M. (2007). Culturally relevant prevention: The scientific and practical considerations of community-based programs. *The Counseling Psychologist, 35,* 763–778.

Reese, L. E., Vera, E. M., & Hasbrouck, L. (2003). Examining the impact of violence on ethnic minority youth, their families, and communities. In G. Bernal, J. E. Trimble, A. K. Burlew, & F. T. L. Leong (Eds.), *Handbook of racial and ethnic minority psychology* (pp. 465–484). Thousand Oaks, CA: Sage.

Reise, S. P., Widaman, K. F., & Pugh, R. H. (1993). Confirmatory factor analysis and item response theory: Two approaches for exploring measurement invariance. *Psychological Bulletin, 114,* 552–566.

Resnicow, K., Baranowski, T., Ahluwalia, J. S., & Braithwaite, R. L. (1999). Cultural sensitivity in public health: Defined and demystified. *Ethnicity & Disease, 9,* 10–21.

Resnicow, K., Soler, R., Braithwaite, R. L., Ahluwalia, J. S., & Butler, J. (2000). Cultural sensitivity in substance use prevention. *Journal of Community Psychology, 28,* 271–290.

Roberts, R. E., Roberts, C. R., & Chen, Y. R. (1997). Ethnocultural differences in prevalence of adolescent depression. *American Journal of Community Psychology, 25,* 95–110.

Roberts, S. (2007). Minorities now form majority in one-third of most populous counties. *New York Times.* Retrieved June 10, 2008, from http://www.nytimes.com/2007/08/09/us/09census.html

Rogoff, B. (2003). *The cultural nature of human development.* New York: Oxford University Press.

Romero, A. J., & Roberts, R. E. (2003). The impact of multiple dimensions of ethnic identity on discrimination and adolescents' self-esteem. *Journal of Applied Social Psychology, 33,* 2288–2305.

Roosa, M. W., Deng, S., Nair, R., & Burrell, G. L. (2005). Measures for studying poverty in family and child research. *Journal of Marriage and Family, 67,* 971–988.

Roosa, M. W., Liu, F. F., Torres, M., Gonzales, N. A., Knight, G. P., & Saenz, D. (2008). Sampling and recruitment in studies of cultural influence on adjustment: A case study with Mexican Americans. *Journal of Family Psychology, 22,* 293–302.

Roosa, M. W., Morgan-Lopez, A. A., Cree, W. K., & Specter, M. M. (2002). Ethnic culture, poverty, and context: Sources of influence on Latino families and children. In J. Contreras, A. Neal-Barnett, & K. Kerns (Eds.), *Latino children and families in the United States: Current research and future directions* (pp. 27–44). Westport, CT: Praeger.

Roosa, M. W., Wolchik, S. A., & Sandler, I. N. (1997). Preventing the negative effects of common stressors: Current status and future directions. In S. A. Wolchick & I. N. Sandler (Eds.), *Handbook of children's coping: Linking theory and intervention* (pp. 515–533). New York: Plenum Press.

Roselló, J., & Bernal, G. (1999). The efficacy of cognitive behavioral and interpersonal treatments for depressed Puerto Rican adolescents. *Journal of Consulting and Clinical Psychology, 67,* 734–745.

Rudner, L. M., Getson, P. R., & Knight, D. L. (1980). Biased item detection techniques. *Journal of Educational Statistics, 5,* 213–233.

Ruiz, S. Y., Roosa, M. W., & Gonzales, N. A. (2002). Predictors of self-esteem for Mexican-American and Anglo youth: A re-examination of the influence of parenting. *Journal of Family Psychology, 16,* 70–80.

Sabogal, F., Otero-Sabogal, R., Pasick, R. J., Jenkins, C. N. H., & Pérez-Stable, E. J. (1996). Printed health education materials for diverse communities:

Suggestions learned from the field. *Health Education Quarterly, 23*(Suppl.), S123–S141.

Safren, S. A., Gonzalez, R. E., Horner, K. J., Leung, A. W., Heimberg, R. G., & Juster, H. R. (2000). Anxiety in ethnic minority youth: Methodological and conceptual isues and review of the literature. *Behavior Modification, 24,* 147–183.

Sanchez-Burks, J., Nisbett, R. E., & Ybarra, O. (2000). Cultural styles, relational schemes, and prejudice against out-groups. *Journal of Personality and Social Psychology, 79,* 174–189.

Santisteban, D. A., Muir-Malcolm, J. A., Mitrani, V. B., & Szapocznik, J. (2001). Integrating the study of ethnic culture and family psychology intervention science. In H. Liddle, R. Levant, D. A. Santisteban, & J. Brays (Eds.), *Family psychology intervention science* (pp. 331–351). Washington, DC: American Psychological Association.

Scott, C. K. (2004). A replicable model for achieving over 90% follow-up rates in longitudinal studies of substance abusers. *Drug and Alcohol Dependency, 74,* 21–36.

Sellers, R. M., Caldwell, C. H., Schmeelk-Cone, K. H., & Zimmerman, M. A. (2003). Racial identity, racial discrimination, perceived stress, and psychological distress among African American young adults. *Journal of Health and Social Behavior, 44,* 302–317.

Sellers, R. M., & Shelton, J. N. (2003). The role of racial identity in perceived racial discrimination. *Journal of Personality and Social Psychology, 84,* 1079–1092.

Sireci, S. G. (1997). Problems and issues linking assessments across languages. *Educational Measurement: Issues and Practice, 16,* 12–19, 29.

Skaff, M. K., Chesla, C., Mycue, V., & Fisher, L. (2002). Lessons in cultural competence: Adapting research methodology for Latino participants. *Journal of Community Psychology, 30,* 305–323.

Slavin, R. E. (1980). Cooperative learning. *Review of Educational Research, 50,* 315–342.

Snowman, J., & Biehler, R. (1997). *Psychology applied to teaching* (8th ed.). Boston: Houghton Mifflin.

Spencer, M. B., & McLoyd, V. C. (Eds.). (1990). Minority children [Special issue]. *Child Development, 61*(2).

Spoth, R., Goldberg, C., & Redmond, C. (1999). Engaging families in longitudinal prevention intervention research: Discrete-time survival analysis of socioeconomic and socio-emotional risk factors. *Journal of Consulting and Clinical Psychology, 67,* 157–163.

Steiger, J. H. (1998). A note on multiple sample extensions of the RMSEA fit index. *Structural Equation Modeling, 5,* 411–419.

Stephens, R. C., Thibodeaux, L., Sloboda, Z., & Tonkin, P. (2007). Research note: An empirical study of adolescent student attrition. *Journal of Drug Issues, 37,* 475–488.

Sue, S., Fujino, D. C., Hu, L., Takeuchi, D. T., & Zane, N. W. S. (1991). Community mental health services for ethnic minority groups: A test of the cultural responsiveness hypothesis. *Journal of Consulting and Clinical Psychology, 59,* 533–540.

Taylor-Piliae, R. E., & Froelicher, E. S. (2007). Methods to optimize recruitment and retention to an exercise study in Chinese immigrants. *Nursing Research, 56,* 132–136.

Temple, B., & Young, A. (2004). Qualitative research and translation dilemmas. *Qualitative Research, 4,* 161–178.

Thompson, T. G. (2001). *Culture, race, and ethnicity: A supplement to* Mental Health: A report of the Surgeon General. Washington, DC: U.S. Department of Health and Human Services, Office of the Surgeon General, Substance Abuse and Mental Health Services Administration.

Tolan, P. H., Gorman-Smith, D., Huesmann, L. R., & Zelli, A. (1997). Assessing family processes to explain risk for antisocial behavior and depression among urban youth. *Psychological Assessment, 9,* 212–223.

Tsai, J. L., Chentsova-Dutton, Y., & Wong, Y. (2002). Why and how researchers should study ethnic identity, acculturation, and cultural orientation. In G. C. Ngayama Hall & S. Okazaki (Eds.), *Asian American psychology: The science of lives in context* (pp. 41–65). Washington, DC: American Psychological Association.

Turner, W. L. (2000). Cultural considerations in family-based primary prevention programs in drug abuse. *Journal of Primary Prevention, 21,* 285–303.

Twinn, S. (1997). An exploratory study examining the influence of translation on the validity and reliability of qualitative data in nursing research. *Journal of Advanced Nursing, 26,* 418–423.

Umaña-Taylor, A. J., & Bámaca, M. Y. (2004). Conducting focus groups with Latino populations: Lessons from the field. *Family Relations, 53,* 261–272.

Umaña-Taylor, A. J., & Fine, M. A. (2001). Methodological implications of grouping Latino adolescents into one collective ethnic group. *Hispanic Journal of Behavioral Sciences, 23,* 347–362.

Umaña-Taylor, A. J, Yazedjian, A., & Bámaca-Gómez, M. (2004). Developing the Ethnic Identity Scale using Eriksonian and social identity perspectives. *Identity, 4,* 9–38.

UNC Carolina Population Center. (n.d.). *Add Health: Social, behavioral, and biological linkages across the life course.* Retrieved January 21, 2009, from http://www.cpc.unc.edu/projects/addhealth

U.S. Census Bureau. (1993a). *We the Americans: Asians: Census 1990 special report.* Washington, DC.: U.S. Department of Commerce, Economics and Statistics Administration.

U.S. Census Bureau. (1993b). *We the Americans: Blacks: Census 1990 special report.* Washington, DC: U.S. Department of Commerce, Economics and Statistics Administration.

U.S. Census Bureau. (1993c). *We the Americans: Hispanics: Census 1990 special report.* Washington, DC: U.S. Department of Commerce, Economics and Statistics Administration.

U.S. Census Bureau. (1995). *Statistical abstract of the United States, 1994.* Washington, DC: U.S. Government Printing Office.

U.S. Census Bureau. (2001a). *The Black population: 2000: Census 2000 brief.* Washington, DC: U.S. Department of Commerce, Economics and Statistics Administration.

U.S. Census Bureau. (2001b). *The Hispanic population: Census 2000 brief.* Washington, DC: U.S. Department of Commerce, Economics and Statistics Administration.

U.S. Census Bureau. (2001c). *Population change and distribution: 1990–2000: Census 2000 brief.* Washington, DC: U.S. Department of Commerce, Economics and Statistics Administration.

U.S. Census Bureau. (2001d). *Poverty in the United States: 2000. Current population reports.* Washington, DC: U.S. Department of Commerce, Economics and Statistics Administration.

U.S. Census Bureau. (2002). *The Asian population: 2000: Census 2000 brief.* Washington, DC: U.S. Department of Commerce, Economics and Statistics Administration.

U.S. Census Bureau. (2003). *Language use and English-speaking ability: 2000. Census 2000 brief.* Washington, DC: U.S. Department of Commerce, Economics and Statistics Administration.

U.S. Census Bureau. (2004a). *Census Bureau projects tripling of Hispanic and Asian populations in 50 years; non-Hispanic Whites may drop to half of total population.* Washington, DC: U.S. Department of Commerce.

U.S. Census Bureau. (2004b). *We the people: Asians in the United States. Census 2000 special reports.* Washington, DC: U.S. Department of Commerce, Economics and Statistics Administration.

U.S. Census Bureau. (2004c). *We the people: Hispanics in the United States. Census 2000 special reports.* Washington, DC: U.S. Department of Commerce, Economics and Statistics Administration.

U.S. Census Bureau. (2005). *We the people: Blacks in the United States. Census 2000 special reports.* Washington, DC: U.S. Department of Commerce, Economics and Statistics Administration.

U.S. Census Bureau. (2006). *Income, poverty, and health insurance coverage in the United States: 2005. Current population reports.* Washington, DC: U.S. Department of Commerce, Economics and Statistics Administration.

U.S. Census Bureau. (2007). *Income, poverty, and health insurance coverage in the United States: 2006.* Washington, DC: U.S. Department of Commerce, Economics and Statistics Administration. Retrieved June 10, 2008, from http://www.census.gov/prod/2007pubs/p60-233.pdf

U.S. Department of Education. (1982). *A study of alternative definitions and measures relating to eligibility and service under Part A of the Indian Education Act.* Unpublished report.

U.S. Department of Education. (2000). *Dropout rates in the United States: 1998* (NCES 2000-022). Washington, DC: U.S. Government Printing Office.

U.S. Department of Health and Human Services. (2001). *Mental health: Culture, race, ethnicity* (Supplement to *Report of the Surgeon General*, Inventory SMA-01-3613). Rockville, MD: U.S. Department of Health and Human Services, Office of the Surgeon General, Substance Abuse and Mental Health Services Administration. Retrieved March 3, 2008, from http://mentalhealth.samhsa.gov/cre/default.asp

Valle, R. (2005). Culturally attuned recruitment, retention, and adherence in Alzheimer disease and associated disorders. *Alzheimer Disease and Associated Disorders, 4,* 261–266.

Vandenberg, R. J., & Lance, C. E. (2000). A review and synthesis of the measurement invariance literature: Suggestions, practices, and recommendations for organizational research. *Organizational Research Methods, 3,* 4–70.

van de Vijver, F. J., & Tanzer, N. K. (1997). Bias and equivalence in cross-cultural assessment: An overview. *European Review of Applied Psychology, 47,* 263–279.

Vera, E. (2007). Culture, prevention, and the politics of disparities. *The Counseling Psychologist, 35,* 860–867.

Verkuyten, M., & Pouliasai, K. (2002). Biculturalism among older children: Cultural frame switching, attributions, self-identification, and attitudes. *Journal of Cross-Cultural Psychology, 33,* 569–609

Wallerstein, N. B., & Duran, B. (2006). Using community-based participatory research to address health disparities. *Health Promotion Practice, 7,* 312–323.

Wang, W. L., Lee, H. L., & Fetzer, S. J. (2006). Challenges and strategies of instrument translation. *Western Journal of Nursing Research, 28,* 310–321.

Warren-Findlow, J., Prohaska, T. R., & Freedman, D. (2003). Challenges and opportunities in recruiting and retaining underrepresented populations into health promotion research. *The Gerontologist, 43,* 37–46.

Werner, E. E., & Smith, R. S. (1992). *Overcoming the odds: High risk children from birth to adulthood.* Ithaca, NY: Cornell University Press.

Widaman, K. F. (1995). On methods for comparing apples and oranges. *Multivariate Behavioral Research, 30,* 101–106.

Widaman, K. F., & Reise, S. P. (1997). Exploring the measurement invariance of psychological instruments: Applicants in the substance use domain. In K. J. Bryant, M. Windle, & S. G. West (Eds.), *The science of prevention: Methodological advances from alcohol and substance abuse research* (pp. 281–324). Washington, DC: American Psychological Association.

Word, C. O. (1992). Cross-cultural methods for research in Black urban areas. In K. A. Burlew, W. C. Banks, H. P. McAdoo, & D. A. Azibo (Eds.), *African American psychology* (pp. 28–42). Newbury Park, CA: Sage.

Yancey, A. K., Ortega, A. N., & Kumanyika, S. K. (2005). Effective recruitment and retention of minority research participants. *Annual Review of Public Health, 27,* 1–28.

Yasui, M., & Dishion, T. J. (2007). The ethnic context of child and adolescent problem behavior: Implications for child and family interventions. *Clinical Child and Family Psychology, 10,* 137–179.

Zambrana, R. E., & Aguirre-Molina, M. (1987). Alcohol abuse and prevention among Latino adolescents: A strategy for intervention. *Journal of Youth and Adolescence, 16,* 97–113.

Zayas, L. H., Lester, R. J., Cabassa, L. J., & Fortuna, L. R. (2005). Why do so many Latina teens attempt suicide? A conceptual model for research. *American Journal of Orthopsychiatry, 75,* 275–287.

Index

Accessible population, 30, 34–35
Acculturation, 8, 21
Adaptation, degree of, 21
Add Health. *See* National Longitudinal Study of Adolescent Health
Advisors, 59–61
Advocacy groups, 60
African Americans
  countries/regions of origin of, 13
  median income of, 14
  pan-ethnic studies of, 47
  population dynamics of, 12–13
Africans, 13, 47
Alaska Natives, 19, 49
American Indians
  collaborative research with, 59
  defining, 19–20, 49
  as ethnic minority, 10
  pan-ethnic studies of, 47
American Psychological Association (APA), 80, 82
American Sociological Association, 80
Anonymous data, 84
Anti-immigration movements, 52, 53
APA. *See* American Psychological Association
Asian Americans
  country/region of origin of, 14–15
  median income of, 14
  pan-ethnic studies of, 46–47
  population dynamics of, 14
Attrition, 37
Authority figures, 52, 55

Back-translation, 142, 145–156
Belmont Report, 79, 81
Beneficence, 81–84
Bias. *See also* Measurement bias
  in research designs, 90
  response, 102–104, 125
  sample, 25–26
  social, 52
Biculturalism, 58–59, 65, 72. *See also* Acculturation
Bilingual fluency, 58–59, 65, 72
Biomedical studies, 47–48
Blind back-translation, 145

Cambodians, 15
Caribbean, 13
Cell phones, 51
Central Americans, 11–13, 66
Certificates of Confidentiality, 83–84
CFA. *See* Confirmatory factor analysis
Chance parameter, 111
Check cashing, 63

Chinese Americans, 14, 61
Churches, recruitment through, 61
Code of Ethics (APA), 82, 85
Coding teams, 159
Collaboration, 59–61, 175–176
Collaboration-as-equals model, 59–60
Collaborative models, 59
Collectivism, 56, 63, 71
College attendees, 41–42
Colloquialisms, 141
Comadres, 140
"Common good," 41
Communication, 61–62
Community advisory boards, 59–61,
    70–71, 74, 176
Community-based participatory research,
    59, 92
Community benefits, 63
Community collaboration, 175–176
Community members, 62
Community partnerships, 65
Comparative research designs, 90–91
Conceptual equivalence, 138–140, 164
Configural invariance, 109
Confirmatory factor analysis (CFA),
    108–112
Consent processes, 82–83, 87–89, 93–94
Constrained SEM, 118
Construct equivalence, 138–140
Construct validity equivalence, 115–120
Construct validity relations, 99–100, 127
Contact information, 67–68, 73
Content modification, 172
Convenience sampling, 40–41, 77–78
Coping styles, 125–126
Cronbach's alpha, 156, 157
Cross-group comparative designs, 16–17
    ethical issues in, 93–95
    measurement/measurement equiva-
        lence in, 128–130
    of prevention interventions, 188–189
    translation issues with, 161–162
Cubans, 11, 46

Cultural adaptation
    dual, 12
    efficacy of, 188–189
    with preventive interventions, 171–173
Cultural competence, 91–93, 167
Cultural context, 174–175
Cultural insiders, 121–122
Cultural priming, 150
Cultural responsiveness hypothesis, 57
Cultural strengths, 180
Cultural validity, 159
Cultural variables, 91
Culture, mainstream, 8n.1

Data analyses, 159–160
Decentering, 148–149
Deep structure adaptation, 172–173
"Deficit model," 45
Degree of measurement error, 101–102
Delivery modification, 172, 180–181
Demographic characteristics, 153–154
Demographic matching, 57–59
Depression prevention program, 184–188
Dialects, 151–152
Diffusion stage (of prevention research
    cycle), 171
Diminished decision-making capacity, 81
Discrimination experience, 13, 52–53
Dissemination of program, 171
Distrust, 60
Diversity, obtaining, 63–64
Dominicans, 11, 12
Double translation/double-back transla-
    tion, 142–143, 145–146
Drivers license records, 69
Dropout rates, 71
Drug trials, 82

Economically disadvantaged populations
    defining, 48–49
    and ethnic minorities, 15–16
    goals for studying, 5
    growing interest in, 6–7

importance of studying, 4
recruitment issues with, 50–52
underrepresentation of, in research, 5–6
Education level, 15–16
Electronic white pages directories, 69
Employers, tracing information from, 68
Enculturation, 8
English fluency, 21, 23
Environmental Protection Agency, 42–43
Ethical issues, 79–96
    in cross-group comparative designs, 93–94
    cultural competence, 91–93
    and ethical principles, 81–85
    in inadvertently diverse samples, 95
    informed consent, 87–89
    methods/designs, 89–91
    in national sample designs, 94–95
    participation, 85–87
    in within-group designs, 94
Ethical principles for research, 81–85
    beneficence, 81–84
    justice, 84–85
    respect for persons, 81
Ethical risks, 82–83
Ethics guidelines, 79–80
Ethnically homogeneous designs, 181–183
Ethnic identity, 8. See also Acculturation
Ethnic minority populations
    African Americans as, 12–14
    Asian Americans as, 14–15
    cultural differences between, 4
    defined, 9
    defining, 49–50
    and economic disadvantage, 15–16
    geographic diversity of, 15–16
    goals for studying, 5
    growing interest in, 6–7
    importance of studying, 4
    Latinos as, 10–12
    recruitment issues with, 50–53
    underrepresentation of, in research, 5–6

Experimental field trials, 170
External validity, 31
Extreme-alternative response bias, 102–104, 125

Face-to-face recruitment, 61, 62, 75
Factor analysis, 156
Factorial invariance, 107–115
    analytic strategies for, 108
    CFA of, 108–112
    defined, 98
    IRT analysis of, 110–113
    model of, 109
    partial, 112–115, 127
Fairness, 84
Familistic values, 31, 56, 63
Family, recruitment of, 56, 67
Family-based interventions, 179–180
Fatalism, 31
Fathers, 72
Financial incentives, 62–63, 68, 72, 73
Firmemente, 139
Fliers, 68, 71–72
Focus groups, 122, 123, 175
Form letters, 73
Forward-translation, 143, 146–147
Frame-switching behavior, 150
Fuertemente, 139
Functional equivalence, 106, 107
Funding agencies, 138, 165, 194

Generative research, 170
Generative stage (of prevention research cycle), 170
Geographic diversity, 15–16
Group membership, defining, 48–50
Group specificity, 124–127

Harm
    assumption of lack of, 42–43
    minimizing possible, 82
    reporting threats of, 83

Head of household
  African American, 14
  Asian American, 14
  and economic disadvantage, 15
  Latino, 11
Health fairs, 61
Health services studies, 47–48
Hispanics. *See* Latinos/Latinas
Hmongs, 15
Hybrid prevention programs, 183

ICC. *See* Item characteristic curve
Idioms, 141
Illegal activity, reporting, 83
Illegal immigrants, 53
Immigrants
  consent issues with, 88–89
  recruitment issues with, 51–53
  retention issues with, 66
Immigration laws, 66
Implementation stage (of prevention
  research cycle), 170–171
Inadvertently diverse designs, 24–26
  ethical issues in, 95
  measurement/measurement equiva-
    lence in, 132–133
  of prevention interventions, 189–190
  sampling/recruitment/retention in,
    77–78
  translation issues with, 163
Incentives. *See* Financial incentives
Income level. *See also* Median income
  and awareness of social bias, 52
  and geographic distribution, 51
  and recruitment methods, 61
Indicated preventive interventions, 170
Indigenous languages, 15, 52
Informed consent, 82–83, 87–89
Initial contacts, 71–72
In-person referrals, 61
Interethnic marriages, 49–50
Internal validity, 31–34
Internet, 68, 69

Intervention studies, 64–65
Interviewer effects, 58
Interview protocol, translating, 158
Invariance, factorial. *See* Factorial invariance
IRT analysis. *See* Item response theory
  analysis
Item characteristic curve (ICC), 110–111
Item difficulty, 111
Item discrimination, 111
Item equivalence, 105–106
Item identification, 99
Item response theory (IRT) analysis, 108,
  110–113

Japanese, 15
Jargon, 87
Journals, 166
Justice, 84–85

Language. *See also* English fluency;
    Translation of measures
  of Add Health study, 22
  of Asian Americans, 15, 46–47
  of informed-consent forms, 87–89
  of Latinos, 12
  in national sample designs, 95
  prevention intervention issues involv-
    ing, 177–178
  recruitment issues involving, 51–52,
    58–59
  retention issues involving, 66
Laotians, 15
Latinos/Latinas
  common language of, 15
  countries/regions of origin of, 11
  discrimination experiences of, 52–53
  language use/capabilities of, 12
  and Likert-type response scales,
    102–104
  median income of, 11
  pan-ethnic studies of, 46
  population dynamics of, 10–11
  promotoras used with, 65

recruitment of, 61–62
suicide attempt rates among, 19
values of, 55
Lead-based paint abatement study, 43, 80
Legal authorities, 84
Letters, 71–72
Likert-type response scales
    extreme-alternative response bias with,
        102–104, 125
    translation of anchors in, 138–139
Limited-partnership models, 60
Literacy, 66
Literal translations, 139, 141, 164
Longitudinal studies, 64–70

Mailings, 68–69
Mainstream culture, 8*n*.1
Maintenance interventions, 170
Measurement, 97–105
    bias in, 102–105
    in cross-group comparative designs,
        128–130
    elements of, 98–100
    errors of, 100–102
    in inadvertently diverse designs,
        132–133
    in national sample designs, 131–132
    and research practices, 124–127
    in within-group designs, 130–131
Measurement accuracy, 18, 20
Measurement bias, 102–105, 135–136,
    162–163
Measurement equivalence, 105–120
    of construct validity, 115–120
    in cross-group comparative designs,
        128–130
    defined, 98
    in inadvertently diverse designs,
        132–133
    in national sample designs, 131–132
    in qualitative research, 121–124
    and research practices, 124–127
    types of, 105–107

of variance, 107–115
    in within-group designs, 130–131
Measurement error, 100–102, 162–163
Measures, 135n1
Median income
    of African Americans, 14
    of Asian Americans, 14
    of Latinos, 11
Medical centers, recruitment through, 61
Medical studies, 48
Methodological information, 35–36
Methodologically driven research, 7–8
Metric invariance, 110
Mexicans, 11, 66
Misrepresentation in research, 43–48
Mobility, 50, 66, 68, 73
Monolingual (in translation process, 151
Moral code, 79
Multigroup CFA, 109
Multiple regression analysis, 115, 117
Municipal water customer records, 69
Muy de acuerdo, 139
Muy en desacuerdo, 139

National clearinghouse, 166
National Institute of Health (NIH),
    48, 83, 84
National Institute of Mental Health
    (NIMH), 169
National Longitudinal Study of Adolescent
    Health (Add Health), 22, 24
National sample designs, 21–24
    ethical issues in, 94–95
    measurement/measurement equivalence
        in, 131–132
    of prevention interventions, 189
    sampling/recruitment in, 75–77
    translation issues with, 163
Naturalized citizens, 15
Nested CFA models, 109
Newsletters, 69, 73
NIH. *See* National Institute of Health
NIMH (National Institute of Mental
    Health), 169

"No estoy de acuerdo para nada," 139
Nonprofessional referral sources, 61
Nonrandom attrition, 37

Official notices, 61
Organizational partnerships, 60–61
Oversampling, 76

Pakistanis, 15
Palma, 159
Pan-ethnic studies, 8, 20, 45–47
Parenting practices, 4, 86
Partial factorial invariance, 112–115, 127
Participants data, translating, 159
Participation issues, 85–87
Participation rate, 35, 36
Partner organizations, 60–61
Pathological portrayal, 45
Penn Resiliency Program (PRP), 184
Permission to contact tracers, 68, 73
Personal benefits, 62
Personal contact, 55–56, 62, 72
Personal experience, 56–57
Pilot testing, 78, 153–157
Police records, 69
Postage-paid envelopes, 68
Poverty
    adaptation to, 9
    rural vs. urban, 44
Poverty guidelines, 49
Poverty levels, 9
Poverty thresholds, 48–49
Practical fit indices, 112
Preventive intervention research, 167–190
    challenges of/future directions for,
        183–184
    community collaboration in, 175–176
    cross-group comparative, 188–189
    and cultural adaptation, 171–173
    and cultural context, 174–175
    defined, 169–170
    depression case study, 184–188
    ethnically homogeneous designs for,
        181–183

inadvertently diverse, 189–190
    language issues in, 177–178
    location of, 178–179
    national sample, 189
    need for, 168–169
    research cycle in, 170–171
    revising target variables/intervention
        design for, 179–181
    within-group, 188, 189
Program development stage (of research
    cycle), 170
Promotoras, 65
Property tax records, 69
PRP (*see* Penn Resiliency Program), 184
Psychosocial intervention studies, 47–48
Public records, 69
Puerto Ricans
    language of, 12
    mobility issues with, 66
    parenting practices of, 123
    region of origin of, 11
    as U.S. citizens, 46

Qualitative interviews, 122–124, 157–161
Quantitative research, 34, 123, 124

Racial profiling, 53
Random attrition, 37
Random measurement errors, 101
Random sampling, 38–39, 75
Reading grade levels, 88
Recruitment, of participants, 30–37
    and assumptions, 41–43
    with benefits/incentives, 62–63
    case study, 70–74
    with community collaborators, 59–61
    and contact/communication methods,
        61–62
    defined, 30
    and definitions of group membership,
        48–50
    with demographic matching, 57–59
    and diversity, 63–64

in inadvertently diverse designs, 78
judging representativeness of sample
    prior to, 35, 36
methodological information about,
    35–36
and misrepresentation in research, 43–48
in national sample designs, 75–77
overcoming challenges to, 53–64
practical issues in, 50–53
problems with, 41–53
terms used with, 35–37
and validity of study, 31–34
and values/belief systems, 55–57
in within-group designs, 74–75
"Reflected glory," 60
Reminders, 69
Replicated studies, 77–78
Representative sampling
    challenges with, 19–21
    importance of, 18
    lack of, 43–48
Reputation, 57, 61, 70
Research designs, 16–26
    cross-group comparative, 16–17
    inadvertently diverse, 24–26
    national sample, 21–24
    types of, 16
    within-group, 17–21
Research misconduct, 80
Research team, characteristics of, 160–161
Respect, 55, 56, 81
Respeto, 88–89
Response bias, 124–125
Retention, of participants, 30–34, 64–70
    case study, 70–74
    defined, 30
    in inadvertently diverse designs, 78
    in intervention studies, 64–65
    in longitudinal panel studies, 65–70
    terms used with, 37
    and validity of study, 31–34
Review committee translation, 144,
    147–148
Rural poverty, 44

Sample bias, 25–26
Sampling, 30–50
    and assumptions, 41–43
    convenience, 40–41
    defined, 30
    and definitions of group membership,
        48–50
    and diversity, 63–64
    in inadvertently diverse designs, 77–78
    judging representativeness of, 36, 37
    and misrepresentation in research,
        43–48
    in national sample designs, 75–77
    problems with, 41–50
    random, 38–39
    stratified random, 39–40
    terms used with, 34–35
    and validity of study, 31–34
    in within-group designs, 74–75
Sampling frame, 34–35
Scalar equivalence, 106–107
Scheduling interviews, 72
Schools
    partnering with, 60, 71
    prevention interventions located in,
        178–179
    tracing information from, 68
Seasonal farm workers, 50
Secondary constructs, 102, 103
Segregation experience, 13
Selective preventive interventions, 170
SEM analysis. See Structural equation
    modeling analysis
Semantic equivalence, 140–141
SES (socioeconomic status), 152
Single-parent households, 15
Small theory of intervention, 170
Snowball sampling, 40
Social service organizations, 60–62
Socioeconomic status (SES), 152
South Americans, 11, 13
Squared validity coefficient, 103
Stratified random sampling, 39–40

Strict invariance, 110
Strong invariance, 110
Structural equation modeling (SEM)
    analysis, 115, 118
Stuttering-inducement study, 80
Suicidal thoughts, 124
Suicide attempt rates, 19
Surface structure adaptation, 171–173
Systematic secondary constructs, 103–104

Target population, 34–35, 59–61
Telephone access, 50–51
Telephone contacts, 72
Telephone surveys, 51
Test construction, 152–153
Toll-free telephone numbers, 68
Tracers, 67–69, 73
Training, in cultural competence, 92–93
Translation of measures, 135–166
    and adaptation, 140
    assessing equivalence of, 156–157
    back-, 142, 145–156
    best practices for, 163–164
    cautions about, 149–151
    conceptual equivalence of, 138–140
    in cross-group comparative designs,
        161–162
    and data analysis of equivalence,
        159–160
    decentering, 148–149
    double translation/double-back,
        142–143, 145–146
    forward-, 143, 146–147
    future directions for, 164–166
    goal of, 164
    importance of, 18
    in inadvertently diverse designs, 163
    and interview protocol, 158
    issues with, 157–161
    and measurement error/bias, 162–163
    in national sample designs, 163
    necessity of, 137–138

and participants' data, 159
pilot testing of, 153–157
with prevention interventions,
    177–178
in quantitative research, 141–151
and research team characteristics,
    160–161
review team/committee approach to,
    144, 147–148
and selecting translators, 151–153
semantic equivalence of, 140–141
timing of, 161
in within-group designs, 162–163
Translation teams, 152–153
Translators, selecting, 151–153
Treatment interventions, 170
Tribal membership, 20, 49
Trust, 175, 176
Tuskegee syphilis study, 19, 42, 47–48, 80

Unconstrained SEM, 118
Universal preventive interventions, 170
University–community partnerships, 59
Urban poverty, 44

Validity, of study, 31–34
Validity coefficients, 101
Values, 55–57
Vietnamese, 15

Water customer records, 69
White pages directories, 69
Within-group designs, 17–21
    ethical issues in, 94
    measurement/measurement equiva-
        lence in, 130–131
    of prevention interventions, 188, 189
    sampling/recruitment in, 74–75
    translation issues with, 162–163
    translations of, 137–138
Within-group diversity studies, 8, 9
Written communication, 61

About the Authors

George P. Knight, PhD, is a professor in the Department of Psychology at Arizona State University, Tempe. He received a bachelor's degree in psychology from Macalester College, St. Paul, Minnesota, and master's and doctorate degrees from the University of California at Riverside. His research interests have focused on the role of culture in prosocial development, acculturation and enculturation processes, the development of ethnic identity, and measurement equivalence in cross-ethnic and developmental research. He is currently involved in three research programs involving ethnic minority adolescents. Dr. Knight has served as an editorial board member for *Child Development, Journal of Research on Adolescence, Journal of Family Psychology, Merrill-Palmer Quarterly, Personality and Social Psychology Bulletin,* and *Review of Personality and Social Psychology* (Vol. 15). He has published widely in developmental, cultural, and social journals.

Mark W. Roosa, PhD, is a professor of social and family dynamics at Arizona State University, Tempe. He received his bachelor's degree from Ohio State University, Columbus, and his master's and doctorate degrees from Michigan State University, Ann Arbor. His career research interest has been the development of children from low-income families, especially the etiological processes that place these children at risk and those that protect them from risk. He is particularly interested in the additive and interactive roles of culture (e.g., parent and child levels of enculturation and acculturation) and context (family, community, and school) in influencing child outcomes in Mexican immigrant and Mexican American families. He is currently conducting a longitudinal, generative research study examining these cultural and contextual processes in a sample of 750 Mexican and Mexican American families with children who were in fifth grade when the study began. Dr. Roosa has published widely in family, community psychology, and developmental journals.

Adriana J. Umaña-Taylor, PhD, is an associate professor of family and human development at Arizona State University, Tempe, in the School of Social and Family Dynamics. She received a bachelor's degree in psychology and a master's degree in child development and family relationships, both from the University of Texas at Austin. She received her PhD in human development and family studies from the University of Missouri—Columbia. Her research has included adolescents from a variety of ethnic groups in the United States, with most of her work focused on Latino adolescents and their families and, more specifically, on ethnic identity formation, familial socialization processes, culturally informed risk and protective factors, and psychosocial functioning. Her work has been published widely in developmental, family, and cultural journals. Dr. Umaña-Taylor currently serves on the editorial boards of *Child Development, Journal of Marriage and Family, Family Relations, Journal of Early Adolescence,* and *Journal of Social and Personal Relationships.*